AGAINST EVERY HUMAN LAW

AGAINST EVERY HUMAN LAW

The Terrorist Threat to Diplomacy

Andrew Selth

Australian National University Press
A division of Pergamon Press Australia

Australian National University Press is a division of Pergamon Press Australia
and a member of the Pergamon Group of Companies.

AUSTRALIA	Pergamon Press Australia, 19a Boundary Street, Rushcutters Bay, N.S.W. 2011, Australia
U.K.	Pergamon Books Limited, Headington Hill Hall, Oxford OX3 OBW, England
U.S.A.	Pergamon Books Inc., Maxwell House, Fairview Park, Elmsford, New York 10523, U.S.A.
PEOPLE'S REPUBLIC OF CHINA	Pergamon Press, Quianmen Hotel, Beijing, People's Republic of China
FEDERAL REPUBLIC OF GERMANY	Pergamon Press, Hammerweg 6, D-6242 Kronberg, Federal Republic of Germany
BRAZIL	Pergamon Editora, Rua Eça de Queiros, 346, CEP 04011, São Paulo, Brazil
JAPAN	Pergamon Press, 8th Floor, Matsuoka Central Building 1-7-1 Nishishinjuku, Shinjuku-ku, Tokyo 160, Japan
CANADA	Pergamon Press Canada, Suite 104, 150 Consumers Road, Willowdale, Ontario M2J IP9, Canada

First Published 1988

Copyright © 1988 Andrew Selth

Typeset in Australia by Post Typesetters
Printed in Singapore by Singapore National Printers Ltd

National Library of Australia Cataloguing in
Publication Data

Selth, Andrew, 1951-
    Against Every Human Law: the terrorist threat to
    diplomacy.

    Bibliography
    Includes index.
    ISBN 0 08 034404 6.

    1. Terrorism. 2. Diplomats — Protection. 3.
    Terrorism — Prevention. 4. Embassy buildings —
    Takeovers. I. Title.

363.3' 2

Almost every page of history offers some remark
on the inviolable rights of ambassadors, and the
security of their persons, a security sanctioned by
every clause and precept of human and revealed law

Grotius
De Jure Belli ac Pacis
(1625)

for Patti

and in memory of

Geoffrey Fairbairn
(1924–1980)
scholar and gentleman

CONTENTS

APPENDICES

ACKNOWLEDGEMENTS

This book stems in large part from work carried out for a Master of Arts degree in international relations at the Australian National University (ANU) between 1984–1985. Its origins, however, can be traced as far back as the early 1970s, when my interest in unconventional conflicts was first aroused by Geoffrey Fairbairn, then a Lecturer in the ANU's History Department. Since that time I have accumulated many debts and to all those who contributed in any way to the preparation of this study go my thanks. Not all can be named here, but there are some to whom special consideration is due.

In Burma, U Myint Thein, Sun Myint, N Hkum Kaw Hpang, Tin Tin San, Khin Myint Myint, Thanegi, Bella Khathing and Sela Khathing all gave valuable advice and encouragement. In the Republic of Korea this role was generously performed by Ron and Julie Stansfield, Marvin and Marilyn Wodinsky, Nigel and Milly Bowie, Steven Searle and Vijayanthi Parthasarty. For their help both in Korea and New Zealand I have to thank Paul and Wendy Tipping. I have also drawn heavily on the wisdom and friendship of Michael Birch, Ann Darvall, Alan Thomas and Clive Williams.

My time at the ANU between 1984–1985 was made possible by the grant of an Australian Public Service Postgraduate Study Award. This award would not have been received without the support of Jeff Benson and for his help I am very grateful. While at the Australian National University I profited from, and greatly enjoyed, my association with the members of the Department of International Relations, the Strategic and Defence Studies Centre, and the Peace Research Centre. Geoffrey Jukes, Jim Piscatori, Tom Millar, Desmond Ball, Paul Dibb, Andrew Mack, Shirley Steer and Richard Agnew all deserve my thanks for their help with different aspects of this project. Mention must also be made of my fellow MA students, in particular Michael Smith, Alan Stephens and Robert Glasser. The library staff of the Department of Foreign Affairs, Australian Defence Force Academy and Australian Federal Police College helped with sources.

I am grateful too, to the United Kingdom's Foreign and Commonwealth Office and the British Council for a scholarship to continue my studies at Oxford University for a period in 1987. My stay there was greatly enriched by Adam Roberts, Richard and Tai-fang Rigby, and the members of St. Antony's College. The former took considerable trouble to read my draft manuscript and his detailed comments were much appreciated. Of the latter, I particularly remember the kindness of William Gaskin, Kathy Funtek, Paul Lalor, Floresca Karanasou and Dave Morray.

Special thanks are due to Garry Woodard and Grant Wardlaw. The former has been a constant source of advice, encouragement and support since our paths first crossed in 1973. Even without his help with this book I would have to call him Sayagyi. First as the supervisor of my MA thesis and later as a colleague, Grant Wardlaw shared his expertise and friendship with equal generosity. Whatever there may be of value in this work must in part at least be credited to him.

As always, I am indebted to Kim Jackson for his unfailing friendship and help with my various literary and academic projects. Throughout the course of researching and writing this book I also received constant support from my family, and from Peg and Al Koorey. Finally, and most importantly, I should like to thank Patti Collins, without whom this book would have never been written.

It goes without saying that, while I gratefully acknowledge the help given by all of the above, I take full responsibility for what I have written. For the record, it should also be noted that this book is based entirely on public sources. It represents my views alone and has no official status or endorsement.

An earlier version of this book was published in January 1986 by the Australian National University's Strategic and Defence Studies Centre (SDSC), as part of its series of Canberra Papers on Strategy and Defence. In addition, edited portions have appeared as articles in journals or been published as SDSC Working Papers. I acknowledge with thanks permission from the following to use them here: the *Australian and New Zealand Journal of Criminology, Australian Foreign Affairs Record, Australian Quarterly, Current Affairs Bulletin, Pacific Defence Reporter, RUSI* (Journal of the Royal United Services Institute for Defence Studies), *Terrorism: An International Journal* and the ANU's Strategic and Defence Studies Centre.

Andrew Selth
Oxford
March 1987

ABBREVIATIONS

ABC	Australian Broadcasting Corporation
ACT	Australian Capital Territory
AFP	Australian Federal Police
AID	Agency for International Development
ALN	*Açao Libertadora Nacional* (National Liberating Action)
ALP	Australian Labor Party
ANC	African National Congress
ANZUS	Australia, New Zealand and United States (Treaty)
ASALA	Armenian Secret Army for the Liberation of Armenia
ASEAN	Association of South East Asian Nations
ASIO	Australian Security Intelligence Organisation
ASIS	Australian Secret Intelligence Service
BR	*Brigate Rosse* (Red Brigades)
BSO	Black September Organisation
CHOGM	Commonwealth Heads of Government Meeting
CHOGRM	Commonwealth Heads of Government Regional Meeting
CIA	Central Intelligence Agency
DETF	Departmental Emergency Task Force
DGI	*Direccion General de Intelligencia*
DPRK	Democratic Peoples Republic of Korea (North Korea)
EOKA	*Ethniki Organosis Kyprion Agoniston* (National Organisation of Cypriot Fighters)
ETA	*Euskadi ta Askatasuna* (Freedom for the Basque Homeland)
FAA	Foreign Affairs Association
FALN	*Fuerzas Armadas de Liberacion Nacional* (Armed Forces of National Liberation)
FAWA	Foreign Affairs Womens Association
FAR	*Fuerzas Armadas Rebeldes* (Rebel Armed Forces)
FBI	Federal Bureau of Investigation

FLNKS	*Front de Liberation National Kanak et Socialiste* (National Kanak Socialist Liberation Front)
FRG	Federal Republic of Germany (West Germany)
GSG-9	*Grenzschutz Gruppe 9* (Federal Border Guard Group 9)
HIRO	*Hrvatska Ilegalna Revolucionarna Organizacija* (Croat Illegal Revolutionary Organisation)
HNO	*Hrvatski Narodni Otpor* (Croat National Resistance)
HRB	*Hrvatsko Revolucionarno Bratsvo* (Croat Revolutionary Brotherhood)
ICAO	International Civil Aviation Organisation
ILC	International Law Commission
IMO	International Maritime Organisation
IRA	Irish Republican Army
IZL	*Irgun Zvei Leumi (*National Military Organisation*)*
JCAG	Justice Commandos of the Armenian Genocide
KGB	*Komitet Gosudarstvennoi Bezopasnosti* (Committee for State Security)
M-19	*Movimiento 19 Abril* (April 19 Movement)
MI5	(British) Security Service
MLN	*Movimiento de Liberacion Nacional* (National Liberation Movement)
Mossad	(Israeli) Central Institute for Intelligence and Security
MR-8	*Movimento Revolucionario do Outubre 8* (Revolutionary Movement of 8 October)
NATO	North Atlantic Treaty Organisation
NSD	National Security Directive
OAS	Organisation of American States
OECD	Organisation for Economic Cooperation and Development
ONA	Office of National Assessments
OPEC	Organisation of Petroleum Exporting Countries
OPM	*Organisasi Papua Merdeka* (Free Papua Movement)
PDRY	Peoples Democratic Republic of Yemen (South Yemen)
PFLP	Popular Front for the Liberation of Palestine
PLO	Palestine Liberation Organisation
PSCC	Protective Services Coordination Centre
PSR	Protective Security Review: Report
RAF	*Rote Armee Fraktion* (Red Army Faction)
RCIS	Royal Commission on Intelligence and Security
ROK	Republic of Korea (South Korea)
SAC-PAV	Standing Advisory Committee for Commonwealth–State Cooperation on Protection Against Violence
SASR	Special Air Service Regiment

SIDC-PAV	Special Inter-Departmental Committee on Protection Against Violence
SRV	Socialist Republic of Vietnam
SWAPO	South West Africa People's Organisation
TAG	Tactical Assault Group
UDBa	*Uprava Drzavne Bezbednosti* (Yugoslav State Security Service)
UHNj	*Ujedinjeni Hrvati Njemaske* (United Croats of West Germany)
UHRO	*Ustasa Hrvatska Revolucionarna Organizacija* (Rebel Croat Revolutionary Organisation)
UK	United Kingdom
UKUSA	United Kingdom-United States (Security) Agreement
UN	United Nations
UNGA	United Nations General Assembly
UPRF	Universal Proutist Revolutionary Federation
URA	United Red Army (*Rengo Sekigun*)
US	United States (of America)
USSR	Union of Soviet Socialist Republics
WPC	Woman Police Constable

FOREWORD

A diplomat is a guest in the country to which he is accredited, even if he represents the strongest government in the world. An embassy staff from the USA or the USSR is totally at the mercy of the host government, even if that government controls a population of under a million and an army of a few thousand.

For this reason, diplomats have generally been regarded as inviolable, and this convention has existed since Roman times. A government which harms or incarcerates a diplomat is rightly regarded with as much revulsion as a family which hurts or kidnaps the child of a neighbour whom it has invited into its care. By common consent 144 countries — almost all the civilised world — are parties to the Vienna Convention of 1961 which spells out the rules for diplomatic immunity.

Perhaps the most flagrant breach of this Convention in history was by the Khomeini Government which condoned the seizure of the US Embassy in Tehran in November 1979, and the holding of 50 of its staff as hostages for over a year. Though the seizure was not ordered by Khomeini, he at once threw the full weight of his police and army behind the organised mob which did it. When his Prime Minister urged that the Embassy staff be released he was summarily dismissed. Ironically, while these diplomatic hostages were still held, the British Government, at Khomeini's request, used soldiers to release the Iranian Embassy staff in London when they were seized by anti-Khomeini terrorists in April 1980.

Almost as flagrant as Khomeini's action was the murder of a British policewoman in London in April 1984 by members of the Libyan Embassy (or 'People's Bureau' as Colonel Qaddafi chose to call it), who were firing from their windows at a crowd of anti-Qaddafi Libyans demonstrating on the street outside. It was again ironical that the British policewoman was one of those protecting Qaddafi's Embassy by keeping the demonstrators on the far side of the street.

The weapons fired from the Libyan Embassy windows were undoubtedly smuggled into London in Libyan diplomatic bags — and out again, with the murderers under diplomatic immunity, after the event. The weapons used to seize the Iranian Embassy in London four years earlier were almost certainly smuggled in similarly in an Iraqi diplomatic bag. In both these cases (and in many other assassinations of Libyans by Libyans in London) their weapons were used in operations carried out, or organised, by officials of the countries concerned. In other cases, weapons and explosive devices were smuggled in by diplomatic couriers to give clandestine support to terrorist movements aiming to destabilise the host country or to fight their own battles with rival Middle Eastern movements on the host country's streets. Syria and Iran, and, again, Iraq and Libya, have been the worst offenders.

It has been suggested that this might be overcome by amending the Vienna Convention to allow the host country to subject diplomatic bags to external search using X-rays or vapour detectors. If such a search were to reveal anything suspicious (eg a metal box which might conceal a gun, or traces of explosive vapour), the customs officials conducting the search could require that the package be opened in the presence of two neutral diplomatic witnesses, one selected by the host country and the other by the parent country owning the bag. These witnesses would ensure that the subsequent search of the contents did not abuse diplomatic privilege (eg by perusal or removal of papers). If, however, the courier refused to agree to the bag being opened at all, then both he and the bag could be returned to the parent country or to its embassy, at the discretion of the host country.

Unfortunately, the countries most likely to abuse their diplomatic immunity would be the least likely to agree to such an amendment to the Convention. Alternatively, if forced to agree to such measures as a condition of retaining diplomatic relations, they would probably take advantage of their reciprocal powers to inflict the maximum of harassment and delay on the movement of diplomats from countries which do respect the Convention, and on their couriers carrying diplomatic bags. Countries like Australia, Canada, Japan, UK, USA, USSR and West Germany conduct a great deal of international commercial, diplomatic and cultural activity all over the world, and they would suffer far more than countries like Libya and Syria from such procedures.

Ultimately the only effective response to governments which abuse the privileges accorded to their diplomats or countries which fail to protect foreign diplomats who are their guests is to withdraw the privileges from offending individuals (making them *persona non grata*) or to terminate diplomatic relations altogether, but this may involve a heavy price for the countries most involved on the international scene.

Most of the attacks on diplomats in the last 20 years, however, have been by independent terrorist movements, albeit sometimes sponsored or supported by foreign governments. In 1968–73, some 50 diplomats were kidnapped in Latin America, and taken to secret hideouts, from which threats to kill them were used as political blackmail to get the parent country to apply pressure on the host country to release other terrorists named by the kidnappers. Some ambassadors and other diplomats were murdered, but by 1973 the staunchness of governments and the heroism of a number of the hostages — notably Geoffrey Jackson, the British ambassador kidnapped in Uruguay in 1971 — had convinced terrorists that this technique was no longer achieving their aims. They then turned to the seizure of embassies, with staffs held as hostages inside (as in Tehran and London in 1979–80), either to extort political concessions or obtain publicity. These seizures reached a peak in the three years 1979, 1980 and 1981, with 102 seizures in all — 46 of them in Latin America, 35 in Europe and 21 elsewhere — and 32 of the hostages were ambassadors. These also, however, generally failed to achieve their objectives (largely because, being surrounded in a known location, the terrorists held few cards) and have been attempted far less often since 1981.

Since then, the focus has shifted to the Middle East, or to Middle East-based terrorist groups. In Lebanon and Kuwait terrorists sponsored by Iran have carried out a number of horrific bombings, assassinations and kidnappings of diplomats and others. Yugoslav and Armenian terrorists have also murdered, or attempted to murder, diplomats and consular staff all over the world, including Australia, in order to apply coercion, or to induce host governments to apply coercion, on the governments of Yugoslavia and Turkey respectively.

All of these cases and many others are examined fully in this book, which provides the clearest and most comprehensive analysis of the subject I have seen; in fact, I know of nothing comparable that has ever been published. C. E. Baumann's *The Diplomatic Kidnappings* (1973) is now fifteen years old and, as I indicated earlier, the techniques of 1968–73 have long since been superceded by others. This book badly needed writing and Andrew Selth was the man to do it. I have kept in touch with him both in Australia and the UK, during the years in which he has been researching and writing it, and I have been enormously impressed by his grasp of the subject. This results from his amalgam of fourteen years' practical experience in Australia and overseas in the Department of Foreign Affairs with exhaustive academic research before, during and after it.

Australia, as he records in his Appendix E, has had more than its share of attacks on diplomatic targets, and as the country continues to expand its international activities and influence, these are likely to increase. His book should become a classic, not only in Australia but all over the world where these most pernicious forms of terrorism are used. The threat is shared by East and West, whose diplomats are equally vulnerable, as has recently been shown in Lebanon. A practical, analytical and constructive book like this should appeal strongly to the new regime in the Soviet Union, and it could have a useful by-product in developing the growing cooperation and common ground across the rapidly eroding Iron Curtain. This may, in the end, be one of its greatest contributions to reducing and controlling international conflict in the world.

Richard Clutterbuck
Exeter, 1 January 1988

INTRODUCTION

The proper study of terrorism should seek to explain a phenomenon, not justify it. And it must be realised by all that explanation does not entail justification.

Grant Wardlaw
Political Terrorism
(1982)

TERRORISM STUDIES

Over the past twenty years, terrorism and counter-terrorism have become subjects for analysis and academic debate in much the same way that guerrilla warfare and counter-insurgency caught the interest of scholars and commentators in the 1950s and 1960s. In 1968 the *New York Times Index* did not even include a subject heading for terrorism, yet by the end of 1976 the United States Central Intelligence Agency (CIA) could compile a bibliography which cited 1277 books and articles on the subject.[1] Only four years later, Edward Mickolus published another bibliography on *The Literature of Terrorism* which listed nearly 4000 entries, including a further twenty-one bibliographies and study guides.[2] By a more recent count, the number of references now exceeds 5600.[3] As the Australian scholar Geoffrey Fairbairn once wrote, the number of written works on international terrorism seems to be in danger of outstripping the number of its victims.[4]

The subject has now been approached from almost every conceivable angle. Some authors have looked at modern terrorism from a historical perspective, while others have concentrated on the sociological and behavioural aspects of the problem. Studies have been made of terrorist organisations, terrorist personalities, terrorist tactics and specific terrorist incidents. There are books and articles on the state sponsorship of terrorist groups, the implications of terrorist acts for domestic and international law, and the impact of these developments on the international political and economic system. Others have examined the challenges posed by terrorism to liberal democratic states and the difficulties of implementing effective counter-measures. Most of these works mention the specific problem of terrorist attacks on diplomats and diplomatic facilities as part of their overall treatment of the subject, but very few examine it in any detail. Even those studies which concentrate on related aspects of international terrorism have tended to treat the terrorist threat to diplomacy only in passing.

The scant attention paid to this particular facet of the terrorist problem is not due to an underestimation of its seriousness. Rather, it is because terrorist attacks on diplomats and diplomatic facilities are usually viewed as part of a global problem and rarely as a discrete subject worthy of examination in its own right. It is not a phenomenon which has been confined to one geographical area or to one political system. While some terrorists, like Armenian and Croatian separatists, have long considered diplomatic targets a high priority, no contemporary terrorist groups have attacked exclusively diplomatic personnel or premises. Nor has any state suffered only this kind of threat. C. Edler Baumann's pioneering study of *The Diplomatic Kidnappings* usefully included an examination of the wider implications of that particular terrorist tactic, but his survey has now been overtaken by events. Baumann did not deal with other kinds of terrorist attacks against diplomats and diplomatic facilities, nor did he foresee the dimensions that this problem would assume after 1973.[5] In the relatively few cases where the terrorist threat to diplomacy has been the subject of close analysis since then, scholars have tended to concentrate on certain specialised aspects of the problem, such as the role of international law in the protection of diplomatic agents.

As might be expected, greater attention has been paid to this problem by governments, the diplomatic services of which have been placed at risk. With its diplomats and diplomatic facilities among the most favoured targets for terrorist attack, the United States Government, primarily through the State Department and CIA, has for a number of years now made efforts to study this aspect of the international terrorist problem and devise appropriate counter-measures. In the ten years between 1975 and 1985 spending on State Department security increased more than twenty-fold, from US$22.6 million to US$497.3 million.[6] In September 1986, after a comprehensive review by a special Advisory Panel, the State Department announced a proposal for a five-year, US$5.5 billion program to overhaul security at US missions overseas.[7] Congress has even called for the issue of diplomatic security to be raised 'to as important a level as diplomacy itself'.[8] As the number of diplomatic services affected by terrorist attacks has grown and as this particular problem has attracted greater attention in international fora, so other governments have begun to consider the safety of diplomats and diplomatic missions more seriously. Academic interest in this subject is also growing but to date few scholars appear to have published their thoughts on the matter.

THE THREAT TO DIPLOMACY

For a number of reasons, the lack of scholarly attention being paid to the threat faced by diplomats is very surprising. Since the problem of international terrorism assumed significant proportions in the late 1960s, attacks on diplomats and diplomatic facilities have been steadily growing, to the point that they now constitute over forty per cent of all international terrorist incidents for the period.[9] According to the State Department, the diplomats of at least 113 countries have either been attacked or threatened with attack since 1968, by the terrorists of more than 100 groups in some 130 countries.[10] As new terrorist groups emerge many are singling out diplomats and diplomatic missions as prime targets. There is clear evidence too that a number of states like Libya, Syria and Iran support these practices and have themselves resorted to terrorism of this kind as a form of 'coercive diplomacy'. One noted British scholar in this field has even suggested that 'the profession of diplomat must now rank as one of the most dangerous in the world'.[11]

As states have resorted to terrorist methods, either directly or through surrogates, there has been growing evidence of the systematic abuse of established diplomatic conventions. While increasingly the 'objects' of terrorism, diplomats (or other officials claiming that status) have also been the 'subjects' of terrorism, by actively assisting or participating in terrorist attacks themselves. Diplomatic bags and diplomatic passports have been used to evade the protective security arrangements of target countries and diplomatic facilities have been used to support terrorist operations. The 1984 shooting of a Woman Police Constable from the Libyan People's Bureau in London starkly revealed the extent to which some governments were prepared to flout international law and manipulate diplomatic conventions in order to pursue such violent policies. Diplomacy has never been pure, nor is ever likely to be, but the abuses seen over the past thirty years mark a significant departure from the practices established over preceding generations and are an important factor in the spread of international terrorism.

Inevitably, terrorist attacks on diplomats and the increasing use of terrorism by states as an instrument of their foreign policies have had profound effects on the conduct of diplomacy and, many would argue, international relations in general. As early as 1970 the Chairman of the US House of Representatives Subcommittee on Inter-American Affairs was warning that 'unless something is done to remedy this situation, international relations may come to be dictated by the whims and self-designated necessities of guerrillas, terrorists and other extreme radical elements.'[12] As demonstrated by events in April 1986, terrorism has been pushed to the forefront of global politics and now figures prominently on the agenda of the world's major negotiating groups. At the same time, diplomatic action seems increasingly to be set aside by some governments in favour of military responses to terrorists and their state sponsors. This has implications for the international order at least as great as terrorism itself.

Consideration of this problem at an international level is greatly complicated by the fact that 'at base, terrorism is a moral problem'[13] and, naturally enough, provokes such emotional reactions. What may be considered justifiable violence by one state can be seen as illegitimate by another, hence the ubiquity of the phrase 'one man's terrorist is another man's freedom fighter'. Differences persist despite the fact, or perhaps even because of the fact, that at various times throughout history most states could be accused of terrorism of one kind or another. It is one of the ironies of international debate on the nature of terrorism that the actions of many states could still be included in their own proposed definitions of the problem. Because assessments of terrorism are usually so subjective, argument has tended to revolve around ideological positions and emotional judgements rather than objective political analysis. Yet wide agreement has been reached regarding terrorist attacks on diplomats and diplomatic facilities, suggesting that in this area at least some further progress might be possible. In addition, the rare international consensus on this particular aspect of the terrorist problem lends weight to the claim that it is worth closer examination.

To date, Australia has remained relatively free from international terrorist violence, yet a number of events in recent years has demonstrated that no country is immune from this problem. Almost half of those attacks which have occurred in Australia have been directed at foreign representatives or their facilities, and much of the risk of another international terrorist incident attaches to the presence in the country of a sizeable diplomatic community. In addition, Australia is now playing an active and sometimes prominent role in international affairs and fields a significant diplomatic presence in nearly eighty countries. Should it ever fall under threat from terrorist attack its officials and official premises abroad would immediately become prime targets. In these circumstances, there would appear to be good arguments for a closer study of Australia's foreign policy approach to international terrorist issues and the threat faced by its diplomats and diplomatic facilities abroad. These subjects, however, have been as much neglected by officials and scholars in Australia as elsewhere and an examination of the issues involved is long overdue.

The following study is intended to help fill these needs. Before it can proceed, however, some comments must be made on the question of methodology, in particular the sources and terms used.

SOURCES AND DEFINITIONS

As noted above, there is now a vast literature on the subject of terrorism, some of it very good, some of it not. Much is highly speculative and asks the reader to take a great deal on trust. Yet many of those works produced to date are weighted to represent a particular ideological perspective and are often more informative about the author than about terrorism *per se*. Given the nature of the subject and the dearth of reliable information on certain aspects of the terrorist problem this is perhaps not surprising, but it means that anyone wishing to attempt an objective study of the phenomenon needs to exercise considerable care in approaching their sources — both official and academic. Terrorists themselves have written comparatively little and even that is often not accessible. The reliability (or otherwise) of the news media as a source of information on terrorism has been described often enough elsewhere and does not bear repetition here.

As several scholars have noted, particular problems arise in trying to quantify and evaluate trends in terrorist behaviour.[14] The major difficulty, as always, lies in determining precisely what constitutes a terrorist attack. Another relates to the unavoidable reliance of researchers on incomplete data and untested sources. While considerable efforts have been made by some collection agencies, such as the Rand Corporation and Aberdeen University, there will always be gaps in information about any clandestine activity. No figures can show the terrorist operations planned but never carried out, begun but aborted before they came to official notice, or which may have taken place in closed societies and never been publicly revealed. Even compilations made by organisations in the same country and with access to many of the same sources, like those of the State Department and CIA, differ markedly in some crucial areas. Figures can in any case provide only part of the picture, as terrorist attacks must ultimately be judged in terms of their effects.

The definition of terrorism has long been a subject of considerable controversy and since 1936 more than one hundred formal attempts have been made by politicians, officials and scholars to devise a form of words that could be universally accepted.[15] To date it has proven impossible to satisfy fully the demands of either politics or scholarship but for practical reasons some working definition is necessary. While still open to argument, a useful starting point for the purposes of this study is that suggested by Grant Wardlaw of the Australian Institute of Criminology:

> political terrorism is the use, or threat of use, of violence by an individual or group, whether acting for or in opposition to established authority, when such

action is designed to create extreme anxiety and/or fear-inducing effects in a target group larger than the immediate victims with the purpose of coercing that group into acceding to the political demands of the perpetrators.[16]

Political terrorism so defined can be divided into four broad categories, depending on its location, its intended victims and those carrying it out: domestic, state, international and state-sponsored terrorism. Some examples can fit into more than one category.

'Domestic terrorism' includes actions initiated by groups or individuals within a state against members or institutions of the same state, such as attacks by Sikh separatists against Hindus in the Punjab, the kidnapping of West German industrialists by the Red Army Faction (RAF) in the Federal Republic of Germany (FRG) or the murder of Italian political figures by the Red Brigades in Rome. Since it became a weapon to be used in international debates, the term 'state terrorism' has often been distorted, but in an academic context it can be taken to mean that 'enforcement terror'[17] employed by totalitarian states and certain kinds of authoritarian governments (already in control of the ordinary institutions of power) to maintain their positions. State terrorism was evident in Brazil after the 1964 coup, Argentina under the Generals and Nicaragua under the Somoza regime. Examples are still plentiful, in Latin America and elsewhere.

Most acts of terrorism have international repercussions of some kind, but the term 'international terrorism' is generally used to describe terrorism conducted with the support of a foreign government or organisation, directed at foreign nationals, institutions or governments, or which in other ways directly transcends national boundaries.[18] All terrorist attacks on diplomats and diplomatic facilities thus by definition constitute examples of international terrorism. One form of international terrorism of rapidly growing importance in the 1980s is 'state-sponsored terrorism', by which is meant either the direct use of terrorist tactics by agents of a state or the employment of more or less independent terrorist groups by a state to pursue its foreign policy aims beyond the bounds of accepted international behaviour. The assignment of a North Korean Army team to assassinate South Korean President Chun Doo Hwan and his retinue in Rangoon in 1983 could be described as an example of state-sponsored terrorism, as could the bombing of the Greenpeace vessel *Rainbow Warrior* by French agents in Auckland in 1985. The assistance given to various terrorist groups by states like Libya, Syria and Iran also falls into this category.

A distinction also needs to be made between the terrorism of governments and that used by political extremists and revolutionary groups. This study includes a brief examination of the (usually clandestine) involvement of states in international terrorism, but is not concerned with 'regimes of terror'.[19] It does not look at the calculated use of terror by states in overt military conflicts such as World War II or the Vietnam War, nor considers at any length the 'balance of terror' which currently governs the nuclear confrontation between the superpowers. Rather, this book concentrates on 'agitational terror'[20] against states and international institutions. In the terms of Noam Chomsky and E. S. Herman's provocative analysis, it is a study not of 'wholesale violence' to maintain order and security, but 'retail violence' to precipitate political and social change.[21]

There have also been numerous attempts to define diplomacy, though with far less controversy. For this book I have relied in the first instance on the definition coined by Hedley Bull in *The Anarchical Society*. To Bull, diplomacy is:

> the conduct of relations between states and other entities with standing in world politics by official agents and by peaceful means.[22]

This definition subsumes the more traditional and now outdated explanations of diplomacy offered by commentators like Sir Ernest Satow and Sir Harold Nicolson. It does not, however, include certain forms of state policy described as 'diplomacy' by scholars like Raymond Aron, Thomas Schelling and Michael Stohl, and which are essential to a discussion of international terrorism. To them 'diplomacy is bargaining'[23] and the terms of the exchange are set by the power of the parties involved. This view of interstate relations is touched upon in Chapter Three.

As Bull and others have pointed out, not everyone engaged in diplomacy is a diplomat.[24] For the purposes of this study, however, the term is taken to include all members of diplomatic and consular posts who enjoy formal, privileged status. It also includes government officials on special diplomatic missions or attached to recognised international organisations. This use of the term in some respects exceeds the scope of various international agreements governing such matters as diplomatic privileges and immunities, and excludes certain other internationally protected persons, but realistically includes all members of the Diplomatic Establishment who are likely to become targets for terrorist attack through virtue of their official positions. It also recognises that since 1945 diplomatic status has been accorded to a wide range of officials and support staff attached to diplomatic and consular missions and international organisations, whether or not they were professional diplomats. Honorary office holders, while occasionally the victims of terrorists, have been excluded from this category.

Following from this broad definition of 'diplomat', the term 'diplomatic facility' has been adopted to cover not only formal diplomatic premises such as embassies and high commissions, but also consulates and consulates-general. At times, where specified in the text, it has also been used to describe such facilities as information offices and cultural centres, where these are recognised extensions of a government's official representation in another country.

NOTES

1. *Annotated Bibliography on Transnational and International Terrorism* (Central Intelligence Agency, Langley, 1976)
2. Edward Mickolus, *The Literature of Terrorism: A Selectively Annotated Bibliography* (Greenwood Press, Westport, 1980)
3. See Amos Lakos, *International Terrorism: A Bibliography* (Westview Press, Boulder, 1986)
4. Geoffrey Fairbairn, 'Terrorism and Defence', *World Review* 18:1 (April 1979), p. 52
5. C. E. Baumann, *The Diplomatic Kidnappings: A Revolutionary Tactic of Urban Terrorism* (Martinus Nijhoff, The Hague, 1973)
6. 'US Embassies Try to Maintain Open Society in Tight Security', *International Herald Tribune*, 2 April 1985. See also Frank Perez, 'Terrorist Target: The Diplomat', Address by Frank Perez, Deputy Director of the Office for Combatting Terrorism, before the conference on terrorism sponsored by the Instituto de Cuestiones Internationales, Madrid, 10 June 1982, *Current Policy* 402 (10 June 1982).
7. 'Chronology: Terrorism', *Foreign Affairs* 64:3 (1986), p. 647. This program included measures against espionage but was primarily to counter the increased terrorist threat.
8. 'Diplomatic Security', *Hearings* before the Committee on Foreign Affairs, US House of Representatives, Ninety-ninth Congress, First Session, 16 and 24 July 1985
9. *Terrorist Incidents Involving Diplomats: A Statistical Overview of International Terrorist Incidents Involving Diplomatic Personnel and Facilities from January 1968 through April 1983* (State Department, Washington, 1983), p.1 and B. M. Jenkins, *New Modes of Conflict*, Rand Report R-3009-DNA (Rand Corporation, Santa Monica, 1983), p.14. In 1984 the State Department estimated that terrorist attacks on diplomats between 1979-1983 constituted some 43 per cent of all international terrorist attacks for the period. See *Patterns of Global Terrorism: 1983* (State Department, Washington, 1984), p.5.
10. *Terrorist Incidents Involving Diplomats*, p.3 and p.5.
11. Paul Wilkinson, 'After Tehran', *Conflict Quarterly* (Spring 1981), p.5.
12. 'Safety of US Diplomats', *Hearings* before the Subcommittee on Inter-American Affairs of the Committee on Foreign Affairs, US House of Representatives, Ninety-first Congress, Second Session, 27 April 1970.
13. Grant Wardlaw, *Political Terrorism: theory, tactics and counter measures* (Cambridge University Press, Cambridge, 1982), p.4.
14. See for example Wardlaw, *Political Terrorism*, pp.50-53.
15. According to one survey, 109 formal definitions of terrorism were offered between 1936–1981. See A. P. Schmid, *Political Terrorism: A Research Guide* (Transaction, New Brunswick, 1984), pp. 119–152.
16. Wardlaw, *Political Terrorism*, p. 16
17. This term was devised by T. P. Thornton, 'Terror as a Weapon of Political Agitation', in H. Eckstein (ed), *Internal War: Problems and Approaches* (Collier-Macmillan, London, 1964), p. 72
18. This definition is drawn from *Terrorist Incidents Involving Diplomats*. It has been expanded, however, to include attacks by terrorists upon nationals or institutions of their own state where these occur in a third country, for example attacks by the Provisional Irish Republican Army (IRA), based in Northern Ireland, against British diplomats and diplomatic facilities abroad.
19. The term comes from E. V. Walter, *Terror and Resistance: A Study of Political Violence* (Oxford University Press, New York, 1969), p. 7
20. Thornton, p. 72. Walter speaks of 'sieges of terror' to describe this kind of terrorist violence. Walter, p. 7

21. Noam Chomsky and E. S. Herman, *The Washington Connection and Third World Fascism* (Vol. 1 of *The Political Economy of Human Rights*) (Hale and Iremonger, Sydney, 1980), pp. 85–95

22. Hedley Bull, *The Anarchical Society: A Study of Order in World Politics* (Macmillan, London, 1983), p. 162

23. T. C. Schelling, *Arms and Influence* (Yale University Press, New Haven, 1966), p. 1

24. Bull, *The Anarchical Society*, pp. 162–167. See also Alan James, 'Diplomacy and International Society', *International Relations* 6:6 (November 1980), pp. 934–935. While the word 'diplomat' was long held to be a solecism, it is now the standard form in the United States and is sufficiently common elsewhere to be preferred to the older word 'diplomatist'.

PART ONE

The Terrorist Threat to Diplomacy

1

DIPLOMACY AND TERRORISM

Violence and war try to settle in a short time, and by a sudden dissipation of energy, difficulties that ought to be dealt with by the subtlest analysis and the most delicate tests—for the object is to reach a state of unforced equilibrium.

Paul Valery
History and Politics (1931)

Diplomacy and terrorism share a number of parallels. Both have their roots in the ancient past and both have developed in response to changes in the international environment. 'The purpose of each is to persuade and prevail, and *both rely heavily on symbolism*'.[1] Yet here the similarity ends. Diplomacy has developed as an organised tool of states within a recognised international system, while terrorism has traditionally been used by disparate non-state actors against established authority. Diplomacy attempts to manage political and socio-economic change through compromise and peaceful negotiation, where terrorism seeks radical change by violent means. Diplomacy has been directed towards adjustment and conciliation, goals largely incompatible with ideology, yet terrorism invariably springs from a strong ideological base rarely sympathetic to such an approach.[2] Diplomatic negotiations have never been far from considerations of power but traditionally diplomacy and terrorism have been found at opposite ends of the political spectrum.

Throughout history, diplomats have been granted special protection from violence and despite a number of isolated incidents the worlds of terrorism and diplomacy have tended to remain poles apart. This situation, however, is now changing. Since the late 1960s, diplomats and diplomatic facilities the world over have become popular targets for terrorist attack and terrorism is now a major topic for discussion on the agenda of international negotiating groups. With the increasing use by some states of agitational terror as an instrument of foreign policy the traditional divisions between diplomacy

3

and terrorism are becoming blurred and the conduct of international relations more dangerous and uncertain. In order fully to appreciate the changes which have taken place and the impact of terrorist attacks on diplomatic targets it is necessary first to consider the development of both diplomacy and international terrorism from an historical perspective.

THE DEVELOPMENT OF DIPLOMACY

As C. Edler Baumann has pointed out, terrorist attacks on diplomats and diplomatic facilities, while a relatively new phenomenon, base their effectiveness on a number of old and very simple realities.[3] Relations of some kind have always been considered necessary between states and have always been conducted through some means of political intercourse. This has required official intermediaries whose status and behaviour have been subject to agreement between the parties involved. Indeed, diplomatic agents are probably the world's oldest international institution and the codes regarding their protection and conduct by custom antedate all other rules of international law.[4] Examples of formal diplomatic exchanges can be found as long ago as 3000 B.C. and the concept of resident envoys was discussed as early as 1380 B.C.. There were a number of precedents in the days of the Greek city states but the evolution of permanent diplomatic missions was a slow process. It was the second half of the 15th century before accredited resident envoys began to make their regular appearance in Renaissance Italy.

Pressures associated with the Italian Wars after 1494, the expansion of trade and the ferment of the Reformation all encouraged the adoption of resident diplomacy. By the 16th century the practice had begun to spread throughout Europe and in some cases the right to maintain permanent legations was the subject of formal treaties. It was not until the Peace of Westphalia in 1648, however, and the evolution of a society of independent sovereign states, that the establishment of embassies or legations became common practice. Even then permanent diplomatic missions were resisted by some influential rulers but, as Sen has observed, the French Revolution, the wars that followed and the demands of the industrial revolution all effectively ended the isolation of independent states.[5] With the resulting multiplication of contacts came changes in the methods and characteristics of diplomacy but eventually it emerged as 'an organising institution, bearing its own distinctive styles and manners, and its own networks and procedures, rules, treaties and other commitments'.[6]

Although the first records of diplomatic activity were to be found outside Europe, resident diplomacy seems never to have developed there. Hebrew, Islamic and Asian rulers all had diplomatic relations with other states and in some regions there developed comprehensive systems of diplomatic rules and procedures. These contacts, however, were conducted largely through envoys sent abroad on short term missions for specific political, commercial, social or religious purposes. The evolving European system was in many ways alien to these other civilisations but as the Western states encroached ever more insistently on their interests (and territories) these other powers found acceptance of European conventions of diplomatic intercourse increasingly difficult to resist. By 1900 Western international law and customs, and as a corollary resident diplomacy, extended throughout the world.

The collapse of the colonial empires after 1945, the emergence of over 80 new states and the proliferation of international organisations all brought pressures for a reconsideration of some of these practices. Many new states in particular viewed with suspicion a system which stemmed primarily from European culture and traditions and in the development of which they had played no part. To the more radical states this was the same system which had permitted the spread of European colonialism and which still worked to prevent the Third World from sharing the power and resources to which they felt all states were entitled.[7] Yet, to a surprising extent, states of all geographical regions, political colours, cultures and stages of development were willing more or less to embrace what Hedley Bull has called 'the often strange and archaic diplomatic procedures that arose in Europe in another age'.[8] The new states have placed considerable reliance on the diplomatic system as an agency through which to achieve quite fundamental changes and calls for amendments to the system itself have almost without exception been made in its own idiom. These calls have not always been received sympathetically by the older states but despite this 'the contemporary global system is gradually evolving new rules and conventions to replace those of its more purely European predecessor'.[9]

DIPLOMATIC INVIOLABILITY

One convention which has always had universal application and is unlikely markedly to change is that regarding the personal inviolability of diplomatic agents. As early as the first century B.C. Cicero could write that:

> the inviolability of ambassadors is protected by divine and human law; they are sacred and respected so as to be inviolable not only when in an allied country but also whenever they happen to be in the forces of the enemy.[10]

As resident diplomacy spread, so the principle of diplomatic inviolability and certain associated immunities also developed. Prompted initially by the fact that the diplomat represented the person of his sovereign, the justification for these privileges soon came to be accepted as one of functional necessity. In 1625 Grotius confidently stated that:

> There are two maxims in the law of nations relating to ambassadors which
> are generally accepted as established rules: the first is that ambassadors must
> be received and the second is that they must suffer no harm.[11]

These fundamental laws and the special duties of protection owed by
receiving states were expressed in the norms of diplomatic reciprocity which
emerged from the Peace of Westphalia and were soon strengthened by
municipal laws in code and practice. Most of the privileges found today
were in existence in some form by 1720. They were further refined at the
Congress of Vienna in 1815, when an attempt was made to resolve the
prevailing confusion over precedence, consistent with the nominal equality
of states. The regulations and codes of behaviour established then soon
became universal and many remain in force today.

International developments did not prompt another major effort to codify
the rights and privileges of diplomatic agents until 1928, when the Sixth
International Conference of American States met in Havana to consider
draft conventions on diplomatic and consular officers. The drafts also
specified the position of personnel representing international organisations
like the newly-formed League of Nations and reaffirmed the principle of
non-interference by diplomats in the affairs of receiving states. Although
agreement was reached on the two Havana Conventions, consideration of
the matters included in them was felt to be incomplete. The new Pan-
American Convention on Diplomatic Officers, for example, described itself
as an interim instrument 'until a more complete regulation of the rights
and duties of diplomatic officers can be formulated'.[12] As a consequence,
the International Law Commission (ILC) at its first meeting in 1949 selected
diplomatic intercourse and immunities as a subject for early attention.
Between 1954 and 1959 draft Articles were produced, governments were
invited to offer their views and a detailed commentary was prepared. This
work by the ILC culminated in the United Nations Conference on Diplomatic
Intercourse and Immunities held in Vienna in 1961. Attended by the representatives of 81 countries (including 24 created since 1945), the Conference
agreed upon a comprehensive multilateral convention which 'codified and
restated the law with regard to the status of the diplomat and all members
of his staff'.[13]

For the purposes of this study, three Articles of the Vienna Convention
on Diplomatic Relations are particularly important. Article 22 states, in
part:

> 1. The premises of the mission shall be inviolable. The agents of the receiving
> State may not enter them, except with the consent of the head of mission.
> 2. The receiving State is under a special duty to take all appropriate steps to
> protect the premises of the mission against any intrusion or damage and to
> prevent any disturbance of the peace of the mission or impairment of its dignity.[14]

Article 29 of the Convention extends this fundamental principle to diplomatic agents themselves:

> The person of the diplomatic agent shall be inviolable. He shall not be liable to any form of arrest or detention. The receiving State shall treat him with due respect and shall take all appropriate steps to prevent any attack on his person, freedom or dignity.[15]

This Article was considered to be completely in accordance with the accepted principles of international law and practice and was adopted without amendment from the draft Articles prepared by the ILC.[16] In addition, it had long been an accepted principle of international law that for the proper discharge of their duties, and hence as a necessary incident of the right of legation, envoys should be entitled to correspond freely and secretly with their governments.[17] This principle was endorsed and strengthened by the Vienna Convention, Article 27 of which provides in part that:

> 1. The receiving State shall permit and protect free communications on the part of the mission for official purposes...
> 2. The official correspondence of the mission shall be inviolable...
> 3. The diplomatic bag shall not be opened or detained.[18]

It also stipulated that:

> 4. ...the diplomatic bag...may contain only diplomatic documents or articles intended for official use.[19]

The Convention entered into force on 24 April 1964 with 63 signatures and, with 144 states now party to it, has become universal practice. Even the few states that are not parties to the Convention are regarded as subject to its rules, since they generally reflect customary law.

The Vienna Convention on Diplomatic Relations was followed in 1963 by a similar Convention on Consular Relations. Under this instrument consular posts were accorded broadly the same measure of inviolability of premises, archives and communications as diplomatic missions. There were, however, two significant exceptions to this rule which limited the inviolability of consular premises in special circumstances, such as an emergency requiring immediate access by the receiving state.[20] Career consular officers also enjoy a slightly more limited measure of inviolability than diplomatic agents. The Convention came into force on 19 March 1967 but, as Poulantzas has observed, there is a growing tendency today for states to entrust their diplomatic representatives with their consular services. As a result, the differences in treatment given to diplomatic envoys and consular officers is gradually diminishing.[21]

Although disagreement over the scope of the proposed convention restricted the Vienna Conference to an examination of formal interstate relations, the 1961 Diplomatic Convention and its companion on Consular

Relations were soon followed by other agreements, such as the 1969 Convention on Special Missions and 1975 Vienna Convention on the Representation of States in their Relations with International Organisations of a Universal Character. These instruments extended broadly similar privileges and rights of protection to members of other kinds of diplomatic groups.[22] The agreements were still open to different interpretations according to the historical traditions and political outlook of states but they 'raised the codification, if not the actual protection, of the personal inviolability of diplomats to a new level of international validity'.[23] It was widely recognised that in times of heightened international competition and growing functional interdependence diplomacy was likely to assume an increasingly important role. This role could only be fulfilled if there was universal agreement about the conditions under which state representatives could work. It is thus ironic that, within only a few years of the most complete exposition of these time-honoured rules and practices, there should be an unprecedented succession of attacks on diplomats, and seizures and bombings of diplomatic facilities.

THE RISE OF TERRORISM

Although terrorism does not enjoy quite the same historical credentials as diplomacy, it is still an ancient practice which has held a firm position in the political calculus within and between states throughout recorded history. Scholars searching for early examples of organised terror have identified antecedents to modern groups in the *sicarii*, a religious sect active in the Zealot struggle against the Romans in Palestine between 66-73 AD, and the *hashshashun*, or Assassins, an Ismaili Muslim sect which between the 11th and 13th centuries sent agents on missions throughout the Islamic world.[24] Because of the nature of totalitarian governments since antiquity the origins of terror organised as a political system are difficult to determine but by wide consensus are attributed first to the French Revolution of 1789-1799, from whence the words 'terrorism' and 'terrorist' are derived.

Examples of insurgent terrorism occurred in the years that followed but the doctrine only found real expression in Russia during the second half of the 19th century, when extremists inspired by the ancient concept of justifiable tyrannicide carried out numerous attacks against representatives of the Czarist state. The *Narodnaya Volya* (or Party of the People's Will), for example, believed that:

> Terrorist activity, consisting in destroying the most harmful person in government, aims to undermine the prestige of the government and arouse in this manner the revolutionary spirit of the people and their confidence in the success of the cause.[25]

One of its more successful operations was the assassination of Czar Alexander II in 1881. Other Russian terrorist movements took this idea one stage further and sought to wear down the capacities and resolve of the Government by a prolonged series of attacks on officials and property:

> The terrorist cannot overthrow the government, cannot drive it from St. Petersburg and Russia, but having compelled it for so many years to do nothing but struggle with them, by forcing it to do so still for years and years, they will render its position untenable.[26]

These tactics were soon emulated by groups elsewhere and by the 20th century terror as an organised political tactic was being used by anarchists in France, Spain, Italy and the United States. Michael Bakunin's ill-fated International Brotherhood believed it was engaged in an international campaign of terrorist violence. More importantly, terror was adopted as a strategy by radical nationalist groups in Ireland, Macedonia, Serbia, Armenia and India. These early examples sometimes made a considerable public impact, but failed to achieve more than minor tactical successes.

From the turn of the century until the mid-1960s, terrorism was largely the preserve of nationalist separatist movements and extreme right wing groups. In Ireland between 1918 and 1921, for example, IRA leader Michael Collins in many ways anticipated the guerrilla and terrorist strategies that were to prove so effective in later struggles elsewhere. The successful campaigns against the British in Palestine between 1944 and 1948 and in Cyprus between 1955 and 1959 were also characterised by the widespread use of terrorist methods on the part of the insurgents. Like the Irish before them, the Jewish terrorists of the National Military Organisation (*Irgun Zvei Leumi*, or IZL) and the Greek Cypriots of the National Organisation of Cypriot Fighters (*Ethniki Organosis Kyprion Agoniston*, or EOKA) knew that they could not win a military victory. They agreed, however, with the approach expounded by earlier Russian radical theorists, which stressed the political and economic costs to the state of a long struggle against committed insurgents. In using such a strategy they were highly successful.[27] Other anti-colonial insurgent groups using these methods achieved similar results.

The revolutionary struggles of the period, on the other hand, were dominated by three schools of thought, none of which viewed terrorism as an effective tool for political change. While fundamentally opposed on certain key principles, both the Soviet and Chinese communists agreed that terrorism should not be accorded an important place in their political-military doctrines. The Bolsheviks were ambivalent about the use of terrorism but to Lenin and Trotsky (and orthodox Marxists still) it was considered elitist adventurism which lowered the political consciousness of the masses. Writing in 1902, for example, Lenin bitterly denounced the terrorist tactics of the Social Revolutionary Party on the grounds that they were 'nothing else than *single combat*, a method that has been wholly condemned by the experience of history'.[28] Organisational and political work was felt to be more important for the ultimate seizure of power.

The Chinese too held misgivings about the use of terrorist tactics. After the disastrous failures of the Canton and Shanghai uprisings in 1925–1927 Mao Tse-tung placed little faith in urban campaigns of any kind. He was prepared to use terrorist tactics as occasion demanded but accorded them a specific, limited, role:

> To put it bluntly, it is necessary to create terror for a while in every rural area, or otherwise it would be impossible to suppress the activities of the counter revolutionaries in the countryside or overthrow the authority of the gentry.[29]

Mao recognised, however, that such tactics could alienate the population and thus prove counter-productive. He placed greatest emphasis on building mass support under the leadership of the party and, in contrast to the Bolsheviks, saw victory arising from a 'protracted war' conducted by guerrilla armies in the countryside.[30] This strategy subsequently enjoyed some authority (and success) with insurgents in the developing countries of Asia and Africa, but after 1959 was displaced in Latin America by the Cuban model of revolution.

Like that of the Chinese, the Cuban model emphasised the primacy of the struggle in the rural areas. Fidel Castro believed that 'the city is a cemetery of revolutionaries and resources'[31] and stressed the development of a rural power base before the 'descent to the city'.[32] Unlike the Soviet and Chinese doctrines, however, little emphasis was given to the initial mobilisation of the population, whose support was expected to flow from the successful establishment of a guerrilla *foco*, or focus. Political considerations were made subordinate to military factors and the armed forces placed at the centre of the revolutionary struggle. According to the French theorist Regis Debray, who was widely taken to represent Castro's views at the time, 'the vanguard of the party can exist in the form of the guerrilla *foco* itself. The guerrilla force is the party in embryo'.[33] In addition, a significant role was given to violence as an act in itself and in Debray's writings at least little concern was shown to relate it to the overall direction of the political struggle. Debray seemed to feel that violent acts had a certain intrinsic value and need not be rationed to specific circumstances. This feeling was not shared by Castro's lieutenant Ernesto (Che) Guevara, however, who cautioned his fellow revolutionaries against the use of purely terrorist tactics. Guevara felt that they were of 'negative value', were liable to cause disproportionate losses and would alienate the population.[34] Yet despite Guevara's greater popular appeal, it was the philosophy of action enunciated by Debray which was to have the greatest impact on Latin American politics over the next decade, and beyond.[35]

While there is little evidence to suggest that Castro and Guevara initially planned to 'export' their revolution, the success of the Cuban guerrillas in 1959 encouraged the adoption of the *foco* theory throughout Latin America and by the early 1960s several insurgencies had erupted on the continent. It also prompted a number of isolated attacks on foreign targets, which during the preceding fifteen years had suffered relatively few such threats. Following the defeat of guerrilla bands in Guatemala, Venezuela, Peru and Colombia, however, and abortive rural uprisings in Paraguay, Ecuador and Argentina, the value of the Cuban model lay in grave doubt. With the help of radical theorists like Frantz Fanon the emphasis on violence and the primacy of the armed revolutionary over the political cadre—the so-called 'subjective will' over the 'objective conditions'—kept their force, but particularly after the failure of Guevara's own Bolivian expedition in 1967 the *foco* theory was largely discredited. In the announcement launching his new urban guerrilla movement the following year, for example, the Brazilian Carlos Marighela stated:

> We are not interested in sending armed men to a certain spot in Brazil and in waiting for other groups to spring up in other parts of the country. This would be a fatal error.[36]

The attention of Latin American revolutionaries turned increasingly to the major population centres.

With the shift in operations to the cities and industrial areas even less emphasis was given to the development of a political infrastructure and the 'mobilisation of the masses'. Attention was increasingly focussed on purely tactical factors and the 'propaganda of the deed', leading in turn to a new form of political struggle. According to Brian Jenkins of the Rand Corporation:

> Urban guerrilla warfare led almost automatically to the use of terrorist tactics. Bombings of political property and other symbolic targets, spectacular bank robberies, attacks on government officials and wealthy businessmen, political kidnappings, audaciously carried out in the heart of the enemy camp are amplified by city communications facilities. Rural guerrillas might win battles nobody would ever hear of, but dramatic acts of violence in a major city win national, perhaps international attention. It was an easy slide from kidnapping or killing local officials to killing or kidnapping foreign diplomats.[37]

Several commentators have correlated the increase in political terrorism with the fall into disrepute of the Cuban model for revolution in the late 1960s, and the consequent shift in focus to the population centres.[38] The development of this kind of political violence, however, was not confined to Latin America.

THE MODERN ERA

The crucial date for this transition is by wide agreement 1968, when 'fires spread across the world in much the same style as 1848'.[39] In a curious confluence of ideological, nihilistic, romantic and sectional passions, there arose almost at the same time in different parts of the world a number of diverse terrorist movements. In Latin America, for example, Marighela formed the National Liberating Action movement (*Açao Libertadora Nacional*, or ALN) and began a campaign of 'violence, radicalism and terrorism' in Brazil.[40] The same year the Rebel Armed Forces (*Fuerzas Armadas Rebeldes*, or FAR) in Guatemala abandoned their struggle in the countryside and began a series of terrorist attacks in the cities of that country. In Uruguay, the Tupamaros turned from occasional shootings and bank robberies to widespread bombings and kidnappings. In the Middle East, the Palestinians finally despaired of conventional military methods after the crushing defeat of the Arab armies in the 1967 Six Day War. They turned completely to guerrilla and terrorist strategies and moved the main focus of their attacks to targets outside Israel.

The 1960s were also a period of social and political turmoil in Europe and North America. While the role of the student movements of that decade have often been misrepresented, it does appear that from them emerged a number of radical, violence-prone groups which later adopted terrorist tactics. Closely following the civil disturbances in Paris in 1968, for example, and the first manifestations of Baader-Meinhof terrorism in the Federal Republic of Germany, the Angry Brigade appeared in Britain and the Weathermen began making their presence felt in the United States. The same ideological ferment and sense of frustration produced the Red Brigades (*Brigate Rosse*, or BR) in Italy. At the same time, the Basque separatists of the Freedom for the Basque Homeland movement (*Euskadi ta Aska-tasuna*, or ETA) launched their first terrorist attacks against the Spanish Government and the seeds were sown in the Irish Republican Army for the doctrinal split that produced the Provisional IRA the following year. Further afield, tensions within the Trotskyist League of Revolutionary Communists led to the emergence of the *Rengo Sekigun* (United Red Army, or URA) in Japan.[41]

Due largely to its visibility and the ease with which it can be performed, 'terrorism is a highly imitable form of political behaviour'.[42] As some terrorists, notably those in Latin America, achieved initial tactical successes, other groups were encouraged to follow and by the early 1970s the world had seen an extraordinary proliferation of terrorist organisations. Between 1968–1981, for example, more than 670 different groups had claimed responsibility for at least one international terrorist incident.[43] The political stance of the more important groups tended to be radically left wing but they were characterised overall by a wide diversity of roots, ideologies and goals. Their specificity was disguised, however, by a superficial similarity in their rhetoric, the tactics adopted and by the fact that they were quick to copy each other's ideas. Also, as they realised the opportunities which lay beyond their national boundaries many groups expanded the scope of their operations and formed loose co-operative arrangements with other terrorist organisations and sympathetic states.

The transition from popularly-supported, rural-based guerrilla struggles to campaigns of violence by smaller, secret, international terrorist cells not only represented disillusionment with traditional theories of revolution, but also the recognition by extremist groups of all political colours everywhere that fundamental changes had taken place in world society. Rapid and widespread urbanisation, technological developments in transport, communications and weaponry, together with changes in political and social attitudes, all contributed to a new global environment. International society was smaller, more sophisticated and more closely interconnected, both permitting and demanding new methods of attack. Because of their reliance on complex technological systems like large passenger aircraft, electric power grids, natural gas pipelines and offshore oil rigs modern states were highly vulnerable to terrorist violence.

The strategy chosen by extremist groups was to use these developments to instil fear and apply political pressure through action of a violent and unexpected kind. Although they frequently issued manifestos and communiques, either to influence public opinion or as ex post facto justification for their attacks, there were few coherent expositions of terrorist ideology or methods. Most groups tended to share an impatience with abstract theorising and a dependence on action, both as a means of strengthening their own organisations and giving expression to their feelings about the existing order. Particularly among the more nihilistic groups there was a feeling that 'writing is shit, now let's make the revolution'.[44] The constraints observed by some of the earlier terrorist groups came no longer to be considered necessary, or sound. Unconsciously echoing the 19th century French anarchist Emile Henry, the leader of the Popular Front for the Liberation of Palestine (PFLP) declared in 1970 that:

> there can be no political or geographical boundaries or moral limits to the operations of the peoples' camp. In today's world, no one is 'innocent', no one is 'neutral'.[45]

Individuals, states and international organisations were all made 'legitimate' targets in a vision of world-wide terrorism.

The tactics used by international terrorists have varied over time. The period 1968–1971 was noteworthy for the number of kidnappings which occurred, mainly in Latin America. The early 1970s also saw a spate of aircraft hijackings, with 1972 recording no less than 61 attempted and successful incidents.[46] As security at airports and on board aircraft increased, so terrorists turned their attention more to the seizure of buildings and the capture of hostages with whom to bargain for various concessions, such as the publication of a political manifesto or the release of fellow terrorists from gaol. Bombs have always been a favourite terrorist weapon, accounting for approximately half of all terrorist incidents before 1983.[47] As explosive devices grew larger and more destructive, terrorists were faced with the problem of transporting and placing them, leading in turn to the appearance that year of large vehicle bombs driven to their targets by zealots willing to martyr themselves in order to cause the highest number of casualties and the greatest property damage. Since the late 1960s there has also been a steady growth in the frequency and deadliness of assassinations and indiscriminate attacks, and the 1980s have already seen a steep increase in the number of casualties resulting from such incidents. Terrorists are now drawing on this entire arsenal of violent tactics in order to apply pressure on governments and to make their causes known.

Despite the higher proportion of people killed and injured this decade, terrorist attacks are still essentially symbolic acts against targets of equally symbolic value. As David Fromkin has noted, 'whereas military and revolutionary actions aim at a physical result, terrorist actions aim at a psychological result'.[48] In this, the terrorists are greatly assisted by the international news media. The tabloid press (and its electronic counterparts) in particular have contributed to widespread public misconceptions and over-reactions by their sensationalist and frequently inaccurate reporting of terrorist incidents. Groups of little or no political power are thus able to reach beyond their immediate environment and achieve effects on a target community out of all proportion to their numbers, popular appeal or capacity for violence. Indeed, 'a very plausible case can be made that the most important difference between past and present terrorism may be traced to the modern, transnational flow of information'.[49]

Taken together, these developments contribute to a coherent strategy of violence that is markedly different from earlier terrorist campaigns. As Brian Jenkins has observed, international terrorism today is:

> an offshoot, the newest branch in the evolution of modern revolutionary and guerrilla warfare theories. It elevates individual acts of violence to the level of strategy...It denigrates conventional military power by substituting dramatic violence played for the people watching. It violates the conventional rules of engagement: it reduces the category of innocent bystanders. It makes the world its battlefield: it recognises no boundaries to the conflict, no neutral nations.[50]

Such a philosophy of action casts aside all traditional restraints on international behaviour—both in peace and war—and exposes the fragility of those laws and conventions, customs and principles on which international society is now based. It also reveals the vulnerability of those officials whose position and protection depend on the universal acceptance of certain aspects of international law. Foremost among these are diplomats who, together with their facilities, were immediately recognised as holding unique symbolic value, both to the terrorists and to the states which they represented.

The increased physical dangers that have accompanied the growth in international terrorism come at a time when the functions of diplomacy are perhaps more important than ever. Technological developments have made the nuclear balance more fragile, power relationships are more fluid than they have been for decades, and both state and non-state actors have grown in number and become more interdependent. While in some respects the role played by traditional diplomacy has decreased since it reached its apogee in 19th century Europe, and there has been a decline in the observance of the rules which govern its workings, professional diplomats continue to have an important place in the conduct of world affairs. As Martin Wight has stated so succinctly:

> Diplomacy is the system and art of communication between powers. The diplomatic system is the master institution of international relations.[51]

Thus any threat to the institution of diplomacy must have serious implications for the international order of which it is such an integral part.

NOTES

1. J. E. Karkashian, 'Too Many Things Not Working', in M. F. Herz (ed), *Diplomats and Terrorists: What Works, What Doesn't: A Symposium* (Institute for the Study of Diplomacy (Georgetown University), Washington, 1982), p.6 (emphasis retained).
2. Maurice Keens-Soper, 'The Liberal Disposition of Diplomacy', *International Relations* 5:2 (November 1975), p.909.
3. Baumann, p.32.
4. J. E. S. Fawcett, 'Kidnappings versus Government Protection', *World Today* 26:9 (September 1970), p.359. See also Ira Stechel, 'Terrorist Kidnapping of Diplomatic Personnel', *Cornell International Law Journal* 5:189 (Spring, 1972), p.190.
5. B. Sen, *A Diplomat's Handbook of International Law and Practice* (Martinus Nijhoff, The Hague, 1979), p.6.
6. Adam Watson, *Diplomacy: The Dialogue Between States* (Eyre Methuen, London, 1982), p.17.
7. Keens-Soper, p.913. See also P.J. Boyce, *Foreign Affairs for New States: Some Questions of Credentials* (University of Queensland Press, St. Lucia, 1977), p.201.
8. Bull, *The Anarchical Society*, p.183.
9. Watson, p.19.

10. Quoted in *Report of The Secretary of State's Advisory Panel on Overseas Security* (State Department, Washington, 1985). (Hereinafter referred to as the Inman Report).

11. Quoted in Sen, p.6.

12. The other instrument negotiated at the time was the Pan-American Convention on Consular Intercourse. See Lord Gore Booth (ed), *Satow's Guide to Diplomatic Practice* (Longman, London, 1979), p.109.

13. Stechel, pp.193–194.

14. The full text of the Vienna Convention on Diplomatic Relations (1961) is included in I. Brownlie (ed), *Basic Documents in International Law* (Clarendon Press, Oxford, 1983), pp.213–229.

15. *op.cit.*, pp.220–221.

16. Stechel, p.195 and J. F. Murphy, 'The Role of International Law in the Prevention of Terrorist Kidnapping of Diplomatic Personnel', in M.C. Bassiouni (ed), *International Terrorism and Political Crimes* (Charles Thomas, Springfield, 1975), p.288.

17. Sen, pp.102–103.

18. See Brownlie, pp.219–220.

19. *ibid.*

20. *Satow's Guide*, pp.222–223.

21. N. M. Poulantzas, 'Some Problems of International Law Connected with Urban Guerrilla Warfare: The Kidnapping of Members of Diplomatic Missions, Consular Officers and other Foreign Personnel', *Annals of International Studies* 3 (1972), p.144.

22. See J. F. Murphy, 'Protected Persons and Diplomatic Facilities', in A. E. Evans and J. F. Murphy (eds), *Legal Aspects of International Terrorism* (Heath and Co., Lexington, 1978), p.279.

23. Baumann, pp.40–41.

24. See for example Walter Laqueur, *Terrorism* (Abacus, London, 1978).

25. Quoted in B. W. Tuchman, *The Proud Tower: A Portrait of the World Before the War, 1890–1914* (Hamish Hamilton, London, 1966), p.66.

26. Stepniak, *Underground Russia* (1891), quoted in Tom Bowden, *The Breakdown of Public Security: The Case of Ireland 1916–1921 and Palestine 1936–1939* (Sage, London, 1977), p.63.

27. For first hand accounts of the strategies behind these conflicts see Michael Collins, *The Path to Freedom* (Talbot Press, Dublin, 1922), Menachem Begin, *The Revolt* (W.H. Allen, London, 1951) and George Grivas, *The Memoirs of George Grivas* (Longmans, London, 1964). The connections between them are discussed in Andrew Selth, 'Romantic Ireland's Dead and Gone', *RUSI* (Journal of the Royal United Services Institute for Defence Studies) 128:1 (March 1983), pp.44–47.

28. V. I. Lenin, 'Why the Social Democrats Must Declare War on the SRs', in Walter Laqueur (ed), *The Terrorism Reader: A Historical Anthology* (Wildwood House, London, 1979), p.210 (emphasis retained).

29. Mao Tse-tung, 'The Question of Going Too Far', in *Selected Works of Mao Tse-tung* (Foreign Languages Press, Peking, 1967), Vol.1, p.29.

30. See in particular Mao Tse-tung, 'Problems of Strategy in China's Revolutionary War', 'Problems of Strategy in Guerrilla War Against Japan' and 'On Protracted War', in *Selected Military Writings of Mao Tse-tung* (Foreign Languages Press, Peking, 1966).

31. Quoted in Regis Debray, *Revolution in the Revolution? Armed Struggle and Political Struggle in Latin America* (Penguin, Harmondsworth, 1968), p.67.

32. *op.cit.*, p.65.

33. *op.cit.*, p.105.

34. Ernesto (Che) Guevara, *Guerrilla Warfare* (Penguin, Harmondsworth, 1969), p.105.

35. Ironically, Debray was to make his most perceptive comments about the nature of terrorist violence in a novel, published by Allen Lane (London) in 1978, entitled *Undesirable Alien*.

36. Quoted in Sanche de Gramont, 'How One Pleasant, Scholarly Young Man From Brazil Became a Kidnapping, Gun-Toting, Bombing Revolutionary', *New York Times Magazine*, 15 November 1970, p.136.

37. B. M. Jenkins, 'International Terrorism: Trends and Potentialities', in 'An Act to Combat International Terrorism', *Hearings* before the Committee on Governmental Affairs, US Senate, Ninety-fifth Congress, Second Session, 1978.

38. See for example Jack Davis, *Political Violence in Latin America*, Adelphi Paper 85 (International Institute for Strategic Studies, London, 1972), p.20.

39. Francois Duchene, 'Introduction', in *Civil Violence and the International System*, Part 1, Adelphi Paper 82 (International Institute for Strategic Studies, London, 1971), p.2.

40. Quoted in Baumann, p.19.

41. The best public guide to these and other terrorist groups is Peter Janke, *Guerrilla and Terrorist Organisations: A World Directory and Bibliography* (Harvester Press, Brighton, 1983).

42. Martha Crenshaw, 'The International Consequences of Terrorism', Paper prepared for delivery at the 1983 Annual Meeting of the American Political Science Association, The Palmer House, 1-4 September 1983. For a more detailed treatment of this theme, see M. I. Midlarsky, Martha Crenshaw and Fumihiko Yoshida, 'Why Violence Spreads', *International Studies Quarterly* 24:2 (June 1980), pp. 262-298.

43. *Patterns of International Terrorism: 1981* (State Department, Washington, 1982), p.12. This figure is probably inflated to some degree by very small and bogus groups.

44. Ulrike Meinhof, quoted by Nathan Leites, 'Understanding the Next Act', *Terrorism: An International Journal* 3:1-2 (1979), p.32.

45. Quoted in John Hamer, 'Protection of Diplomats', *Editorial Research Reports* 11:3 (October 1973), p.766.

46. See David Phillips, *Skyjack: The Story of Air Piracy* (Harrap, London, 1973), pp.269-281.

47. Gail Bass and B. M. Jenkins, *A Review of Recent Trends in International Terrorism and Nuclear Incidents Abroad*, Rand Note N-1979-SL (Rand Corporation, Santa Monica, 1983), p.6.

48. David Fromkin, 'The Strategy of Terrorism', *Foreign Affairs* 53:4 (July 1975), p.693.

49. Wardlaw, *Political Terrorism*, p.31. For a perceptive and useful study of this question, see also A.P. Schmid and J. de Graaf, *Violence as Communication: Insurgent Terrorism and the Western News Media* (Sage, London, 1982).

50. B. M. Jenkins, *High Technology Terrorism and Surrogate War: The Impact of New Technology on Low-Level Violence*, Rand Paper P-5339 (Rand Corporation, Santa Monica, 1975), p.8.

51. Martin Wight, *Power Politics* (Leicester University Press, Leicester, 1978), p.113.

2
DIPLOMATS AND DIPLOMATIC FACILITIES AS TERRORIST TARGETS

the title of ambassador ought to be held in such respect as to be safe not only under the laws of allies, but even amid the weapons of the enemy. These facts have been so thoroughly ascertained, are so certain and well known that one of the oldest proverbs is said to have been: 'An ambassador is neither killed nor outraged'.

Gentili
De Legationibus Libri Tres (1585)

Despite the universal acceptance by states of the principle of diplomatic inviolability, the profession of diplomacy has always held its dangers. Throughout history diplomats have been exposed to insults, harassment and violent attack, sometimes at the hands of state authorities but more often from mobs and individuals with a grievance. Diplomats have been strangers in foreign lands, symbolising different political and economic systems, different races, religions and standards of living. As interstate contacts grew and their official representative status came to be accepted as an integral part of international society, so diplomats were increasingly identified as vehicles through which protests might be registered against the sending states. Only this century, however, have diplomats been viewed as worthwhile targets for terrorist attack.

THE THREAT BEFORE 1968

A number of scholars have cited the murders of the German Minister and the Chancellor of the Japanese Legation in Peking in 1900 as the first examples of terrorist attacks against diplomats this century. Both were killed by rebellious Chinese troops, however, not Boxers as often supposed, and the circumstances surrounding their deaths are still unclear.[1] It was in fact Russian terrorists who once again showed the way. After the Bolshevik coup in October 1917 the Social Revolutionary Party assassinated the German Ambassador to the new Soviet Republic in an attempt to disrupt relations between Moscow and Berlin. In 1923 a Soviet diplomat at the Lausanne Peace Conference was shot by White Russians and four years later another monarchist killed the Soviet Minister to Poland. In the 1930s the Counsellor of the German Embassy in Paris was murdered by an anti-Nazi emigre and not long afterwards the German Counsellor in Moscow suffered the same fate. The period immediately before the Second World War and the years that followed its end saw an increasing level of threat to diplomats and diplomatic facilities. There was a trend towards large, often violent demonstrations against diplomatic missions and, particularly during the Cold War years, the beginnings of state-directed harassment, again often violent, of diplomats themselves. Clifton Wilson, who has carried out perhaps the most detailed study of this subject, could count the deaths of at least 13 people attached to diplomatic missions between 1945-1967. 'Many more' were injured.[2]

Most of those diplomats killed during this later period, however, appear to have died not as a result of any particular terrorist intent but from events related to the general social turmoil and political unrest of the time. There was a small number of isolated incidents, such as the abduction of the United States Ambassador to Brazil in 1949 and the attempted murder of the US Ambassador to Japan in 1961, but with few exceptions none of the anti-colonial or revolutionary groups of the time seem to have had any policy specifically to attack diplomatic targets.[3] No doubt because the mobilisation of international support was an integral part of their strategies they appear deliberately to have eschewed attacks which risked the alienation of the diplomatic community. For example, General George Grivas, leader of the EOKA terrorists, declared in his 1953 Preparatory General Plan:

> The British must be continuously harried and beset until they are obliged by international diplomacy exercised through the United Nations to examine the Cyprus problem and settle it in accordance with the desires of the Cypriot people and the whole Greek nation.[4]

When a US Vice-Consul in Nicosia was killed by an EOKA bomb in June 1956 the terrorists expressed their 'deep regret' to the US Government and explained that the bomb was meant for representatives of the island's British administration.[5]

It was not until the late 1960s that attacks on diplomats and their facilities were made a significant part of terrorist campaigns. As described by the

Inman Report, the world saw:

> an expansion of the threat from physical violence against diplomats—often
> private, incidental, even furtive—to the beginnings of calculated terror campaigns,
> psychological conflict waged by nation or sub-group against nation, with an
> ever-broadening range of targets, weapons and tactics.[6]

While it is not possible to divide such complex phenomena into neatly
defined periods, four broad phases can be discerned in these sorts of terrorist
attacks over the last 15 years. Following global trends, they were kidnappings, letter bombings, embassy seizures and assassination attempts. Indiscriminate violence against diplomatic targets—usually in the form of bomb
attacks—remained a feature throughout the period.

ATTACKS SINCE 1968

The initial spate of kidnappings seems to have been a direct product of
the collapse of rural-based insurgencies in Latin America. The Deputy Chief
of the US Military Mission in Venezuela was kidnapped by members of
the Armed Forces of National Liberation (*Fuerzas Armadas de Liberacion
Nacional*, or FALN) in 1963, and another American military officer was
taken by the FALN in 1964. No demands were made in either case and
both captives were released unharmed after only a few days. Four years
later two Military Attaches from the US Embassy in Guatemala City were
killed in what appears to have been an abortive kidnapping attempt. Two
other members of the American Military Assistance Advisory Group were
injured. This attack was followed in August 1968 by the death of the US
Ambassador to Guatemala, John G. Mein, who was shot while attempting
to escape a group of terrorists which had held up his car. The day after
the incident the FAR announced that Mein had been killed 'while resisting
a political kidnapping'.[7]

It was in Brazil, however, that the tactic of abducting diplomats was
first used successfully by terrorists to win concessions from a receiving
government. In September 1969 the US Ambassador, C. Burke Elbrick,
was kidnapped in Rio de Janeiro by members of the Revolutionary Movement of 8 October (*Movimento Revolucionario do Outubre 8*, or MR-
8), a group associated with the the ALN. For the Ambassador's safe return
the terrorists demanded the publication of their political manifesto and
the release of 15 political prisoners from Brazilian gaols. ALN leader Carlos
Marighela declared that:

> By kidnapping the American Ambassador we wish to demonstrate that it is
> possible to triumph over the dictatorship and exploitation if we are properly
> armed and organised.[8]

The Brazilian Government responded with massive searches and increased military controls over the population but three days later agreed to the ALN's demands and the Ambassador was released without harm. Elbrick subsequently described his captors as 'young, very determined, intelligent fanatics' who would have acted on their threat to kill him if their demands had not been met.[9]

The success of this operation encouraged Brazilian terrorists to try again. In March 1970 the Japanese Consul-General in Sao Paulo, Nobuo Okuchi, was abducted by a group calling themselves the Popular Revolutionary Vanguard. He was later released in return for five political prisoners and permission for them to leave for asylum in Mexico. The following month an attempt to seize the US Consul in Porto Allegre failed, but in June the same year terrorists successfully kidnapped the Federal Republic of Germany's Ambassador to Brazil, Ehrenfried von Holleben. A communique left at the scene stated that 'the terrorists would no longer confine themselves to kidnapping the representatives of the major powers: all foreign diplomats would be considered fair game'.[10] Von Holleben was later set free in return for the release of 40 political prisoners. Only six months later, when the Swiss Ambassador to Brazil was kidnapped (also by members of the ALN) the price of a diplomat's safe return had risen to 70 political prisoners, yet it was still paid. As Robert Moss has observed, it was 'runaway inflation'.[11] It was also the successful manipulation of forces both within the Brazilian Government and outside it, as explained by the leader of MR-8 in 1970:

> We orient our armed actions in such a way as to make them politically profitable. For instance, the kidnapping of a foreign diplomat creates political problems for the regime. Either the regime agrees with the Minister of the Interior not to give in and allows the diplomat to be killed—which creates difficulties with the foreign power the diplomat represents, and with which the regime has economic ties—or the regime meets the demands of the kidnappers and the diplomat is set free, then the army and police criticise the leniency of the Government and that creates dissension within the regime. In our case, we only carried out kidnappings when we were fairly sure our demands would be met. We chose diplomats from countries on which Brazil is dependent and we knew the Minister for the Interior was not in a position to adopt a tough stance.[12]

The success of the diplomatic kidnappings in Brazil ensured that the tactic would be quickly taken up by terrorist groups elsewhere. Between August 1968 and May 1971 there were no less than 21 kidnappings or attempted kidnappings of diplomatic personnel, in ten countries. All but four occurred in Latin America[13]. Most of the hostages were released unharmed but three, the FRG Ambassador to Guatemala and a US AID Advisor in Uruguay in 1970, and the Israeli Consul-General in Turkey a year later, were killed by their captors after ransom demands were refused.

After the death of the US AID Advisor, Dan Mitrione, a terrorist was reported to have told a Cuban newspaper that the murder was necessary for the kidnappers to retain their credibility. It was also carried out 'because the success or failure of one urban guerrilla group in using diplomatic kidnapping as a form of political blackmail would influence other extremist movements that might be tempted to use the same weapon'.[14]

The kidnapping and murder of Count Karl von Spreti, the FRG Ambassador to Guatemala, was significant for other reasons. It was the first time that money had been demanded as part of the ransom and the first time that a diplomat had been killed by his captors. Perhaps most importantly, it was the first time that a sending government had publicly criticised the receiving government for its inability both to protect the diplomatic personnel for which it was responsible and to recover them safely in the event that they were abducted. The West German Government sent a special envoy to Guatemala to press for accession to the terrorists' demands and even offered to pay the US$700 000 wanted as part of the ransom. Yet the Guatemalan Government refused to release 25 political prisoners also sought by the kidnappers. After von Spreti's murder the FRG Government lodged a strong protest and reduced its diplomatic relations with Guatemala to a bare minimum. West German Chancellor Willy Brandt went as far as to suggest that concerted international action be taken to investigate this latest threat to diplomats, thus for the first time removing the entire problem 'from the realm of newspaper headlines to the realm of international law and politics'.[15]

Diplomatic kidnappings reached a peak in 1970, when there were 17 separate incidents. They then sharply dropped away until 1972 when the number began slowly to rise again. According to the US State Department, diplomats from some 47 countries were kidnapped in the 15 years between 1968 and 1983.[16] This problem continues to occupy governments, particularly those with representatives in areas of serious unrest like the Lebanon, where French, American, South Korean, Saudi Arabian and Soviet diplomats have been kidnapped in recent years.[17] Personnel of all ranks have been involved in diplomatic kidnappings, including a number of honorary consuls. A study conducted by the Rand Corporation in 1977 showed that, of the 43 successful kidnappings carried out in the period August 1968–June 1975, terrorists managed to abduct an ambassador or at least a consul-general 11 times.[18] From 1972, however, this tactic was overshadowed by an increased number of bomb attacks and seizures of diplomatic facilities.

On 19 September 1972 Dr Ami Shachori, the Agricultural Counsellor of the Israeli Embassy in London, was killed when he opened a letter addressed to him, containing explosives. Warnings were immediately sent to other Israeli missions around the world and, as a result of this prompt action, two letter bombs addressed to members of the Israeli Embassy in

Paris were discovered. Another four such devices were found addressed to members of the Israeli Embassy in London. The following day 17 letter bombs postmarked Amsterdam and addressed to Israeli diplomats in different parts of the world were discovered and defused in Brussels, Geneva, Jerusalem, Montreal, New York and Vienna. A week later it was announced that five more letter bombs had been detected in Canberra and Sydney. Two more letter bombs, also addressed to Israeli officials in Sydney, were detected by the Australian postal authorities on 3 October. In November yet another five letter bombs addressed to Israeli officials and other prominent Jewish figures were intercepted at a Geneva postal centre. They were postmarked New Delhi, prompting the Indian Government later to claim that it had detected and defused more than 50 such devices. While there was no definitive evidence, it appeared that the bombing campaign was directed by the Palestinian Black September Organisation (BSO).[19] Since then, letter bomb attacks against diplomats have continued, but are less common as postal authorities and embassy staff have become more proficient at the detection of such devices.

In February 1955 six gunmen stormed the Romanian Legation in Berne and demanded the release of five anti-communist resistance fighters held in Romanian prisons. Fifteen years later Croatian emigres seized the Yugoslav Consulate in Gothenburg, but neither incident seemed to capture the imagination of the world's terrorists. In December 1972, however, a significant new threat to diplomats emerged when the Israeli Embassy in Bangkok was seized by four members of the BSO and its six occupants (including the Israeli Ambassador to Cambodia) taken hostage. The terrorists demanded the release of 36 Palestinian prisoners held in Israel but, after 19 hours, were persuaded by Thai authorities to free their own captives in return for safe passage to Egypt. Less than three months later, on 1 March 1973, eight members of the same terrorist group stormed the Saudi Arabian Embassy in Khartoum and seized ten hostages. The terrorists demanded the release of other Palestinians held in Israel and Jordan, and members of the Red Army Faction imprisoned in the FRG 'because they supported the Palestinian cause'.[20] All their demands were rejected, but before surrendering to the Sudanese authorities the terrorists killed two senior United States diplomats and a Belgian diplomat who had been in the Saudi Embassy at the time it was seized. In their tactics, the nature and scope of their demands, their ruthlessness and their use of one state's diplomatic assets to apply pressure on other states, the terrorists responsible for these two attacks set a pattern for further seizures of diplomatic facilities in the years that followed.

Between 1972 and 1982 armed extremists took over embassies and consulates more than 50 times, 'generally to demand the release of prisoners or other political concessions, sometimes just to register disapproval of a particular policy'.[21] There was a dramatic increase in such incidents after 1979. This was no doubt due in part to the example provided by the American hostage 'crisis' in Iran, but also stemmed from political struggles like that between Iraq and Iran, or that continuing in El Salvador. By the end of 1982 the diplomatic premises of 38 states had been seized by terrorists in some 27 countries, with the missions of the United States and Egypt the most popular targets for this form of terrorist attack.[22] After 1981, however, the number of seizures each year declined as diplomatic facilities became more secure and as terrorists came to accept the limited results that such operations usually achieved. Seizures of diplomatic premises were not eliminated from the terrorists' tactical inventory, but were replaced as the most prevalent threat to diplomats by a greater frequency of personal attacks.

As both sending and receiving states began to take measures to guard against kidnappings and the seizure of diplomatic facilities, so terrorist groups turned increasingly to bombings and assassination attempts against more vulnerable targets. In 1970 about half the total number of international terrorist incidents was directed against people, half against property. By 1981 some 80 per cent of attacks were against people and there seems to have been a corresponding rise in the proportion directed against diplomatic personnel and their families.[23] In addition, the overall level of terrorist attacks on diplomats increased. Many were made with handguns but bombs were responsible for many more casualties. Between 1968–1982, 381 diplomatic and consular officers were killed in terrorist incidents, and 824 were wounded.[24] Over the past few years attacks have become more destructive and less discriminating in their victims. The car bombing of the US Embassy in Beirut in April 1983, for example, resulted in the deaths of 57 people (including 17 Americans) with 120 people injured.[25] Among those diplomats killed by terrorists since 1968 were 23 ambassadors from 13 countries, including the US Ambassadors to Lebanon, Cyprus, Sudan, Guatemala and Afghanistan, the Turkish Ambassadors to France, Spain, Austria and Yugoslavia and the British Ambassadors to Eire and the Netherlands.

THE SCOPE AND FREQUENCY OF ATTACKS

Bearing in mind all the problems involved in trying to quantify terrorist violence, it is nevertheless still possible to survey the levels of attacks on diplomats and diplomatic facilities over the past 20 years and make some general observations. Between 1968 and 1982 the Rand Corporation recorded 574 attacks against diplomats and diplomatic facilities, in total more than 25 per cent of all terrorist attacks for the period.[26] By 1983 the level of attacks against diplomatic targets had risen sharply to nearly 40 per cent of the total.[27] At that time the Corporation stated that diplomats were 'the most common target in incidents of international terrorism and this trend is increasing'.[28] In 1983 the US State Department, which at that time included threats, hoaxes, arms smuggling incidents and other kinds of terrorist-related data in its statistics, reckoned that the level of attacks against diplomatic targets between 1968–1983 stood at 52 per cent of the total.[29] Both collection agencies agreed that the number of attacks against diplomats and diplomatic facilities grew steadily almost every year, jumping dramatically to reach a peak in 1981. According to preliminary figures issued by the State Department in 1986, the number of terrorist incidents aimed at diplomats and diplomatic facilities between 1968–1985 had risen to 2081.[30] This represented a smaller proportion of the total than before, but attacks on diplomatic targets still accounted for more incidents than in any other single category. On present indications 1987 is already well on the way to recording similar figures, suggesting that despite a wider range of terrorist victims in recent years, diplomats and diplomatic facilities will remain popular targets for some time to come.

Not only are terrorists attacking diplomatic targets more often but they are attacking the diplomats of more states. To date terrorists have carried out operations against the personnel and premises of at least 66 states,[31] with ten nationalities the target in more than half the incidents. Those states most threatened with this kind of violence have been the United States, Turkey and Yugoslavia, followed by France, Cuba, the Soviet Union and the United Kingdom. Attacks are also taking place in more countries, although more than 40 per cent of all incidents have occurred in North America and Western Europe, with most of the remainder in Central America and the Middle East. The most favoured location for terrorist attacks against diplomats is the United States, particularly New York which in the United Nations offers a plethora of targets for extremist groups.[32] Other popular locations for such terrorist attacks include France, Lebanon, El Salvador, Guatemala, Argentina, Colombia, Italy and the FRG. In all, the US State Department has listed over 100 groups claiming responsibility for attacks on diplomatic targets over the last 15 years.[33] The number is increasing each year and many new terrorist groups are singling out diplomats as one of their primary targets.

The motives behind these attacks are almost as diverse as the groups responsible for them. While several attempts have been made to devise typologies for such incidents, perhaps the most useful is that suggested by Brian Jenkins in 1982. In a study published by the Rand Corporation that year he identified five major types of terrorist attack involving diplomats, as follows;[34] terrorist attacks on diplomats that are associated with current insurgencies, such as those in Central America—this is one of the largest categories; attacks by ethnic, emigre or exile groups against the representatives of the state they oppose, such as those carried out by Croatian separatist groups against Yugoslav diplomats and diplomatic missions; world-wide attacks on foreign diplomats by terrorists operating as part of a wider campaign against a government, such as those operations carried out by various Palestinian groups; isolated terrorist attacks against diplomats by indigenous groups to protest the actions of a foreign government, one example of which would be the bombing of the French Embassy in Lima to protest against French nuclear tests in the Pacific; and finally, the government use of terrorist tactics, or employment of terrorist groups to attack foreign diplomats and diplomatic facilities abroad as the continuation of a local armed conflict, or as a form of surrogate warfare. The rash of attacks by Iran and Iraq against the diplomats of the other since the war between those two countries began in 1980 would fall into this category.

No terrorist group concentrates exclusively on attacks against diplomats and diplomatic facilities, but a number have given a high priority to these targets. Since their latest terrorist campaign began in 1975 Armenian separatists, for example, have carried out more than 70 attacks on Turkish diplomats, resulting in the deaths of nearly 30, including members of their families.[35] Various Croatian groups too have singled out diplomatic targets for special attention, directing attacks against Yugoslav officials and official facilities in the United States, Europe and Australia. Since it was formed in 1968, 62 per cent of all attacks by the Jewish Defence League have been directed against Soviet diplomats and diplomatic facilities, mainly in the United States and Western Europe.[36] Iranian exiles opposed to the Khomeini regime have tended to concentrate their violent attacks against Iranian missions and officials abroad, and Jordanian diplomatic officials have often been the victims of extremist Palestinian groups. In 1974 a number of Latin American terrorist groups established a so-called Junta of Revolutionary Coordination (*Junta de Coordinacion Revolucionaria*) in Paris, one of the main purposes of which seems to have been to facilitate the assassination of Latin American diplomats in Europe. A number of anti-Castro groups have singled out Cuban diplomatic personnel and premises for attack. Diplomatic targets are still popular with extremists in Central and Latin America.

THE VALUE OF DIPLOMATIC TARGETS

Despite some superficial similarities, these terrorist attacks are in many ways unique, arising from and taking place in circumstances that can never be repeated. Yet here again some general observations can be made. Diplomats and diplomatic facilities might be chosen as primary or instrumental targets, attacked either because of their perceived immediate value to the terrorists (such as the assassination of the British Ambassador to the Netherlands in July 1979 by the IRA, or the bombing of the US Embassy in

Beirut by the Islamic Jihad in 1983) or because they may be used as a means to induce certain responses in other governments. This was the case, for example, in August 1975, when Japanese terrorists seized the Consular Sections of the United States and Swedish Embassies in Kuala Lumpur in order to pressure those Governments into persuading the Japanese Government to release five URA prisoners from gaol. Often elements of both are present, as occurred in February 1980 when members of Colombia's April 19 Movement (*Movimiento 19 Abril*, or M-19) occupied the Dominican Embassy in Bogota and used the 18 high-ranking diplomats captured there at the time (including the US Ambassador) to bargain with the Colombian Government.[37]

In these ways, terrorists have been able to register protests against particular states and win various concessions, such as the release of political prisoners, the publication of political statements or simply additional operating funds. In some cases terrorist actions against diplomats have prompted responses by states that have either been repressive, and thus counterproductive, or else of such a nature as to disrupt the societies and threaten the very liberties which the states claimed to defend. Attacks have embarassed receiving governments by exposing their inability to protect diplomats and their facilities, and in other ways caused friction with the sending states. The latter in their turn have been obliged to divert scarce resources to protect their missions abroad and have suffered additional difficulties in the conduct of their international relations. Rifts in alliances have been exposed and delicate negotiations compromised. These victories for the terrorists, however, have been largely tactical. The real value of diplomatic targets for terrorist groups lies in their ability to promote wider strategic objectives.

Diplomats and diplomatic facilities are uniquely valuable targets for any terrorist group. After centuries, the diplomat is now 'the most purely representative figure of his time. Behind him stands his whole country and its aims...He is the point of contact between policy and the world outside'.[38] By attacking one official or one office a terrorist group which is not structurally or logistically equipped for a larger scale conflict can in effect assault an entire state, group of states or world system in miniature. Terrorists can attack a policy, an alliance or a world view. Thus the American Ambassador kidnapped in Brazil in 1969 represented the 'big North American capitalists'[39] and the British Ambassador kidnapped by Tupamaros in Uruguay in 1971 was seen as 'the notional symbol of institutional neo-colonialism'.[40] Soviet missions have been attacked because they represent the communist system and US missions because they represent the capitalist system. Egyptian missions have been seized because Egypt supported the Camp David Accords in 1978 and Saudi Arabian missions have been bombed because that country supported more recent Western peace initiatives in

Lebanon. Israeli missions have been attacked by groups aiming at that country's overthrow, while Cuban and Iranian missions have been attacked by supporters of others who have been overthrown. Yugoslav diplomats have been assassinated because their government has refused to grant Croatians a state of their own and Turkish officials are threatened because of repressive Turkish Government policies toward the Armenian population over 70 years ago. Because of their uniquely representative function diplomats and diplomatic facilities are seen as potent symbols through the manipulation of which terrorists can seize the initiative in a psychological war.

Such attacks also ensure the terrorists of an immediate and wide response. By openly flouting the time-honoured principle of diplomatic inviolability terrorists 'automatically engage the attention and concern of the entire diplomatic community as well as the states directly involved'.[41] Just as importantly, the blatant contravention of such well-established legal and ethical norms gives the terrorists' actions additional shock value, which in turn guarantees them greater publicity. For, as one observer has noted, 'terrorism is theatre'[42] and targets are chosen in large part because of the attention they are likely to attract in the international news media. Even after 20 years of such incidents the murder of a diplomat or attempted seizure of an embassy is still considered newsworthy, as has been demonstrated on numerous occasions in recent years. Should public interest begin to wane more spectacular operations, such as the car bomb attacks on diplomatic missions in Beirut and Kuwait in 1983 and 1984, can quickly regain the world's attention.

All these factors have combined to make diplomatic targets peculiarly attractive to terrorist groups and seem assured to keep diplomats and their families in the 'front line' for the foreseeable future. Yet in recent years another reason has been suggested for the increased number of attacks on diplomatic personnel and premises. This is the use of terrorist tactics, and the employment of terrorist groups, by states themselves to attack the diplomats of other states abroad, either as an extension of a particular foreign policy or as a form of surrogate warfare.

NOTES

1. See for example Lancelot Giles, *The Siege of the Peking Legations: A Diary*, edited with an introduction 'Chinese Anti-Foreignism and the Boxer Uprising' by L. R. Marchant (University of Western Australia Press, Nedlands, 1970), pp.71–72.
2. C. E. Wilson, *Diplomatic Privileges and Immunities* (University of Arizona Press, Tucson, 1967), p.52.

3. The Viet Cong attack on the US Embassy in Saigon during the 1968 Tet offensive hardly qualifies as a terrorist attack on a diplomatic facility, but is worthy of note as a deliberate attack by insurgents on a diplomatic mission for its symbolic value in a propaganda war.

4. Reproduced as Appendix 1 in Grivas, pp.204-205.

5. Another US Foreign Service staff member was injured in the incident. Wilson, p.54.

6. Inman Report, p.9.

7. Quoted in *Satow's Guide*, p.199.

8. Carlos Marighela, 'Declaration by the ALN October Revolutionary Group', in *For the Liberation of Brazil* (Penguin, Harmondsworth, 1971), p.25.

9. Quoted in *Satow's Guide*, p.200.

10. Robert Moss, *Urban Guerrillas: The New Face of Political Violence* (Alister Taylor, Wellington, 1971), p.206.

11. *op.cit.*, p.245.

12. Quoted in Sanche de Gramont, p.140.

13. The four incidents which took place outside Latin America were the kidnappings of the US Political Secretary in Jordan in June 1970, the British Trade Commissioner in Canada in October 1970, the West German Honorary Consul in Spain that December and the Israeli Consul-General to Turkey in May 1971.

14. Moss, p.228.

15. Baumann, p.101.

16. *Terrorist Incidents Involving Diplomats*, p.4.

17. Since January 1984 more than 65 foreigners have been kidnapped in Lebanon. See 'Free-lance terrorism undercuts Syria', *Christian Science Monitor*, 6 November 1986.

18. Brian Jenkins, Janera Johnson and David Ronfeldt, *Numbered Lives: Some Statistical Observations From 77 International Hostage Episodes*, Rand Paper P-5905 (Rand Corporation, Santa Monica, 1977), p.12.

19. L. M. Bloomfield and G. F. Fitzgerald, *Crimes Against Internationally Protected Persons: Prevention and Punishment: An Analysis of the UN Convention* (Praeger, New York, 1975), p.19.

20. Quoted in *op.cit.*, p.21. The demand for the release of the RAF prisoners was later withdrawn because the West German Ambassador, who was in the Embassy when it was seized, managed to escape.

21. B. M. Jenkins, *Diplomats on the Front Line*, Rand Paper P-6749 (Rand Corporation, Santa Monica, 1982), p.3.

22. B. M. Jenkins, *Embassies Under Siege: A Review of 48 Embassy Take-overs, 1971-1980*, Rand Report R-2651-RC (Rand Corporation, Santa Monica, 1981), p.v.

23. *Patterns of International Terrorism: 1981*, p.4.

24. *Terrorist Incidents Involving Diplomats*, pp.1-4.

25. 'Victims of Terrorism', *Department of State Newsletter* (May 1983), p.2. See also *Terrorist Bombings: A Statistical Overview of International Terrorist Bombing Incidents from January 1977 through May 1983* (State Department, Washington, 1983), p.1.

26. Jenkins, *Diplomats on the Front Line*, p.1.

27. Jenkins, *New Modes of Conflict*, p.14.

28. Bass and Jenkins, p.v.

29. *Terrorist Incidents Involving Diplomats*, p.1. This indexing system has since been refined to permit a more subtle and accurate analysis of terrorist incidents. See also R. M. Sayre, 'International Terrorism: A Long Twilight Struggle', Address by Robert M. Sayre, Director of the Office for Counter-Terrorism and Emergency Planning, before the Foreign Policy Association, New York, 15 August 1984, *Current Policy* 608 (15 August 1984), p.1.

30. 'International Terrorist Incidents by Victim, 1968–1985', statistics issued by the Office for Counter-Terrorism and Emergency Planning, US State Department, 1986.

31. Jenkins, *Diplomats on the Front Line*, p.4. With its wider data base, the State Department lists incidents involving the diplomats of 113 countries. See *Terrorist Incidents Involving Diplomats*, p.3.

32. Approximately half the terrorist attacks on diplomats in the United States have taken place in New York and have involved diplomatic missions to the United Nations. Only 20 per cent have taken place in Washington, with the remainder scattered throughout the country, reflecting the distribution of various ethnic communities and minor diplomatic posts. Jenkins, *Diplomats on the Front Line*, p.6.

33. *Terrorist Incidents Involving Diplomats*, p.5. The State Department has warned that some of these claims may be false and some groups may have been invented to disguise the involvement of states or organisations in particular incidents.

34. The following draws heavily on Jenkins, *Diplomats on the Front Line*, pp.8–10.

35. Grant Wardlaw, 'The Year of the Bomb—And More to Come', *Pacific Defence Reporter* Annual Reference Edition (December 1983/January 1984), p.33.

36. Bruce Hoffman, 'The Jewish Defense League', *Terrorism Violence and Insurgency Journal* 5:1 (Summer 1984), p.13.

37. When M–19 attacked the Dominican Embassy a reception was being held, attended by the ambassadors of ten countries including the Papal Nuncio. The terrorists demanded the release of 311 political prisoners, a US$50 million ransom and safe conduct out of the country..

38. J. D. B. Miller, *The World of States* (Croom Helm, London, 1981), p.35.

39. Carlos Marighela, 'On the Organisational Function of Revolutionary Violence', in *For the Liberation of Brazil*, p.38.

40. Geoffrey Jackson, *Concorde Diplomacy: The Ambassador's Role in the World Today* (Hamish Hamilton, London, 1981), p.116. Sir Geoffrey Jackson's account of his capture and eight-month imprisonment is given in *People's Prison* (Faber, London, 1973).

41. Baumann, p.110.

42. Brian Jenkins, quoted in Philip Schlesinger, Graham Murdock and Philip Elliott, *Televising Terrorism: Political Violence in Popular Culture* (Comedia, London, 1983), p.12.

3
STATE-SPONSORED TERRORISM AND DIPLOMACY

How should you govern any kingdom that knows not how to use ambassadors?

William Shakespeare
King Henry VI, Part 3 (16th Century)

The growing scope and complexity of international terrorism, particularly the threat to diplomats and diplomatic facilities, has caused widespread concern among members of the international community and prompted a lively debate on the measures appropriate for their protection. Consideration of this matter, however, has been greatly complicated not only by differing interpretations of the nature of terrorism but by the involvement of states themselves in terrorist activities. Once again, this problem is not new but since the 1960s, when terrorism emerged as an identifiable doctrine of unconventional warfare and a myriad groups sprang up around the world to capitalise on the increased vulnerability of modern society, the involvement of governments in terrorism has greatly increased. The problem has also been the subject of considerable attention by individual states and international organisations.

In recent years the debate over this matter has been heightened by the open admission of some states that they were prepared to sponsor terrorist groups as a means of extending their foreign policy options and by the Reagan Administration's insistence that state-sponsored terrorism has become a global issue with the potential to undermine world stability and threaten civilisation itself.[1] In taking these extreme positions, both sides have drawn attention to the breakdown of the international system which has prevailed since 1945, in which the two great powers and their allies could indulge in activities of all kinds without upsetting the basic framework of world order which they established as a victorious alliance at the end

31

of World War II. With the emergence of other states less prepared to acquiesce in this system and independent groups active outside it the ability of the great powers to control events has greatly diminished. The conventions of international behaviour have been increasingly threatened and there has developed a less ordered and stable political environment in which it has become increasingly obvious that, to most states, self interest remains the ultimate appellate jurisdiction.

For the purposes of this study, the problem of state involvement in terrorist activities can be approached at three levels. The first level is that at which encouragement—either active or passive—is given by governments to groups or mobs which threaten diplomats and diplomatic facilities within their own national boundaries. The second level is that of support—either direct or indirect—by governments for so-called 'independent' terrorists operating in other states, while the third is that at which states actually conduct terrorist operations themselves, either using their own operatives or by enlisting terrorist groups directly to act on their behalf. All three constitute a significant challenge to the normal processes of interstate contact and pose a growing threat to diplomats and diplomatic facilities.

STATE COMPLICITY IN MOB VIOLENCE

Under international law, governments have a responsibility to take full account of the expression of 'hostile views, contempt or even dis-approbation of a foreign state'.[2] States are also obliged to exercise 'due diligence' to prevent the commission on their territory of acts by private persons against other states or their representatives. Under Article 44 of the Vienna Convention on Diplomatic Relations a receiving state retains its formal responsibilities for the protection of diplomatic representatives and their facilities regardless of any differences which might be at issue between it and the sending states. This remains the case even in the event of an irreparable breach in relations, including war.[3] Yet there have been innumerable cases in the past where governments have knowingly failed to show respect to, or provide protection for, the diplomats and diplomatic facilities for which they were responsible. It is not the place here to investigate the record of harassment, insult or minor injury suffered by diplomats at the hands of state officials, nor is it appropriate to survey the long history of violations of diplomatic premises and communications. It is useful, however, briefly to consider some instances of government complicity in attacks on diplomats and their facilities by violent mobs.

The first and one of the most celebrated instances of this practice this century occurred in 1900. The Chinese Empress Dowager Tzu Hsi formed a loose alliance with a rebellious coalition of soldiers and millenarian elements to besiege the Legation Quarter in Peking for 55 days. Almost as well known, perhaps, is the assault on the British Embassy in Petrograd by Bolsheviks in 1918, which resulted in the death of the Naval Attache, who offered resistance. Another example occurred in March 1956, when several hundred French settlers sacked the US Consulate-General and Information Office in Tunis, protesting alleged American support for Tunisian independence. Two years later the British Military Attache was killed when a mob attacked the UK Ambassador's Residence in Baghdad. On 9 December 1964, after several violent assaults by mobs on United States diplomatic establishments abroad, Secretary of State Dean Rusk stated that:

> The U.S. Government has noticed the tendency of these violent assaults to recur in certain countries. And it is especially concerned about violent acts which appear to be connived at or acquiesced in by the authorities of the host state, or in which the authorities are slow in taking action to control mobs of rioters. Resort to riot and violence against foreign missions strikes at the heart of the system of diplomatic intercourse, the established channel by which one nation communicates with another.[4]

It was a protest that was to be heard more frequently in the years that followed.

There were a number of violent attacks on diplomatic missions in Indonesia during the 1960s, most of which were clearly carried out with the approval of the local authorities. In September 1963, for example, the British Embassy in Jakarta was attacked on two occasions. On the second the Chancery was sacked and a number of diplomatic staff injured by a mob protesting against the formation of the Federation of Malaysia (which included the disputed territory of Sabah). Formal Notes sent to the Indonesian Ministry of Foreign Affairs were ignored, despite strong expressions of concern by the Secretary-General of the United Nations, U Thant. It was six days before the British staff were permitted to reoccupy their Chancery building. The Malaysian Embassy was also attacked, leading in turn to the storming of the Indonesian Embassy in Kuala Lumpur by a Malaysian mob. Three Indonesian diplomats were siezed as hostages.[5] The Suharto regime later inspired or at least condoned a number of attacks on Chinese diplomatic personnel and facilities between 1965–1970 and probably had a part in attacks on two United States consulates in Indonesia during the same period.[6]

During the Cultural Revolution in China between 1966–1967 Red Guards assaulted the diplomats of several states and attacked a number of missions. Over 20 serious violations of diplomatic immunity were recorded. Because of alleged 'fascist measures' against Chinese demonstrators in Hong Kong, the United Kingdom was singled out for particularly violent treatment. In May 1967 the British Consulate-General in Shanghai was invaded and damaged by a large crowd. The following month there was a number of officially inspired anti-British demonstrations in Peking. In August the British Embassy compound was invaded and the Chancery burnt down by a violent mob. Some members of the mission staff were assaulted. These attacks were made with the full knowledge of the local authorities who did nothing to prevent or stop them. In reply to formal protests from the diplomatic community the Chinese Foreign Ministry, temporarily under the sway of leftist extremists, refused assistance, declaring that 'diplomatic immunity is a product of bourgeois norms'.[7] The threat to diplomatic personnel and premises in China only receded in September when Prime Minister Chou En-lai reportedly issued a directive that, in relation to the diplomatic community, the Red Guards should 'demonstrate but not penetrate'.[8] Ironically, while the Chinese Government was rejecting requests for protection from the diplomatic community in Peking, the Burmese Government had called out armed troops to protect the Chinese Embassy in Rangoon from a violent mob which had attacked it, killing one Chinese diplomat.

The tactic of exploiting violent mobs to register grievances against another government has also been clearly demonstrated by the Cambodians. In 1965, for example, a large crowd attacked the United States Embassy in Phnom Penh with the obvious knowledge of Prince Sihanouk's Administration. In 1970, shortly after the Prince was deposed in a military coup by the pro-American General Lon Nol, a similar attack was organised, but on this occasion was directed against the North Vietnamese Embassy. (The same year the Chinese and DPRK Ambassadors to Cambodia were held hostage by the Lon Nol Government pending the safe evacuation of Cambodian diplomatic staff from Pyongyang and Peking). Other cases of such state behaviour can easily be found. In 1979, for example, the United States held the Libyan Government responsible when the American Embassy in Tripoli was attacked by a violent mob. The mission suffered severe structural damage.

Because of the international repercussions of obvious state complicity in such attacks the fiction has usually been maintained that they occurred either without the knowledge of the local authorities or that the security forces of the receiving government had been unable to prevent them. In many cases where serious mob violence occurred official apologies were later offered and in some cases reparations made to the sending state. In December 1966, for example, the Suharto Government agreed to compensate the British for the damage done to their Chancery in Jakarta, and the Chinese subsequently restored the British Embassy burnt down in Peking, with formal apologies. Thus the seizure of the United States Embassy in Tehran in November 1979 and the holding of its American occupants for over a year[9] shocked the international community not so much because

Iran had signally failed to protect them—that had happened often enough before—but because the regime of the Ayotollah Khomeini openly 'adopted' the attack as its own.[10] As US President Jimmy Carter later wrote (somewhat inaccurately) of the seizure:

> We were deeply disturbed, but reasonably confident that the Iranians would soon remove the attackers from the embassy compound and release our people. We and other nations had faced this kind of attack many times in the past, but never, so far as we knew, had a host government failed to attempt to protect threatened diplomats.[11]

Both the Iranian Prime Minister and Foreign Minister had given the US a firm pledge that American staff and property would be protected, but in blatant disregard for these undertakings, traditional norms, international law and world opinion the militants who had stormed the US compound were subsequently given official blessing.

The hostage crisis in Iran gave new emphasis to the significance of diplomatic rules and conventions for the conduct of international relations. In its pronouncement on the case, the International Court of Justice made this abundantly clear:

> There is no more fundamental prerequisite for the conduct of relations between States than the inviolability of diplomatic envoys and embassies, so that throughout history nations of all creeds and cultures have observed reciprocal obligations for that purpose.
> ...The institution of diplomacy, with its concomitant privileges and immunities, has withstood the test of centuries and proved to be an instrument essential for effective cooperation in the international community and for enabling States, irrespective of their differing constitutional and social systems, to achieve mutual understanding and to resolve their differences by peaceful means.[12]

In its judgement of 24 May 1980, the Court made an uncharacteristic exhortation which also deserves to be quoted in full:

> The Court considers it to be its duty to draw the attention of the entire international community, of which Iran has been a member since time immemorial, to the irreparable harm that may be caused by the events now before the Court. Such events cannot fail to undermine the edifice of law carefully constructed by mankind over a period of centuries, the maintenance of which is vital for the security and well-being of the complex international community of the present day, to which it is more essential than ever that the rules developed to ensure the ordered progress of relations between its members should be constantly and scrupulously respected.[13]

Sadly, this plea appears not to have been heard by many states.

Between 1970 and 1980 'there were some 70 forcible incursions into diplomatic facilities'. Fifty per cent occurred after the Iranian hostage siezures.[14] While strictly speaking assaults on diplomats and diplomatic facilities of this kind do not constitute state-sponsored terrorism as defined earlier, they are nevertheless a form of symbolic attack by one state upon another through the agency of non-state actors. In demonstrating the receiving state's displeasure and applying pressure for policy changes they act as an extension of that state's foreign policies. As such they have quite correctly been included by Herman Kahn in his controversial analysis of the progressive intensification of political conflict.[15] These attacks also highlight the fragility of diplomatic conventions and are illustrative of the failure of some states to observe the customary rules regarding the protection of diplomats and their facilities. By extension, they suggest too that such international instruments can never be sufficient in themselves to commit states to the peaceful settlement of disputes and restrain them from other forms of attack on diplomatic targets.

STATE SUPPORT FOR TERRORIST GROUPS

The second level at which states can become involved in attacks upon diplomats and diplomatic facilities is that at which active encouragement, material assistance or other forms of support are provided to terrorist groups which conduct such operations in other countries. This is a highly complex and controversial subject with state sponsorship being given directly and indirectly, in many different forms, to a wide range of groups of diverse backgrounds, aims and ideologies. It can include moral support or formal diplomatic sponsorship in international fora, the offer of temporary shelter, the free use of national airspace or political asylum. Usually, and often secretly, it is given in the form of training, logistical support, arms and ammunition, funds and information. Almost always, at some stage and at some level, such sponsorship involves the state's diplomatic service or facilities.

The support of terrorist groups by states is not new. 'In former times mercenary soldiers provided a near approximation of terrorism'[16] and the use of proxy forces also has a long history. The Assassins could be described as the first known example of organised international terrorism by a state, threatening several Islamic regimes over two centuries. In the 1920s Fascist Italy supported Macedonian and Croatian terrorist groups and was indirectly linked to the assassination of King Alexander I of Yugoslavia by *Ustasa* terrorists in Marseilles in 1934.[17] Since World War II the vast majority of internationally significant conflicts have been internal wars or revolutionary civil wars of some kind, most of which included considerable covert or indirect foreign involvement. Few of the states sponsoring participants in these struggles appear to have been particularly concerned about the tactics used and in a number of cases were themselves directly involved in terrorist-style operations. With the growth of international terrorism in the late 1960s and early 1970s, however, the sponsorship of extremist groups increasingly involved states in tactics of a markedly different kind. A popular base and international diplomatic support were no longer prized and in the search for a greater public impact many traditional restraints on action well nigh disappeared. At the same time there arose a number of groups without any specific national or political constituency whose ideologies contained a significant nihilistic element. States were quickly implicated in the hijacking of aircraft, kidnappings, assassinations and indiscriminate violence against civilian targets far from the central focus of the conflict and in direct violation of all established conventions of international behaviour. They also became deeply involved in attacks against diplomats and diplomatic facilities.

It is easy to find lists of countries accused of sponsoring international terrorism, but these tend to be compiled by Western observers concerned exclusively with agitational terror which is felt to serve the interests of their opponents. Most Soviet bloc and radical Third World states have been condemned at different times as 'subversive centres' or 'terrorist states'.[18] In a speech to the American Bar Association in July 1985, for example, President Reagan denounced Iran, Libya, North Korea, Cuba and Nicaragua in particular as 'outlaw states', describing them as a 'new international version of Murder, Inc'.[19] The US State Department has also compiled a list of 24 countries which it claims has offered political asylum to known terrorists.[20] Such lists must be treated with caution, however, as they can be greatly lengthened or drastically reduced depending on the definition of terrorism used and, often, the ideological persuasion of the person or agency compiling them. There is considerable room for the application of double standards. No Western list, for example, includes the names of those countries which provide aid to regimes which depend on enforcement terror to maintain power, and can thus be accused of 'surrogate terrorism'.[21] Rarely are countries like Saudi Arabia or China included despite their past support for, or tolerance of, known terrorist movements. Political sensitivities apparently decree that the same consideration now be extended to Iraq and (since it helped secure the release of the TWA hostages in Beirut in June 1985) even at times to Syria. Support for groups like the *contras* in Nicaragua is ignored while comparable Eastern bloc support for insurgent groups in Central America is included. Certain kinds of clandestine operations by Western intelligence services are overlooked while those of the West's adversaries are not.

Even if consideration of this problem was confined to the most obvious, and popular, targets for criticism it would be difficult to be specific. Because of its largely clandestine nature, the extent of this assistance is hard to determine. It covers a wide range of activities and is constantly changing.

Not all states are as open as Libya, whose Secretary of Information was reported to have stated in 1980 that:

> We are proud to be used...We assert to the whole world that we provide material, moral and political support to every liberation revolution in the world.[22]

As William Gutteridge has reminded observers, 'the tireless fanaticism attributed to the Libyan leader can easily be overdrawn'[23], but since the mid-1970s Colonel Qaddafi has certainly been generous in the provision of funds, facilities and material support to international terrorists. While claims that the Soviet Union is at the root of world terrorism cannot be sustained, it is true that the USSR, its allies and a number of other radical states have provided various extremist organisations with considerable amounts of arms, funds, training, and logistical support, both directly and through intermediaries. Iran, for example, has been less open than Libya about its aid to terrorist groups but probably wider in its reach, giving support to groups in Europe, the Middle East and Asia. Syria's role has been more complicated, with the Assad Government publicly condemning terrorism and helping resolve particular incidents, while secretly sponsoring attacks on selected targets through Palestinian proxies like the Abu Nidal and Abu Musa groups. Although its support has diminished since 1980, Iraq has been a major sponsor of terrorist organisations, including the Abu Nidal group when it operated under the name 'Black June'. Some less wealthy countries, like the PDRY and DPRK, appear to have concentrated their efforts on the provision of training facilities and since the 1960s are reputed to have trained thousands of terrorists from around the world. Cuba too is reported to have provided support for terrorist groups in Latin America, both in its own right before 1968 and on behalf of the Soviet Union after that time.[24]

STATES AS TERRORISTS

Not only are states providing greater support for international terrorist groups, but to an increasing extent they are becoming directly involved in specific terrorist attacks. States have carried out covert intelligence operations before, a category which has included kidnappings, bombings and even assassinations,[25] but rarely have they participated in a concerted campaign of international terrorist violence. Individuals and groups have been enlisted to carry out attacks on behalf of certain states and there appears to be a growing tendency for states themselves to send agents abroad in a terrorist role. The Qaddafi regime is one of the most notorious offenders in this regard, having made numerous attempts to assassinate Libyan dissidents in exile and to attack Western interests abroad. Despite widespread condemnation of these practices and the deportation of some of the Libyans involved there is no sign that Libya's support for these 'suicide commandos' will cease in the near future.[26] Indeed, it can be argued that since the bombing of Libya by the United States in April 1986, the threat to Western interests from Libyan terrorism has markedly increased. One of the most spectacular recent examples of state-sponsored terrorism occurred in Rangoon in October 1983, when members of a DPRK Army team were responsible for a bomb attack on the party of the visiting South Korean President. Twenty-one people died in the incident, including four Korean Cabinet Ministers. Forty-eight people were injured[27]. Such attacks have also been carried out by Western countries. In July 1985, for example, French secret service agents sank the Greenpeace vessel *Rainbow Warrior* in Auckland harbour, killing one member of the ship's crew.

The frequency of state-sponsored terrorist attacks seems to be growing rapidly. Between January 1968 and June 1982 the United States Government counted at least 129 incidents which it felt had included some form of state support.[28] Yet Iran alone is reported to have been involved in some 50 attacks in 1983, and about 60 in 1984.[29] According to the State Department in 1986, Syria has been linked to almost 50 terrorist incidents since 1983, resulting in over 500 casualties. In an accompanying statement, the State Department said that this list was not intended to be all-inclusive but was illustrative of Syria's involvement in and support for terrorism and terrorist groups.[30] All statistics on terrorism must be used with great care, but these and other figures published by Western analysts in recent years are undoubtedly correct in suggesting a greater willingness on the part of terrorist groups to serve state interests and a growing tendency on the part of some states to use terrorism to pursue their foreign policy goals. These trends are important for a number of reasons, one of which is the impact such practices are having on the conduct of diplomacy.

DIPLOMATS AS THE 'SUBJECTS' AND 'OBJECTS' OF STATE-SPONSORED TERRORISM

The 1961 Vienna Convention on Diplomatic Relations specifically enjoins the representatives of sending states to respect the laws and regulations of the receiving states and not to interfere in their internal affairs. Article 41 reads in part:

> The premises of the mission must not be used in any manner incompatible with the functions of the mission as laid down in the present Convention or by other rules of general international law or by any special agreements in force between the sending State and the receiving State.[31]

Yet there have always been cases where the provisions of this Article have been ignored, either in spirit or in practice. Diplomats have often strayed close to the edges of propriety and diplomatic missions have long been used to shelter and support intelligence agents. This has entailed support for various covert activities, ranging from contacts with opposition groups and simple intelligence gathering to more serious operations posing a threat to the sovereignty of the receiving state.[32] As early as 1584 the Spanish Ambassador in London was expelled for plotting against Queen Elizabeth I. A major diplomatic incident occurred in 1896 when the Chinese nationalist leader Sun Yat Sen was abducted by members of the Manchu Secret Service and held captive in the Chinese Embassy in London for twelve days. Thayer cites the case of Franz von Papen, the German Military Attache in Washington during the First World War, who was declared *persona non grata* after being implicated in plots to destroy US ammunition dumps.[33] In 1966 the Chinese Embassy in The Hague was accused of abducting a Taiwanese national and the two Koreas have levelled similar charges at each other on a number of occasions since.

While the use of diplomatic missions for intelligence purposes may no longer be considered unusual, there appears no precedent to the current widespread use of diplomatic facilities by some states for the purpose of conducting terrorist operations abroad, whether they be against expatriates or foreign governments. Over the past 20 years or so diplomatic bags have been used extensively to smuggle arms and ammunition, and diplomatic premises have often become centres for the storage and distribution of terrorist literature and materials. Diplomatic communications have been used to coordinate operations between terrorists and their state sponsors and diplomatic credentials have been provided both for state assassins and 'independent' terrorist groups. In addition to this use of diplomatic facilities, diplomats themselves, or at least officials masquerading in that role, have been responsible for liaison with terrorist groups, providing them with arms, intelligence about their targets, accommodation and guidance.

Once again, Libya provides perhaps the clearest illustration of the systematic abuse of diplomatic systems for terrorist purposes. Libya's diplomatic service was used, for example, to assist those Palestinians responsible for the Munich Olympic massacre in 1972, and the weapons used in the BSO seizure of the Saudi Arabian Embassy in Khartoum the same year were taken to Sudan in Libyan diplomatic bags. Since 1981, more than 50 Libyan diplomats have been expelled from their assigned countries for terrorist and related offences. When the US Government closed the Libyan People's Bureau in Washington that year it claimed that Libyan diplomatic staff were providing support for assassination squads operating in the United States. The Libyan Chargé d'Affaires in Switzerland was expelled in April 1983 after being accused of passing arms to local terrorists. In 1984 Libyan agents travelling to Saudi Arabia claimed 'diplomatic immunity' when it was discovered that their baggage included weapons destined for extremists in Mecca. The United Kingdom severed diplomatic relations with Libya in April 1984 and expelled all members of the Libyan People's Bureau, after one of them murdered a British policewoman in London. In September 1985 Tunisia also broke off diplomatic relations with Libya, following the expulsion of four Libyan diplomats suspected of having posted over 100 letter bombs. In December that year two Libyan diplomats were forced to leave Spain after it was discovered that they were planning a terrorist attack, and a Turkish court has since formally charged the Libyan Consul in Istanbul for a similar offence. The American bombing of Libya in April 1986 was publicly justified by evidence that the Libyan People's Bureau in East Berlin was directly implicated in the bombing of a West Berlin nightclub.[34]

Libya is not alone, however, in violating diplomatic conventions in this way. In February 1973, for example, it was reported that a cache of arms found hidden in the Iraqi Embassy in Islamabad consisted of some 300 automatic weapons, 60 000 rounds of ammunition and grenades, all sealed in diplomatic bags.[35] According to Seymour Hersh, the CIA smuggled weapons into Chile in United States diplomatic bags before the overthrow of President Salvador Allende in September 1973.[36] Calls in April 1982 for a 'purge of the embassies' in Paris followed the discovery that the officials of a number of countries represented there were implicated in a series of terrorist incidents and on numerous other occasions 'diplomats' have been declared *persona non grata* because of similar behaviour in other states. The assassination attempt against ROK President Chun Doo Hwan in October 1983 provides another clear example of this behaviour, with the discovery by Burmese authorities that the North Korean 'hit team' received close assistance from members of the DPRK Embassy in Rangoon.[37] Members of Syria's ruling Ba'ath party stationed in Syrian embassies in Western Europe have also used diplomatic privileges and facilities to conduct terrorist activities. In April 1986 Britain broke off diplomatic relations with Syria and expelled its diplomats from the United Kingdom, when it was proven that the Syrian Embassy in London was deeply implicated in the attempted sabotage of an El Al airliner at Heathrow Airport. A number of Syrian diplomats were expelled from the FRG in November 1986, for similar abuses of diplomatic privileges in that country. In March 1987 it was announced that Tunisia had severed diplomatic ties with Iran, following the discovery of evidence linking the Iranian Embassy in Tunis with terrorist attacks in Tunisia and elsewhere.[38]

Not only have diplomats been party to state-sponsored terrorism, but they have figured prominently among its victims. A high proportion of terrorist attacks instigated by states have been directed against the diplomats and diplomatic facilities of other states. One early example of this could be seen in 1960, when Fidel Castro reportedly assigned agents to assassinate the US Ambassador to Mexico, who had suggested that Mexico's sugar quota to the United States be increased (presumably at Cuba's expense). Mexican police were assigned to protect the Ambassador for over a year.[39] After the Gulf of Sidra incident in August 1981[40] US intelligence agencies reported that Libya had planned terrorist attacks against the American Embassies in London, Paris, Rome and Vienna.[41] The Secretary of State has also claimed that Libya planned attacks on more than 23 US missions before the April 1986 bombing raids. Since the 1978 Camp David Accords Libya has joined with other 'confrontation states' in sponsoring terrorist attacks against Egyptian diplomatic missions. Iranian and Syrian-supported organisations like Islamic Jihad openly threatened the US, UK and France after those countries agreed to participate in a multinational force in Lebanon in 1983, and were probably responsible for the car bomb attacks against US and French missions in Beirut which occurred that year. According to the State Department, Syria and Iran were directly involved in the bomb attacks against the American and French Embassies in Kuwait, also in 1983.[42] Responsibility for the attack on the US Embassy Annexe in East Beirut in September the following year, in which 23 people were killed and over 50 people wounded, has also been laid at the door of these countries.[43] After it moved its operational base from Iraq to Syria in 1983 the Abu Nidal Organisation carried out an assassination campaign against Jordanian representatives, to obtain the release of imprisoned Palestinian extremists and to undermine Jordanian peace initiatives with Israel and moderate factions of the PLO. The diplomatic services of both Iran and Iraq have become prime targets for terrorist attack since the war between those two states began in 1980.

Given their preference for attacks on diplomatic targets, state aid to groups like the Armenian Secret Army for the Liberation of Armenia (ASALA) and the Croatian Revolutionary Brotherhood (HRB) directly increases the risks to all Turkish and Yugoslav diplomats and their families. Indeed, it could be argued that as diplomats and their facilities are now viewed as 'legitimate' targets by most groups then any support given to terrorists, whether it be direct or indirect, contributes to the dangers faced by all members of the diplomatic profession. Similarly, any abuses of the diplomatic system by states assisting terrorists must raise the doubts in peoples' minds about the legitimacy of all diplomatic activity and help erode the fragile consensus on which the principle of diplomatic inviolability is based.

STATE-SPONSORED TERRORISM AND 'SURROGATE WARFARE'

States appear to support terrorist operations for a number of reasons. Ideological considerations play a significant role and are often accompanied by a desire to challenge the dominance of the United States (and the West) in international politics. Such involvement also tends to include the export of enforcement terror found in the sponsoring state. Attacks might be prompted by simple vengeance, as in the cases of the Letelier assassination in Washington in 1976 or the assassination of former General Oviessi in Paris in 1984.[44] They might also be to silence critics of the regime, a practice at least as old as the Stalinist campaign against dissident Soviet exiles in the 1920s. Other cases, like those sponsored by Iran, seem to be inspired by a mixture of religious and political motives. It is possible too that support for terrorist groups is felt by some of the smaller and weaker states to give them an influence in world affairs that would otherwise be denied them. Whatever the reason, the sponsorship of international terrorism represents the rejection of conventional diplomacy and to a degree at least a preference for coercion over peaceful negotiation. However slight, this is a movement along the political continuum towards open conflict. Indeed, such is the scope of state-sponsored terrorism and so significant are the differences between it and earlier social and political struggles by terrorist groups that some observers have come to see the curent phenomenon, for all practical purposes, as a form of 'surrogate warfare', the latest man-ifestation of the 'camouflaged wars' predicted by Sir Basil Liddell-Hart and Andre Beaufre in the 1950s and 1960s.[45]

In a thesis first proposed in 1975 and elaborated further in 1983[46], Brian Jenkins of the Rand Corporation has argued that because of the nuclear stalemate between the two superpowers opposing states have been obliged to choose between conventional wars and piotracted unconventional wars. As a general rule, however, the former are becoming increasingly impractical. They are too costly, too destructive and too unpopular in domestic and world opinion. Short 'lightning' wars, like the 1967 Six Day War or the Turkish invasion of Cyprus in 1974 are still an option but are often incon-clusive. Protracted conflicts have other drawbacks, as demonstrated by the Vietnam War. An alternative mode of warfare, Jenkins has argued, is a campaign of low level terrorist violence. By taking advantage of devel-opments in modern society, in particular arms technology and the legal ambiguities of international terrorism, states can wear down the capacities and resolve of their enemies through a series of clandestine attacks. These can be made on targets within the state or, as in the case of attacks on diplomats and dipomatic facilities, against the assets of a state beyond its national borders. Jenkins apparently believes not only that such a conflict is likely but that it would jeopardise the present system of international order based on a community of sovereign states, even the concept of nationhood itself. 'War will cease to be finite, the distinction between peace and war will dissolve', leaving states in an environment not unlike the anarchy of Renaissance Italy.[47]

While this argument is persuasive, it contains a number of flaws. It is true that the current nuclear balance which constrains the major powers from total war has produced a kind of stability in which lower level conflicts can flourish, but however costly and unpopular conventional wars are still seen as a real option, as evidenced by the Iran-Iraq war. Nor is it likely that protracted guerrilla campaigns will ever disappear for, quite apart from indigenous considerations, they continue to serve the wider strategic purposes of the superpowers themselves, as seen in Afghanistan and Central America. 'International terrorist attack is a different mode of war, not an alternative to war as such'.[48] There is a trend towards the development of terrorist violence as part of the world's strategic composition but not all such campaigns can be included within the pattern outlined by Brian Jenkins. As Grant Wardlaw pointed out in 1984, for example:

> Resort to the tactics of terrorism, or the formation of alliances with terrorist groups, provides an option which allows such [small] nations, which would otherwise be unable to mount challenges using conventional force, to carry out surrogate warfare against their opponents.[49]

In such cases, terrorism is seen as a cheap weapons system and while it may be used in conjunction with wider conflicts it should not automatically be viewed as part of one. Jenkins does not distinguish between terrorist activities in this way, however, nor does he seem to allow for terrorist acts unrelated to significant political contests. His vision of surrogate warfare between states is really only applicable to conflicts between major powers and even then fails to accord sufficient weight to the readiness of the international community to take steps against universally disruptive political violence.

Despite its shortcomings, or perhaps even as a result of them, this thesis seems to have been readily adopted by the US Government. As early as 1975 the Special Assistant to the Secretary of State and State Department Coordinator for Combatting Terrorism testified to a US Senate Subcommittee in terms very similar to those used by Jenkins in his first paper on this subject.[50] The idea of a global power shunning outright war but still pursuing its strategic objectives through terrorist surrogates has also found a receptive audience among senior members of the Reagan Administration, who have cited with approval Claire Sterling's claims that the Soviet Union is operating a 'terror network' through its Eastern European satellites, the PLO and Cuba. Congress too has given credence to suggestions that there is 'a large Communist terrorist force, a Communist army which . . . is not yet fully deployed'.[51] This 'low intensity warfare' by the Eastern bloc is seen as part of a concerted effort to expand its influence around the world and is purportedly aimed at everything from the West's strategic interests in Western Europe, the Middle East and the Caribbean to weakening liberal democracy and undermining world stability.

As Grant Wardlaw and others have pointed out, 'the evidence of Soviet support for destabilising influences in the Western-aligned world is overwhelming, but it indicates a capacity for opportunistic exploitation of situations rather than their specific creation and direction'.[52] To view the Soviet Union as the 'puppet master' of world terrorism is to ignore the many, often subtle differences between terrorist groups, their aims and ideologies. In many countries the radical right poses as great a threat as the revolutionary left and the political commitment of many terrorist groups is weak and inconsistent. Despite rhetorical flourishes and short-term alliances terrorists (like states) have tended to remain stubbornly independent and have consistently refused to submerge their differences in a 'sea of world revolution'.[53] Obviously, any weakening in political stability and social cohesion in the West can affect the overall 'correlation of forces' between the two major blocs[54], but the simplistic and misleading picture of world terrorism painted by Sterling and others serves only to reinforce the prejudices of the Reagan Administration, which has already displayed a tendency to view complex world problems in simple East-West terms. Such an approach also ignores America's own involvement in terrorism of different kinds and its selective approach to the terrorist activities of other countries.

Over the years the United States too has 'hired gunmen, mobs and private armies with which to protect her foreign policy interests'.[55] American efforts have included offensive operations but in recent years have been largely reactive. In particular the US has provided considerable support for regimes which have relied on enforcement terror to remain in power, a practice which has been justified publicly by a double standard that has in effect made anti-communist terror acceptable while terror used by the United States' opponents has usually been deemed worthy of universal condemnation. This approach is perhaps exemplified best by the essay written in 1979 by the former US Permanent Representative to the United Nations (and now Presidential hopeful) Jeanne Kirkpatrick, on 'Dictatorships and Double Standards'. In that paper Mrs Kirkpatrick drew a distinction between 'revolutionary autocracies' such as the Soviet Union and 'traditional authoritarian' governments such as those military dictatorships supported by the US. This same distinction was drawn when Mrs Kirkpatrick spoke about terrorism to the Jonathan Institute in Washington in June 1984. On that occasion her argument was essentially the same, that motives were crucial and that while terror used in defence of a society was acceptable, terror used to destroy it was not.[56] The major difficulty with this argument, however, lies in the fact that such distinctions rely on subjective moral judgements as much as those made by the US's opponents when they describe terrorists as 'freedom fighters'. Inevitably, ideological and partisan political factors quickly assume a major role and durable diplomatic solutions become more elusive.

Such considerations are also apparent in the selective approach sometimes taken by the Reagan Administration towards the terrorist activities of other states. In February 1982, for example, it was announced that Iraq was being removed from the official list of nations that supported international terrorism.[57] Iraq, however, not only provides sanctuary for known terrorists but itself conducts terrorist operations, often through its diplomatic agents. Yet, 'rapprochement with Iraq having been determined to be necessary for reasons of Persian Gulf *realpolitik*, legal sanctions against terrorism were abandoned'.[58] It is hard to escape the conclusion that, more recently, Libya has been singled out for particular condemnation and action by the US because it is a relatively weak and isolated country, not having the capabilities, international support, or importance to wider American strategic interests enjoyed by other, more powerful terrorist sponsors. One Australian observer expressed the concerns of many when he told the US Defense Intelligence Analysis Center in 1985:

> The dropping of Syria from the official list of terrorist sponsoring states, the confusion over the U.S. position on the bombing by Israel of the PLO headquarters in Tunis and the reluctance to comment on the bombing of the Greenpeace ship 'Rainbow Warrior' in New Zealand by French agents are all equivocations which detract from the effort to gain international agreement to counter *all* forms of terrorism.[59]

The United States' secret arms shipments to Iran in 1985 and 1986 demonstrated the extent to which the Reagan Administration was prepared to deal with terrorists and their state sponsors. As US Senator Daniel Moynihan has observed, such behaviour seriously undermines the Reagan Administration's credibility and exposes it to accusations that the United States' opposition to terrorism is not rooted in principle or in law, but in self interest. Whether or not this is true, the US is not alone in following such practices, which have a long history.

TERRORISM AND 'COERCIVE DIPLOMACY'

The use of terror and dealings with terrorists have always been seen as options by states whenever their national interests seem to have required it, so much so that in some respects terror has almost become 'acceptable'. Such is the history of repressive state policies, support for dictatorships, clandestine interventions and covert operations against individuals that, as Michael Stohl has shown, 'policies of terrorism in the international system have grown to the status of legitimate (ie considered to be legitimate) behaviour'.[60] As such they sometimes figure prominently in states' foreign relations. Raymond Aron made the point over 20 years ago that the distinction between diplomacy and strategy was purely relative:

> These two terms are complimentary aspects of the single art of politics—the art of conducting relations with other states so as to further the 'national interest'.[61]

Drawing on Thomas Schelling's analysis of the nuclear 'balance of terror', Stohl has gone further and suggested that terrorism has now become part of the 'coercive diplomacy' which states have always used to produce changes in their opponents' political positions through symbolic violence and the fear that non-compliance will bring punishment 'terrible beyond endurance'.[62] Thus a campaign of international terrorism can become a tool of states, an extension of foreign policy by other means, placed on a scale between absolute peace and outright war. In such a situation, diplomacy can be regarded as being more or less effective depending on the ability of states to manipulate the threat of terrorist violence as a means of exerting pressure and winning desired policy changes. As Michael Stohl has written, 'the threat is quite explicit, even if it is non-verbal'.[63]

If seen in such a light, such 'tacit negotiation'[64] challenges the asssumptions in the traditional definition of diplomacy as 'the conduct of business between states by peaceful means'[65] and gives greater weight to the arguments of the Realist School whose 'diplomacy of violence' is discussed by Schelling and Stohl. To the Realists, diplomacy has never been a matter of 'pure persuasion', but has always contained an element of symbolic or clandestine violence. This view has clearly been accepted by the Reagan Administration. In December 1984, for example, Secretary of State Shultz gave a speech entitled 'The Ethics of Power' in which he stated:

> Americans have sometimes tended to think that power and diplomacy are two distinct alternatives. This reflects a fundamental misunderstanding. The truth is, power and diplomacy must always go together, or we will accomplish very little in this world. Power must always be guided by purpose. At the same time, the hard reality is that diplomacy not backed by strength will always be ineffectual at best, dangerous at worst.[66]

Schelling put the same case more bluntly when he wrote that 'the power to hurt is bargaining power. To exploit it is diplomacy—vicious diplomacy, but diplomacy'.[67] Long understood and accepted in terms of conventional power ('gunboat diplomacy') and the nuclear balance, this relationship between terrorism and diplomacy is only now becoming plain.

Such a development has caused considerable concern, not only because of the increased threat to lives and property, but also because of fears that the international system itself cannot survive such a challenge. The United States in particular has warned of the threat to the institution of diplomacy, to world stability and even to civilisation itself.[68] With its perception of international terrorism as being essentially an attack on Western values, the US has tended to blame this impending catastrophe on the USSR and those apparently allied with it, but once again the situation is a great deal more complex than that portrayed by members of the Reagan Administration. Whereas in the past the international system could be controlled to a significant degree by the superpowers and their allies, this is no longer the case. The system is much more fluid, with a greater number of states and non-state actors, many of which act independently of the major blocs. Some have chosen to indulge in activities that are inimical to the interests of all the major powers, regardless of their political persuasion. Terrorist activities that have been 'legitimate' in the past are no longer taking place in a system controlled by these powers and are thus considered more threatening to the world order. New forms of terrorist attack, such as those against diplomats and diplomatic facilities, challenge norms of international behaviour that affect all states. This has resulted in a growing sense of shared danger and, particularly with regard to diplomacy, a rare consensus on the need to take concerted action against violence of this kind.

NOTES

1. This is a recurring theme in statements by members of the Reagan Administration. See in particular G.P. Shultz, 'Terrorism: The Challenge to the Democracies', Address by the Secretary of State before the Jonathan Institute's Second Conference on International Terrorism, Washington, 24 June 1984, *Current Policy* 589 (24 June 1984).
2. Sen, pp.97-98. See also J.L. Brierly, *The Law of Nations* (Oxford University Press, Oxford, 1984), p.289.
3. See Brownlie, p.227.
4. Quoted in Bloomfield and Fitzgerald, p.6.
5. J.A.C. Mackie, *Konfrontasi: The Indonesia-Malaysia Dispute, 1963-1966* (Oxford University Press, Kuala Lumpur, 1974), pp.181-193.
6. Boyce, p.203.
7. Quoted in Boyce, p.207.
8. *Satow's Guide*, p.196.
9. There were 100 people in the US Embassy compound when it was seized on 4 November 1979. The 34 locally-engaged staff members were immediately released and after two weeks the 13 black and female Americans held hostage were also permitted to leave. One other member of the Embassy staff was released because of illness in July 1980, leaving 52 hostages held for the total 444 days of the 'crisis'. They were finally released on 21 January 1981. A detailed chronology of these events is given in Pierre Salinger, *America held Hostage: The Secret Negotiations* (Andre Deutsch, London, 1981), pp.311-319.
10. One earlier example of a state openly embracing terrorism on its own soil (though not for a terrorist act committed within its own borders) was the support given by Ugandan President Idi Amin to the Palestinian and German hijackers of an Air France Airbus at Entebbe in June 1976. See William Stevenson, *90 Minutes at Entebbe* (Corgi, London, 1976), p.ix.

11. Jimmy Carter, *Keeping Faith: Memoirs of a President* (Bantam Books, Toronto, 1982), p.457.

12. Case Concerning United States Diplomatic and Consular Staff in Tehran, Provisional Measures Order of 15 December 1979. *ICJ Reports of Judgements, Advisory Opinions and Orders, 1979* (ICJ, The Hague, 1979), p.16. See also Oscar Schachter, 'International Law in the Hostage Crisis: Implications for Future Cases', in Warren Christopher *et al, American Hostages in Iran: The Conduct of a Crisis* (Yale University Press, New Haven, 1985), p.346.

13. Case Concerning United States Diplomatic and Consular Staff in Tehran, Judgement of 24 May 1980. *ICJ Reports of Judgements, Advisory Opinions and Orders, 1980* (ICJ, The Hague, 1980), pp.42–43. See also Schachter, *op.cit.*.

14. Perez, 'Terrorist Target: The Diplomat', p.2.

15. Herman Kahn, *On Escalation: Metaphors and Scenarios* (Penguin, Baltimore, 1968), p.73.

16. Lauran Paine, *The Terrorists* (Robert Hale, London, 1975), p.163.

17. More correctly, the *Ustasa Hrvatska Revolucionarna Organizacija*, the Rebel Croat Revolutionary Organisation, or UHRO. Established in 1932, UHRO claimed a membership of 550 when King Alexander I was assassinated. See Janke, p.114.

18. See, for example, 'Terrorist Activity: International Terrorism', *Hearings* before the Subcommittee to Investigate the Administration of the Internal Security Act and other Internal Security Laws of the Committee of the Judiciary, US Senate, Ninety-fourth Congress, First Session, 14 May 1975. Also, *Soviet Military Power* (US Government Printing Office, Washington, 1986), pp.124–128.

19. 'The New Network of Terrorist States', President Reagan's address before the American Bar Association, 8 July 1985, *Department of State Bulletin* 85:2101 (August 1985), p.8.

20. *Patterns of International Terrorism: 1981*, p.2.

21. Michael Stohl, 'National Interests and State Terrorism in International Affairs', *Political Science*, 36:1 (July 1984) p.51. See also E.S. Herman, *The Real Terror Network: Terror in Fact and Propaganda* (South End Press, Boston, 1984).

22. Quoted in R.S. Cline and Y. Alexander, *Terrorism: The Soviet Connection* (Crane Russak, New York, 1984), p.69.

23. William Gutteridge (ed), *Libya: Still a Threat to Western Interests?* Conflict Studies 160 (Institute for the Study of Conflict, London, 1984), p.3.

24. 1968 is the year the Soviet KGB is reputed to have taken control of its Cuban counterpart, the *Direccion General de Intelligencia* (DGI). 'The Role of Cuba in International Terrorism and Subversion', *Hearings* before the Subcommittee on Security and Terrorism of the Committee on the Judiciary, US Senate, Ninety-seventh Congress, 26 February–12 March 1982. See also Claire Sterling, *The Terror Network: The Secret War of International Terrorism* (Holt, Rinehart and Winston, New York, 1981), p.247.

25. There has been a spate of books dealing with this subject in recent years, the better known of them including John Barron, *KGB: The Secret Work of Soviet Secret Agents* (Transworld, London, 1975); Phillip Agee, *Inside the Company: CIA Diary* (Penguin, Harmondsworth, 1975); and Thomas Plate and Andrea Darvi, *Secret Police: The Inside Story of a Network of Terror* (Abacus, London, 1982). While there is considerable controversy over the apparent revelations in such works, there seems little doubt that the covert operations of some intelligence and security services have included activities normally associated with terrorist groups.

26. Grant Wardlaw, 'Terrorism: State involvement adds new dimension', *Pacific Defence Reporter*, Annual Reference Edition (December 1984/January 1985), p.59.

27. See *The Bomb Attack at the Martyrs' Mausoleum in Rangoon: Report on the findings by the Enquiry Committee and the measures taken by the Burmese Government* (Rangoon, 1984).

28. G. W. Hopple and B. W. Watson (eds), *The Military Intelligence Community* (Westview Press, Boulder, 1986), p.190.
29. R. B. Oakley, 'International Terrorism: Current Trends and the U.S. Response', Statement by Robert B. Oakley, Director, Office for Counter-Terrorism and Emergency Planning, before the Senate Committees on Foreign Relations and on the Judiciary, Washington, 15 May 1985, *Current Policy* 706 (May 1985).
30. 'Syrian Support for International Terrorism: 1983–86', US Department of State *Special Report* 157 (December 1986). See also 'List links Syria to world-wide terrorism', *Canberra Times*, 17 November 1986.
31. See Brownlie, p.226.
32. See for example N. P. Ward, 'Espionage and the Forfeiture of Diplomatic Immunity', *International Lawyer* 11:4 (1977), pp.657–671.
33. C. W. Thayer, *Diplomat* (Michael Joseph, London, 1960), pp.211–212.
34. This evidence was derived mainly from intercepted radio communications between the Libyan People's Bureau in East Berlin and Tripoli. According to President Reagan, a message to the East Berlin mission ordered an attack on Americans. On 4 April the Libyan People's Bureau reported that an attack would take place the next day. The bomb attack on the 'La Belle' discotheque in West Berlin occurred on 5 April and the Bureau subsequently reported to Tripoli on the success of this mission.
35. *Canberra Times*, 12 February 1973.
36. S. M. Hersh, *The Price of Power: Kissinger in the Nixon White House* (Summit Books, New York, 1983), p.289. See also *Alleged Assassination Plots Involving Foreign Leaders*, Senate Report 465, Select Committee to Study Governmental Operations with Respect to Intelligence (the Church Committee), Ninety-fourth Congress, First Session (1975).
37. *The Bomb Attack at the Martyrs' Mausoleum in Rangoon.*
38. It was claimed that the Iranian Embassy served as an intermediary between Iranian and Tunisian extremists, and helped enlist Tunisians to conduct terrorist operations in Western Europe. 'Tunisia cuts diplomatic ties with Iranians', *Guardian*, 27 March· 1987.
39. Wilson, p.60.
40. In 1973 Libya insisted that the Gulf of Sidra was entirely Libyan territory. Almost as soon as he was inaugurated, President Reagan announced that the Sixth Fleet's summer manoeuvres would be held in the Gulf, within the area claimed by Colonel Qaddafi. When they took place in August 1981, Libyan jets converged on the US fleet and two were shot down. Gutteridge, p.18.
41. Bass and Jenkins, p.22.
42. Sayre, p.1.
43. Ariel Merari and Yosefa Braunstein, 'Shi'ite Terrorism: Capabilities and the Suicide Factor', *Terrorism Violence and Insurgency Journal* 5:2 (Fall 1984), pp.7–10.
44. Former Chilean ambassador and Defence Minister Orlando Letelier was killed in Washington by agents of DINA, the secret police force of the Pinochet Government. Former Iranian General Gholam Ali Oviessi (the so-called 'Butcher of Iran') was assassinated by Iranian agents in Paris in 1984.
45. Basil Liddell-Hart, *Strategy: The Indirect Approach* (Faber, London, 1967), pp.373 *et.seq.*, and Andre Beaufre, *Introduction to Strategy—With particular reference to problems of defence, politics, economics and diplomacy in the nuclear age* (Faber, London, 1965), pp.107 *et.seq.*.
46. *High Technology Terrorism and Surrogate War: The Impact of New Technology on Low-Level Violence* (1975) and *New Modes of Conflict* (1983).
47. *High Technology Terrorism and Surrogate War*, p.3 and pp.24–25, and *New Modes of Conflict*, p.16.

48. Paul Wilkinson, *Terrorism and the Liberal State* (Macmillan, London, 1986), p.194.

49. Grant Wardlaw, 'Strategic Aspects of Political Terrorism', Address to the Joint Services Staff College, Canberra, 29 February 1984.

50. 'Terrorist Activity: International Terrorism', *Hearings*.

51. 'Historical Antecedents of Soviet Terrorism', *Hearings* before the Subcommittee on Security and Terrorism of the Committee on the Judiciary, US Senate, Ninety-seventh Congress, First Session, 11-12 June 1981.

52. Wardlaw, *Political Terrorism*, p.56.

53. J. B. Bell, 'Contemporary Revolutionary Organisations', in R. O. Keohane and J. S. Nye (eds), *Transnational Relations and World Politics* (Harvard University Press, Cambridge, 1981), p.167.

54. W. S. Thompson, 'Political Violence and "the Correlation of Forces"', *Orbis* 19:4 (Winter 1976), pp.1270-1287.

55. Thompson, p.1282. Seymour Hersh's study of former Secretary of State Henry Kissinger, for example, suggests that the US was responsible for, or at least implicated in, the assassinations or attempted assassinations of Fidel Castro, Salvador Allende, Patrice Lumumba, Rafael Trujillo and Nguyen Van Thieu. Hersh, pp.274-277. See also *Alleged Assassination Plots Involving Foreign Leaders*.

56. See J.J. Kirkpatrick, *Dictatorships and Double Standards—Rationalism and Reason in Politics* (Touchstone, New York, 1983), pp.23-52, and J.J. Kirkpatrick, 'Defining Terrorism', *Catholicism in Crisis* (September 1984), pp.41-44.

57. The US Export Administration Act imposes export controls on countries that support or participate in acts of terrorism.

58. Senator Daniel Moynihan, 'Nuturing Terrorism', *Harper's* 268:1606 (March 1984), p.18. Abu Abbas, the man thought to be responsible for the *Achille Lauro* seizure, was carrying an Iraqi diplomatic passport when the Egyptian plane on which he was travelling was forced down by US jet fighters in 1985.

59. Grant Wardlaw, 'State Response to International Terrorism: Some Cautionary Comments', Paper prepared for a Symposium on International Terrorism, Defense Intelligence Analysis Center, Washington, 2-3 December 1985 (emphasis retained).

60. Stohl, 'National Interests', p.40.

61. Raymond Aron, *Peace and War: A Theory of International Relations* (Praeger, New York, 1970), p.24.

62. Schelling, p.15.

63. Stohl, 'National Interests', pp.41-42.

64. The term is former US Secretary of State Dean Acheson's, quoted in J. Eayrs, *Diplomacy and its Discontents* (University of Toronto Press, Toronto, 1971), pp.71-72.

65. *Satow's Guide*, p.1.

66. G. P. Shultz, 'The Ethics of Power', Address at the Convocation of Yeshiva University, New York, 9 December 1984, *Department of State Bulletin* 85:2095 (February 1985), p.2.

67. Schelling, p.2 and Aron, p.61. The British Admiral Horatio Nelson (1758-1805) is reputed to have claimed that a man o' war was 'the best negotiator in Europe'.

68. See in particular Shultz, 'Terrorism: The Challenge to the Democracies' and K.W. Dam, 'Terrorism in the Middle East', Address by Kenneth W. Dam, Acting Secretary of State, to the leaders of the National United Jewish Appeal, Washington, 1 October 1984, *Current Policy* 618 (1 October 1984).

4

COUNTER-TERRORISM AND INTERNATIONALLY PROTECTED PERSONS

The state of peace among men who live together is not a natural state; for the natural state is one of war, ie if not a state of open hostilities, still a continuous threat of such. The state of peace must be established.

Immanuel Kant
Perpetual Peace: A Philosophical Proposal (1795)

Before the 1960s, diplomats could usually rely on the host country's laws, international custom and other traditional restraints to protect them from violence. The increasing frequency of attacks on diplomats and diplomatic facilities by terrorists after that time, however, made it necessary for both sending and receiving states to reassess the measures normally taken for the protection of the personnel and property for which they were responsible. Matters which had formerly been examined only occasionally and on a piecemeal basis required much deeper and broader consideration. As a consequence, a number of complex political and legal issues were raised over the measures required and the states responsible for their implementation. In addition, there were differences in perceptions and capabilities between the older, established and often wealthier states and the newly-constituted non-European states with fewer resources and a shorter history of participation in the formal diplomatic process. The fragility of diplomatic relations was exposed and the tactical advantages held by the terrorists made clear. Above all, the international scope of terrorist activities emphasised the interdependence of modern states and the need for cooperation if the terrorist threat to diplomats and diplomatic facilities was to be countered effectively.

As John Murphy has stated, 'the proper strategy and tactics for governments to employ in response to kidnappings and other attacks on diplomats are key elements in any policy designed to enhance diplomatic protection'.[1] Of necessity, most states have now formulated broad policy positions on the terrorism issue. Many have also devised contingency plans for use in the event of terrorist attacks on targets within their spheres of responsibility. There is considerable controversy, however, over the different approaches that have been adopted. For the sake of argument, these approaches can be divided roughly into the 'hard line' and the 'soft line'.

THE 'HARD LINE' AND 'SOFT LINE' APPROACHES

The so-called 'hard line' states, led by the United States, Britain and Israel, have argued that only by firmly resisting terrorism can it be shown that such violence will not pay. As described by the Vice President's Task Force on Combatting Terrorism in February 1986, for example:

> The U.S. Government will make no concessions to terrorists. It will not pay ransoms, release prisoners, change its policies or agree to other acts that might encourage additional terrorism.[2]

Among the hard liners themselves, there may be considerable differences. These arise in part through different perceptions of the strategic threat posed by terrorism but can also reflect different traditions of conflict resolution. The United Kingdom, for example, has emphasised long term policies which concentrate on careful police work, the prosecution of terrorists in the courts and action against terrorist sponsors through established channels of international law. Military operations are considered only in specific circumstances and as a last resort. The United States, on the other hand, has in recent years tended to favour shorter term military options.

In April 1984 President Reagan signed a secret National Security Directive (Number 138) authorising the establishment of US counter-terrorist forces 'capable of mounting pre-emptive or retaliatory raids against terrorist groups'. The formation of officially sanctioned assassination squads was also seriously debated but apparently did not proceed. The same day that NSD 138 was signed, the Secretary of State gave a major foreign policy address in which he made clear the Reagan Administration's conviction that the only way effectively to combat terrorism was to use force. Mr Shultz criticised the Long Commission for its belief that 'diplomatic alternatives' could be separated from 'military options' and pointed out that 'diplomatic success often rests on perceptions of military power'.[3] The United States in effect declared war against an unspecified terrorist foe 'to be fought at an unknown place and time with weapons yet to be chosen'.[4] In a speech made in October 1984 the Secretary of State again referred to the need to:

> reach a consensus in this country that our response should go beyond passive
> defense to consider means of active prevention, pre-emption, and retalia-
> tion...We should take steps toward carrying out such measures. There should
> be no moral confusion on this issue.[5]

As demonstrated by subsequent events, the kind of measures considered
for inclusion in the Reagan Administration's new policy of 'active defence'
were disinformation campaigns in the Western news media, the kidnapping
of suspected terrorists, the covert training and support of foreign operatives
able to carry out pre-emptive attacks against terrorist groups,[6] the bombing
of terrorist bases and training centres, and possibly even the forcible removal
of regimes sponsoring terrorist groups.

Nor has the United States been alone in adopting such an approach.
Israel and South Africa, for example, have long carried out reprisal raids
for terrorist attacks. Even the 1982 Israeli invasion of Lebanon was publicly
justified on these grounds, after the Abu Nidal group attempted to assassinate
Shlomo Argov, the Israeli Ambassador in London.[7] Only one month after
the United States bombing raids on Tripoli and Benghazi in April 1986,
themselves in retaliation for Libyan terrorist attacks in Europe, South Africa
launched a series of attacks on three neighbouring states accused of assisting
the African National Congress (ANC). The South Africans specifically cited
the US raids as a precedent. Such military reprisals are different, however,
from the use of terrorist methods against terrorists themselves.

Since 1972 Israel's Central Institute for Intelligence and Security (known
by its Hebrew initials as Mossad) has sent so-called 'hit teams' throughout
Western Europe and the Middle East to assassinate terrorists believed
responsible for attacks against Israeli targets. Similar operations have been
carried out by the Spanish Government against Basque terrorists in France
and the FRG has reportedly sent small *zeilfahndung* (target squads) to
abduct terrorists living abroad and return them to Germany for trial.[8] The
Yugoslav Security Service (UDBa) has apparently sent assassins to locate
and kill Croatian dissidents abroad, often with the help of Yugoslav diplomatic agents. A number of Latin American governments, including those
in Argentina and Venezuela, are thought to have sent agents abroad to
kill terrorists who had escaped capture in their own countries.[9] There is
also evidence to suggest that, like their terrorist opponents, the governments
of Israel, Portugal and Spain have resorted to car and letter bombs against
selected targets. Other considerations aside for the moment, such measures
reflect a profound distrust, if not outright rejection of conventional diplomacy as an option in the settlement of terrorist problems.

Officially, diplomacy is seen by hard line states, at best, as a technique
which is useful in broad conceptual areas of policy formulation and in
the coordination of approaches with friends and allies. It is recognised

too that negotiations can help defuse some dangerous situations and provide tactical advantages to counter-terrorist forces. The declared policies of such states, however, rule out any 'deals' or settlements with terrorists or their alleged sponsors. There is even a school which claims that diplomacy is positively harmful to the resolution of specific terrorist incidents. The British Ambassador to Uruguay may have felt in 1971 that the Tupamaros 'had moved by kidnapping him into "the diplomatic world of negotiations" ',[10] but these extreme advocates of a hard line would claim that:

> To the degree that diplomacy becomes a more prominent factor in the management of an incident, *it tends to add stature to the terrorist group* and thereby helps promote their cause.[11]

Under President Nixon, the United States Government refused even to speak with terrorists, and summarily dismissed one US ambassador who agreed to hear the demands of a group holding American hostages.

The so-called 'soft line' states, on the other hand, have seen considerable value in 'diplomatic solutions' to terrorist incidents. Not only is diplomacy considered useful in the co-ordination of responses from the various governments and security forces that might be involved, but traditional diplomatic skills have also been used to explore options with the terrorists themselves, particularly when the lives of hostages have been at stake. At times intermediaries have played a prominent role. Concessions have been made and deals struck to obtain the release of hostages or a more general respite from terrorist violence. While other factors are often important, the soft liners have usually argued that there is no evidence that a strong stand against negotiations helps significantly to reduce the frequency of terrorist attacks, which are often made for reasons additional to those included in any stated demands. The publicity given to an incident is usually justification enough, something that would be achieved regardless of the policies of the governments involved.[12] It is felt too that, by holding the host governments solely responsible for the resolution of certain terrorist incidents the hard line states in effect contribute to the success of the operation by adding to the pressure and embarassment those governments might feel. Moreover, by discarding their options before an incident has even occurred, hard line states effectively nullify their own capacities to react when one does.

Since terrorist attacks against diplomats and diplomatic facilities first reached significant proportions some twenty years ago, there has been a tendency for more and more states to adopt a hard line approach, at least as their declared policy. As Martha Crenshaw has pointed out:

> Of the states that occasionally made concessions to terrorists, including Austria, Bolivia, Haiti, Brazil, the Dominican Republic, France, Guatemala, West Germany and Mexico, four (Mexico, Guatemala, the Dominican Republic, and West Germany) officially changed their policies.[13]

This change of attitude is perhaps most graphically illustrated in the case of the Federal Republic of Germany. In 1970 the FRG bitterly opposed the hard line approach taken by Guatemala after the kidnapping of its Ambassador, Count Karl von Spreti. When the West German Ambassador to Brazil was also kidnapped later that year, Bonn pressed hard for accession to the terrorists' demands and was 'pointedly ostentatious'[14] in thanking the Brazilian Government for doing so. Yet by the time the FRG Embassy in Stockholm was seized by members of the RAF in 1975 the German Government's policy had changed. Its response to this seizure was to refuse the terrorists' demands and authorise the Swedish police to rescue the hostages. Other states have followed this lead and, as suggested by the consensus at the Commonwealth Heads of Government Meeting (CHOGM) in Nassau in 1985, the trend (in public at least) towards a hard line policy is increasing.

There will always be occasions, however, when the imperatives to negotiate with terrorists will appear to outweigh even the most rigid state policies against doing so. There is evidence to suggest, for example, that the Israelis were initially prepared to negotiate a deal with the hijackers of the Air France Airbus at Entebbe in 1976, just as they had been forced to do with other terrorists at least twice before.[15] More recently, the United States and Israel faced a similar dilemma in regard to the hijacking of a TWA Boeing 727 to Beirut in June 1985. As R. H. Kupperman has pointed out:

> Once the decision had been made to ensure the safety of every passenger, then retaliatory options virtually disappeared. Instead we entered into a 'diplomatic minuet', the US and Israel trying to keep a non-concessionary policy toward terrorism intact, and the United States having concurrently entered into unstated negotiations with Nabih Berri and Syria's President Assad. Berri and Assad, both of whom had been previously accused of sponsoring terrorism, had somehow become virginal.[16]

Despite a great deal of political rhetoric designed to disguise the fact, it was clear to most observers that the US (and possibly Israel) had in this instance effectively come to terms with the terrorists.

Should a hard line state eventually feel obliged to negotiate with terrorists it risks losing more prestige and international bargaining power than if it had initially taken a more flexible approach. This was demonstrated vividly in November 1986, when it was discovered that the United States had been secretly selling arms to Iran in return for the release of American hostages being held in Lebanon. The US had covertly negotiated with terrorists before, both directly and through intermediaries, but the collapse of the Reagan Administration's much publicised 'hard line' policy was a major blow to its credibility and international reputation. It is now likely to be exceedingly difficult for the US to persuade its friends and allies of the value of a firm policy when it has shown that it too is prepared to negotiate in certain circumstances. One such result was apparent in January 1987, when an FRG Government spokesman cited the US arms deal as evidence of the need to consider each terrorist incident on its own merits. At the time, Bonn was holding a Lebanese terrorist sought by the US for the 1985 TWA hijacking to Beirut and murder of an American serviceman. Those who stand to gain most from such disunity and lack of confidence are of course the terrorists and their state sponsors. Apart from any immediate advantages, they receive a propaganda boost of enormous value, and seize the psychological initiative in a way that is always difficult to recover.

Intangible factors such as these play an important part in the formulation of state responses to terrorist violence. The high symbolic content of any attack usually means that questions of 'face' or national prestige quickly become of paramount concern. The terrorists see themselves as representatives of their cause before the world, while their adversaries are symbols of systems or policies which they oppose. To the states, however, the terrorists represent a public challenge to their ability to manage their own affairs, fufil their legal responsibilities and protect their citizens. Terrorism tests their resolve and their reputation for action in pursuit of their own interests. Thus neither side wishes to appear weak or vaccillating, nor to accord to the other a status to which it is not felt entitled. By their actions, each side attempts to establish its own legitimacy and the illegitimacy of its opponent. These symbolic duels are invariably conducted in the full glare of world-wide publicity, making both sides highly sensitive to the effect their actions might have on their public image. As Robert Jervis, Martha Crenshaw and others have noted, such perceptions of strength and resolve are crucial factors in international relations on which depend issues much wider than the resolution of a particular terrorist incident.[17] Thus the stakes are quickly raised and responses by states to international terrorism become part of global politics, with all the added complications and dangers which that brings.

PROTECTIVE SECURITY MEASURES

In addition to broad strategic approaches towards terrorist violence, considerable attention has also been paid to more detailed, tactical questions of prevention, protection and response. Over the past 20 years most states have taken steps to upgrade the physical security of their missions abroad, the level varying with the threat perceived, the political will of the government and the resources available. Perimeter defences have been strengthened and protective screens added to approach roads and buildings. Surveillance and alarm systems have been installed and various other measures taken both to prevent unauthorised access to diplomatic facilities and to protect those working inside them. Since the 1979 Iranian hostage crisis additional precautions have been taken by many states to guard against violent crowds, including the erection of special barriers and the stocking of tear gas for use in the event of an attack on embassy premises.[18] More recently, there have been reports that some states facing particularly high levels of threat are giving greater consideration to the relocation and even the redesign of diplomatic facilities in order to make them more secure.[19] Many missions are now protected by armed police or military personnel from the sending state and it is likely that the attachment of guards and security officers to such facilities will become more common in the future.

The increased security of mission premises, however, can encourage attacks on more vulnerable targets. According to one estimate, 95 per cent of all terrorist attacks on individual diplomats take place outside embassy premises, usually in front of their homes.[20] Their families are also at risk. Accordingly, many states now try to house their staff and families within specially protected compounds or housing estates, and take various measures to forestall attacks upon them when they are outside these relatively secure areas. In 1970, for example, after the rash of kidnappings and murders of diplomatic personnel in Latin America, the US State Department sent all its embassies and consulates in the region a directive calling for a dramatic reduction in travel and greater secrecy in the planning of any essential trip. Diplomatic staff were urged to travel to and from work either in convoys or in inconspicuous vehicles. The use of diplomatic number plates and car pennants was temporarily abandoned. Staff were also advised to vary their daily routines in order to reduce the risk of seizure.[21] Other measures since implemented by the US, and by many other states threatened with terrorist action, include the introduction of staggered working hours and the preparation of contingency plans to be followed in the event of an attack. Secure 'safe havens' have been built into many diplomats' homes and special arrangements made for their children to travel to and from school. The senior diplomats of many states now travel in specially armoured vehicles and are often accompanied by personal bodyguards.

All these elaborate counter-measures count for very little, however, unless they are accompanied by a fundamental change in the way that diplomatic staff perceive themselves and their position as representatives of a foreign country abroad. Governments are now obliged to consider ways in which to effect radical changes in the culture of their Foreign Services and to make official personnel and their families more sensitive to the risks they may face from terrorists while on a posting. Brief training courses are now given by many states to make diplomats more aware of the possible dangers and advise them on how to respond to a terrorist attack. Diplomats' spouses are warned to take special precautions in employing domestic staff and in carrying out certain tasks about their homes. Some governments even give diplomatic staff and their spouses rudimentary instruction in defensive driving. Clifton Wilson cites a State Department report that American diplomats in Southeast Asia in the 1950s were instructed to carry firearms but despite recent calls for the reintroduction of this provocative and risky practice it does not appear to be widespread now.[22] In some cases these measures may appear extreme, but they are felt to be warranted by the increased threats now faced by members of the diplomatic profession and their families.

Particular security burdens are carried by those sending states which have a high level of representation abroad, or which are most often subject to terrorist attack. In the early 1980s the United States, for example, as both a superpower and a favourite terrorist target, spent around 15 per cent of its State Department budget and over 2 000 man-years annually on security for its 262 missions abroad. As Paul Wilkinson noted, however, this was still not enough to provide adequate protection for them all, the cost of which would be prohibitive.[23] While generally sympathetic to calls for increased security overseas, Congress has shown some reluctance to accede to the State Department's latest requests for higher levels of funding for protective security programs. Following a comprehensive review of security at US missions overseas, an Advisory Panel led by retired Admiral Robert Inman recommended that 139 posts were in need of replacement or significant overhaul.[24] In March 1986 the US House of Representatives passed a US$4.4 billion, five year program to upgrade the security of American missions abroad and compensate the victims of the Tehran hostage seizure. US$2.7 billion was earmarked for the construction of some 60 new, bomb-resistant embassies and the upgrading of some older structures. The Senate, however, would only agree to a US$1.1 billion package. In August, after reconsideration by a joint conference committee, this was increased to US$2.5 billion. The initial request contained a number of questionable items and the State Department's multi-billion dollar embassy security program had been severely criticised by the US General Accounting Office for inefficiency. There was still a marked reluctance on the part of Congress, however, to accept the significantly higher security costs of maintaining a large diplomatic presence overseas in the current climate of terrorist violence.[25]

In some countries, where the risk of terrorist attack is considered particularly high, the size of diplomatic staffing establishments (including officers' families) has been reduced to provide fewer potential targets and from time to time there have been reports of missions being withdrawn because the receiving government was not able to provide them with adequate protection. These were the grounds, for example, on which the FRG Embassy in Guatemala was closed after Count von Spreti's kidnapping and murder in 1970, and similar reasons have been put forward for the departure of a number of missions from El Salvador and Lebanon in recent years. Since the completion of the Inman Report the US State Department has decided to examine the possible closure of 50 of its consulates because of the cost of providing adequate protection from terrorist attack. Generally speaking, however, the closure of a mission is rare outside of a complete breakdown in civil order and even then might not be an option for a large power or one with vital interests at stake. At the beginning of 1979, for example, there were some 1400 US diplomatic and consular staff in Iran. By the time of the Embassy seizure in November this number had been reduced to less than 100 but despite the obvious dangers faced by the mission America's global interests were considered such that a presence had to be maintained.[26] In 1984, during an upsurge in the fighting between militant factions in Lebanon, Australia closed its Embassy in Beirut and withdrew all its expatriate personnel. Although it too reduced the number of its diplomatic and consular staff and their family members in the country, the United States kept its mission open. US staff numbers were further reduced in March 1985, but there was no question of the US mission closing, regardless of the danger, given American interests in the region and the need to maintain a presence for symbolic reasons.

THE RESPONSIBILITIES OF RECEIVING STATES

While vague about the actual level of protection required, the Vienna Conventions on Diplomatic and Consular Relations both clearly place primary responsibility for the safety of official representatives and their facilities on the receiving states. Yet the rapid expansion in the size and number of missions since 1945 has placed a considerable burden on such states, particularly in areas of high risk such as Central America and Western Europe. At the height of the kidnapping problem in the early 1970s, for example, more than ten per cent of the entire Guatemalan armed forces was assigned to act as bodyguards for foreign diplomatic personnel, at an annual cost of US$1–2 million for each mission.[27] Similar strains were felt during the Montonero threat in Argentina. According to one report, the US Ambassador was assigned a security guard of 70 people. Even then the difficulties of protecting him were so great that by agreement with the Argentine Government he only travelled to his office in the Embassy twice a week, spending the rest of the time in his well-guarded Residence.[28] At the other end of the scale, the United States is responsible for over 16000 accredited diplomatic personnel, their families and some 1500 consuls and honorary consuls. Most are based in New York but many live in cities scattered across the country. Even with a substantial allocation from Congress (US$9.5 million in 1985) the US government agencies responsible cannot hope to provide close protection for them all.[29]

Such is the extent of this problem now that some of the smaller states have suggested that a distinction be made in international law between those countries able to offer adequate security for diplomatic missions and those which cannot. This problem was in fact foreseen by some of the newer states present at the 1961 Vienna Conference. They were loath to see the extension of diplomatic status to non-diplomatic personnel attached to the larger embassies and sought to restrict the extension of privileges to professional diplomats.[30] The older and more prosperous states, however, successfully resisted such a move. It is true that host governments carry an unequal burden for the protection of diplomats and diplomatic facilities, but arguments for different levels of responsibility ignore the fact that, in practice, the degree of protection already varies considerably according to a host state's capacities and level of adherence to international law. Very real difficulties would arise in determining which states were legally entitled to abrogate certain of their responsibilities to sending states. More importantly, perhaps, such arguments presuppose the attainability of complete protection against terrorist (and other) attacks, something that could never be guaranteed by any state, rich or poor.

One solution to this problem has been offered by the United States, although not without a certain amount of controversy. In 1983 the US established an Anti-Terrorism Assistance Program which, in addition to high level consultations on anti-terrorist measures, provides practical training for foreign civilian law enforcement agencies, focussing on such areas as bomb disposal, hostage negotiation and rescue. By 1 January 1986 the program had included almost 2000 participants from 32 countries, and was felt to be 'paying big dividends in improved cooperation and support from foreign governments'.[31] While of real benefit to the US in terms of the increased abilities other governments may have to protect American missions and citizens abroad, the program has been criticised for its obvious 'collateral benefits' to the US, and potential abuses. Although Congress requires that participating countries are screened for their human rights record, the fear has been expressed that any counter-terrorist training given to law enforcement agencies in some Third World countries will serve only to permit them greater controls over their civilian populations. Considerations like these have caused other Western countries investigating such schemes to proceed very cautiously.

Since the terrorist threat to diplomats reached serious proportions most states have taken steps to fulfil their obligations to resident diplomatic missions. Particular importance has been placed on increased intelligence capabilities and cooperation with the law enforcement agencies of friendly countries. A number of states have amended their domestic legislation to permit the local authorities greater freedom in trying to prevent a terrorist incident and in responding should one occur. Improved passport and immigration procedures have reduced the ease with which international terrorists can travel and tighter Customs controls have made it more difficult for them to transport their arms and explosives. Postal services have been alerted to watch for bombs in the mail and devices for their detection have been installed in many post offices and diplomatic missions. Special arrangements have been negotiated to enable governments to extradite suspected terrorists for trial elsewhere. In a number of countries specialised government agencies have been created to coordinate any action required against terrorists. Such agencies usually have access to personnel with special skills, such as intelligence analysts, communications officers, trained negotiators, bomb disposal teams and tactical response experts. In some countries there are specialised units in the Foreign Ministry to handle the international aspects of an incident. In addition, many states have developed specialised police and military capabilities for use in a counter-terrorist role.

More than 40 states are known to have developed specially-trained units capable of mounting armed assaults against terrorist-held premises and it can be assumed that most, if not all, have prepared for missions to rescue diplomats held hostage in their own facilities.[32] The assault on the Iranian Embassy in London in May 1980 by a team from Britain's Special Air Service Regiment (SASR) was a spectacular example of the kind of option that is available to governments with such units at their disposal.[33] The success of this operation, however, and similar assaults against diplomatic missions in Paris, Stockholm, Baghdad and elsewhere must be weighed against the equally spectacular failure of operations against captured embassies in places like Kabul and Guatemala City. The risks involved in such operations are extremely high. As the assault on the Iranian Embassy in London demonstrated in its own way, even the best laid plans can go wrong, jeopardising not only the lives of the attacking force but also those of the hostages. The use of special forces to assault hijacked aircraft have produced the same mixed results.[34] In addition, there can be no guarantee that circumstances will permit such units to be used, particularly if the operation needs to take place in another country.[35] Even if the government of that country is friendly, it may prefer to handle the incident in a different way, or use its own counter-terrorist forces. Should the government of the country prove hostile, a great many other difficulties would arise. In many respects the successful Israeli raid on Entebbe Airport was a special case. Future incidents are more likely to pose the sorts of difficulties encountered by the US in April 1980, during its disastrous Operation 'Eagle Claw'.[36]

The practical and international legal constraints on action of this kind are particularly strong where diplomats or diplomatic facilities are involved.

While the Vienna Convention on Consular Relations permits the host country to enter consular premises without permission in the case of an emergency, such liberty is not extended in the case of diplomatic premises. Permission from the sending state is required before the host country can enter, even if the aim is to capture terrorists and rescue hostages. Failure to observe the wishes of the sending state (and international law) can result in a serious breach in relations. In January 1980, for example, when a group of armed protesters seized the Spanish Embassy in Guatemala, the Guatemalan police assaulted the building despite the Spanish Ambassador's plea that force not be used. During the fighting a Molotov cocktail was thrown and 39 people (including seven of the hostages) died in the resulting fire. Outraged at the assault, Spain broke off diplomatic relations with Guatemala.[37] In most circumstances, units like Britain's SASR and West Germany's Federal Border Guard Group 9 (*Grenzschutz Gruppe* 9, or GSG-9) would not be used except in the last resort and with great reluctance. The stakes involved in such operations are considerable, however, and states anxious to display their resolve, satisfy the demands of their allies or test their counter-terrorist skills may mount an assault without due care and forethought, with dire results.

THE AMENDMENT OF THE VIENNA CONVENTION

In recent years there have been a number of calls for a revision of the Vienna Convention on Diplomatic Relations, in order to make it more difficult for states to use diplomatic privileges and immunities to support or conduct terrorist activities, and for receiving states to act in the event that such abuses should occur. These considerations were given greater urgency in 1984 after a member of the Libyan People's Bureau in London opened fire on a crowd of demonstrators in front of the mission, and killed a Woman Police Constable. In addition, some states (such as Kuwait, Italy and France) have announced at different times that diplomatic bags entering the country may be X-rayed for weapons and other prohibited imports.

These and related questions were carefully examined by the British Government after the shooting incident in St James' Square. The Parliamentary Committee charged with the task reported that there was scope within the existing bounds of the Vienna Convention to enforce greater restrictions against the abuse of diplomatic immunities. Stricter standards could be applied, for example, with regard to the notification and accreditation of diplomatic staff, the designation of diplomatic premises and the size of diplomatic and consular missions. Certain other administrative measures could also be enforced which, while still within the bounds of international law, could help restrict abuses of diplomatic privilege. Legal opinion differed over the question of whether or not the electronic scanning of diplomatic bags constituted a breach of diplomatic inviolability. The British Government eventually decided that, in certain circumstances, such practices could be accommodated under the existing Convention.[38]

In making its detailed study of all the factors involved, the British Government came to the conclusion that it would neither be easy, nor in its own best interests, to try and change the Convention itself. There was no formal mechanism for changing the Convention and little likelihood of ever achieving a similar consensus as had occurred in Vienna in 1961. To introduce new, discretionary clauses of any kind would only open the way for less scrupulous states to use them mischeviously and result in an instrument that was worse than that already in force. In a White Paper published in April 1985 the British Government accepted the Committee's conclusion that:

> Given the difficulties in the way of achieving any restrictive amendment to the Convention, and the doubtful net benefit to the UK of so doing, it would be wrong to regard amendment of the Vienna Convention as the solution to the problem of abuse of diplomatic immunities.[39]

While left unstated, it was no doubt also recognised that there were bound to be occasions when Britain too may wish to use its diplomatic bags for purposes not authorised in the Convention.[40] At their London meeting in June 1984 the seven Summit countries confirmed this view and most other states appear to support the British position. In February 1986 the US Vice President's Task Force on Combatting Terrorism recommended that the question of abuses be pursued in the United Nations General Assembly, but did not propose the Vienna Convention be changed.

The fact that the Convention is unlikely to change does not mean, however, that states are bound rigidly to apply it in every case, particularly if their own vital interests are threatened. It represents the formal position regarding their behaviour in this field, but states have always exercised a degree of flexibility in its interpretation and implementation. As noted earlier, differences have arisen through historical and cultural circumstances, but practical considerations also play an important role. There have been numerous instances when states have violated the strict legal letter of the Convention for one reason or another. These have often occurred during attempts to take action against officers or states abusing diplomatic privileges. The 1973 invasion of the Iraqi Embassy in Islamabad by Pakistani authorities, for example, was an example of just such a case. This particular action was subsequently justified by the discovery of a large weapons cache in the mission. Providing such exercises are demonstrably successful, formal breaches of this kind are rarely the subject of serious protests. The sending states usually recognise that in any argument it could be shown equally to have offended against the letter of the Convention. Thus precedents are set and a certain level of customary law established, which can then be cited by other states forced to take unusual action of this kind.

THE VULNERABILITY OF DIPLOMACY

In the final analysis, it must be accepted that while firm policies and comprehensive security measures may help deter terrorists there can never be complete protection from an imaginative and determined attack. This is particularly the case if the terrorists are prepared to martyr themselves in the attempt or are supported by the host state. As Brian Jenkins explained to the Long Commission in December 1983, terrorist operations are very hard to predict. Also, there is an inescapable asymmetry between the two sides:

> Terrorists can attack anything, anywhere, anytime. Governments cannot protect everything, everywhere, all the time.[41]

There will always be potential targets which remain vulnerable to attack. As protection is increased in one area, so the attention of terrorists will turn to others. Jenkins believes, for example, that embassy seizures grew out of the increasing difficulty of hijacking aircraft, due to tighter security measures introduced at airports in the early 1970s. The increased level of bombings and assassination attempts in recent years appears to be a response in turn to better security measures to protect diplomats and their facilities from seizure. Another option for the terrorists is simply to increase the scale and violence of the attack, with a greater likelihood of casualties. The Islamic Jihad's 1983 attack on the US Embassy in Beirut was a major psychological victory for the terrorists not only because of the Embassy's importance as the US's headquarters in Lebanon, and therefore the symbol of the Reagan Administration's Middle Eastern policies, but also because of the elaborate measures taken to protect it. Only months before, it had been described as a 'fortress'.[42] The same could be said of the group's attack on the US Embassy Annexe in East Beirut in September 1984. A delicate balance needs to be struck between those measures which will help deter attacks and those which, by the nature of the commitment made and the prestige invested, may invite them.

The greatest problem faced by states in this area lies in the nature of diplomacy itself. For to be truly effective, diplomacy must be conducted openly, with ready access to other diplomats, a wide range of officials and members of the local population. To some areas of a diplomatic mission, such as the consular and commercial sections, free access by the public is crucial. The same problem is faced by official aid, cultural and information services abroad, to which the attention of terrorists would inevitably turn if an embassy or consulate was believed secure. In its 1985 report on the implications of terrorism for the US Information Agency, the United States Advisory Commission on Public Diplomacy stated plainly that:

> The Inman Panel recommends relocating and "hardening" our overseas missions so as to give them maximum protection against car-bombing attacks. This recommendation is a logical and pragmatic result of threat analyses and recent tragic events involving some U.S. embassies and consulates. But the "relocation-and-hardening" principle runs directly against the "accessibility-and-openness" principle of public diplomacy.[43]

Such openness and freedom of movement provides opportunities for the terrorists which they have been quick to exploit. To restrict the access of the public to official facilities and for diplomats to have fewer contacts with people outside them might add to the security of the mission but would also greatly reduce its value. It would also have a detrimental effect on the morale of the mission staff and their families. Paradoxically, it is often in precisely those countries where the terrorist threat is highest that diplomacy has the greatest role to play, demanding a larger staff, freer movement and wider contacts outside the mission. Once again, a balance needs to be struck between the interests of security and the requirements of diplomacy, but ultimately the balance will always favour the terrorists.

REGIONAL AND OTHER MULTILATERAL RESPONSES

As the scope and seriousness of the international terrorist problem grew, it quickly became apparent that no national government would be able to combat it alone. Steps were soon taken by a number of states to share intelligence on terrorist groups and activities, counter-terrorist techniques and equipment, and to cooperate at various levels of law enforcement. Yet effective action against international terrorism was constantly blocked by the ability of terrorists to claim political asylum from sympathetic states, or in other ways to evade prosecution by crossing national boundaries. International law recognised the right of all states to grant territorial asylum, with provisions for the extradition of common criminals, but that extradition did not have to be granted in the case of people accused of political offenses. The definition of the latter being left to the states themselves, there was wide scope for abuses of the system and for states sympathetic to the terrorists' motives to grant them refuge of this kind. Even where no such intention was present the law could be used to provide terrorists with sanctuary.[44] Such discretion could not be removed without impinging on the sovereignty of the states in question, but terrorist actions could by international law (and bilateral treaty) be deemed common crimes and thus denied political status. Significantly, the development which first prompted states to consider concerted action on this matter was the growing number of attacks on diplomats and diplomatic facilities in Latin America.

On 2 February 1971 the Organisation of American States (OAS) approved a Convention to Prevent and Punish Acts of Terrorism Taking the Form of Crimes Against Persons and Related Extortion that are of International Significance. It 'both condemned and classified certain acts of terrorism against foreign officials as international crimes'[45] rather than political acts, thus theoretically denying those responsible asylum in any state party to the Convention. These states were bound either to prosecute the perpetrators of such crimes themselves, or extradite them for trial elsewhere. It was, however, a rather loosely worded document which in some respects offered diplomatic personnel less protection than already promised by the 1961 Vienna Convention. Many Articles were deliberately left imprecise in order to encompass the differing views of the OAS members, who were unable to reach agreement on a number of important issues. The greatest difficulty was encountered in attempts to reconcile the wish of some states (such as Brazil, Argentina and Guatemala) for a strong definition and denunciation of terrorism with the equally strong traditional beliefs of some other American states (such as Bolivia and Mexico) in the concept of political asylum. In the event, six states refused to sign the Convention, feeling that it did not go far enough towards combatting terrorism, but with 13 signatures the Convention was approved. It entered into force on 16 October 1973.

Only nine states eventually became full party to the Convention. Cuba, the country in the region most often accused of being sympathetic towards terrorism, did not even participate in the negotiations. The OAS Convention was thus in some respects a rather ineffectual instrument, but it was significant for a number of reasons. It demonstrated above all that, whatever other differences they may have had, all members of the OAS shared a concern for the continuing integrity of diplomatic processes. The Convention was also 'the first international legal instrument to deal directly with the protection of diplomats and . . . served as a primary model for the United Nations Convention' which followed three years later.[46] Even before that, it prompted other multilateral groups to consider measures for the safety of diplomats threatened by international terrorism.

In December 1970, shortly after the OAS first began consideration of the issue, the Council of Europe meeting in Strasbourg examined 'The Protection of Members of Diplomatic Missions and Consular Posts'. The Council's Committee of Ministers considered terrorist attacks against diplomats and diplomatic facilities 'grave violations' of 'the most sacred international traditions' and unanimously condemned all attacks on diplomatic and consular personnel, the current spate of kidnappings in particular.[47] A resolution passed by the Committee recommended member states to survey the security measures then in force for the protection of diplomats and, if necessary, to strengthen them. Members of the Council were also enjoined to examine their national laws to ensure that they adequately provided for the punishment of anyone found guilty of such attacks and states were urged to cooperate in the protection of diplomats and their facilities from terrorist action.[48] In January 1974 the Committee of Ministers passed another resolution on international terrorism which *inter alia* identified offenses against diplomats as being of particular note.[49]

Three years later, the Council of Europe formally agreed to a Convention for the Suppression of Terrorism, which listed attacks on the 'life, physical integrity or liberty' of diplomats as one of those crimes for which political asylum could not normally be claimed. These concerns were again expressed by the Council of Europe meeting in Madrid in 1984. With the example before them of the Libyan People's Bureau shooting in London that April, the Council unanimously approved:

> a concerted campaign against terrorism and abuse of diplomatic privileges, and agreed to set up, under the aegis of the Council of Europe, an ad hoc Ministerial body to consider ways of improving the exchange of information on terrorism, including abuses of diplomatic privilege as well as violence against diplomats.[50]

At a meeting of European Ministers of Justice in Strasbourg between 4–5 November 1986 the Council issued a formal Declaration which called on member states to 'act firmly against terrorism involving abuse of diplomatic or consular privileges and immunities and terrorism directed against diplomatic or consular representatives'. This Declaration was supported by a Resolution which emphasised the Council's concern and spelt out a number of measures by which the Declaration could be put into effect.[51]

The deliberations of the Council of Europe were mirrored in turn by the European Community (EC), which has repeatedly expressed concern over international terrorism and the abuse of diplomatic immunities. In May 1984, for example, a Political Committee on Terrorism and Diplomatic Immunity was established to examine ways in which the then ten members of the EC could increase cooperative measures against the abuse of diplomatic immunities by terrorist sponsors. In September that year agreement was reached on a set of principles, including the need for a joint response in the event of a serious terrorist attack involving the abuse of diplomatic immunity. In particular, EC members undertook strictly to apply the provisions of the Vienna Convention regarding the size and use of diplomatic missions and diplomatic bags. There was to be a greater exchange of information about diplomatic personnel known or suspected to be engaged in terrorist activities. Subsequent meetings have further strengthened this resolve. After the United States bombing raids on Libya a number of measures were taken to reduce the size of the Libyan People's Bureaux in Europe and to restrict the freedom of movement of Libyan diplomats.

The British Foreign Secretary, Sir Geoffrey Howe, expressed the feelings of the EC when he described the Bureaux, which had replaced Libya's conventional diplomatic missions, as 'the command posts and the transmission posts for acts of State terrorism'.[52] One significant obstacle to further European cooperation was removed (at least for a period) in September 1986 when a series of bomb attacks in Paris persuaded the French Government to join other EC countries in applying certain counter-measures.

As the seven Summit countries (the US, UK, FRG, Italy, France, Canada and Japan) expanded their periodic economic consultations to include terrorist issues, so they too have shown a deep concern to preserve and protect the integrity of diplomatic conventions. At the Summit in Venice in 1980 the Seven issued a Statement on the Taking of Diplomatic Hostages which vigorously condemned 'the taking of hostages and the seizure of diplomatic and consular premises and personnel in contravention of the basic norms of international law and practice'.[53] At Ottawa in 1981 and London in 1984 attacks on diplomatic and consular representatives were again strongly condemned. At the latter conference serious concern was also expressed over the abuse of diplomatic privileges by states sponsoring terrorism. The Seven stated that they:

> viewed with serious concern the increasing involvement of States and Governments in acts of terrorism, including the abuse of diplomatic immunity.[54]

The Seven agreed to cooperate over the expulsion from their countries of known terrorists, including those of diplomatic status, and to use to the full the powers they possessed as receiving states under the Vienna Convention. The 1986 Summit, held in Tokyo, also considered the question of international terrorism and resulted in an undertaking to place strict limits on the size of diplomatic missions which engaged in terrorist activities.

While all of these resolutions, conventions and communiques were made with significant majorities, and most of them unanimously[55], they shared a number of shortcomings with the OAS Convention. Because they were all based on consensus they tended to be statements of widely held political principles rather than practical measures for the suppression of terrorism. All were worded sufficiently loosely to permit the states responsible for their implementation considerable latitude in deciding what action should be taken in the event of a terrorist incident in their territories. None of the instruments were completely binding and none included measures to enforce their application. As with the American states there was still a notable reluctance on the part of European states to abrogate their sovereign right to handle a terrorist attack as they saw fit at the time. In addition, many states still placed fear of reprisals and the loss of commercial opportunities above the need to take concerted action against the terrorist threat. The escape clause in Article 13 of the European Convention, for example, has been invoked by five states to date and France, Greece and Ireland have yet to agree to ratification. Well might scholars like Amos Yoder ask, 'if countries with the close political relationships of the European Community can not agree on a strong anti-terrorist agreement, how can there be much hope for a worldwide agreement'.[56]

Similar problems have been encountered in other spheres. French reluctance to be associated with a binding and more effective commitment against international terrorism resulted in a significant weakening of the communique issued after the London economic Summit in 1984. While a demonstration of shared concerns, it was hardly the 'heartening consensus' described by the US Secretary of State.[57] Despite similar claims by Mr Shultz in 1986 the Tokyo Summit was also marked by a reluctance on the part of some participants, the French in particular, to commit themselves to concerted action against terrorism. Nor has France been alone in these concerns. Britain, the FRG and Japan were all quick to join France in its attempts to fill the economic vacuum left in Iran by the US withdrawal in 1980, despite calls by President Jimmy Carter for trade sanctions against the Khomeini regime while it held US diplomats hostage.[58] Despite compelling evidence of Libyan involvement in international terrorism, European and other Western states resisted American calls in early 1986 for comprehensive sanctions against the Qaddafi regime. A number of measures of varying effectiveness were taken against Libyan People's Bureaux by European states after the April bombing raids, but these seemed to be inspired more by fear of further violent unilateral action by the US than any real consensus on the need to cooperate in the fight against international terrorism. Similar equivocation was displayed by the EC when Britain sought support for action against Syria in October 1986.

Yet despite such obvious manifestations of national self-interest, the record of European and Summit commitments against terrorist attacks on diplomatic targets should not be seen in a purely negative light. The consistent and overwhelming support given to the principle that diplomatic institutions deserved special protection is itself significant. Whatever hesitations they may have felt about opposing terrorism itself or the actions of certain terrorist sponsors, the European states (and their Western allies) like those of the Organisation of American States, were all agreed that attacks on diplomats and diplomatic facilities were a cause for particular concern. This aspect of the terrorist problem at least attracted a real consensus, not just at a regional level, or among political allies, but at the global level as well. The growing number of attacks on diplomats and their facilities, and the albeit qualified success of the 1971 OAS Convention led a number of states to press for its universal application. In its 1971 Annual Report, the International Law Commission addressed this issue and expressed its willingness to prepare draft Articles on the subject.

MEASURES IN THE UNITED NATIONS

The ILC's proposal came shortly before a request from the Secretary-General of the UN, Kurt Waldheim, for the UN General Assembly (UNGA) to consider 'measures to prevent international terrorism and other forms of violence which endanger innocent human lives or jeopardise fundamental freedoms'.[59] A draft convention prepared by the United States, however, quickly foundered on the perennial problem of the politically ambiguous nature of terrorist activities. By concentrating on the export of agitational terror and ignoring enforcement terror by states the draft provoked the opposition of the Eastern bloc and Third World. Many of these UN members had achieved their independence through revolution and liberation movements of various kinds and were reluctant for a number of reasons to agree to measures that might, in theory at least, deny others the same option. In addition, a number of states like South Africa used the rubric of 'anti-terrorism' to justify repressive policies toward their own populations. It was also pointed out that a number of terrorist leaders and sympathisers like Menachem Begin and Regis Debray now enjoyed international respectability, thus demonstrating the transience of political values in the West.[60] Indicative of the problems faced by those seeking a global convention against terrorism in the UN was the title of the agenda item, which was later amended to read:

> Measures to Prevent International Terrorism Which Endangers or Takes Innocent Human Lives or Jeopardises Fundamental Freedoms and Study of the Underlying Causes of Violence Which Lie in Misery, Frustration, Grievance and Despair, and Which Cause Some People to Sacrifice Human Lives, Including Their Own, in an Attempt to Effect Radical Changes.[61]

Consideration of this matter soon became bogged down in an Ad Hoc Committee. Like the League of Nations before it, it seems unlikely that the UN will ever be able to agree on a broadly based convention on terrorism that will serve any practical purpose.[62]

Significantly, such problems as were encountered with regard to the proposed UN convention on the protection of diplomats, could be overcome. In a Resolution passed in December 1971 the UNGA requested the ILC to study the question of the protection of diplomatic personnel, with a view to submitting draft Articles on the subject to the General Assembly. These were prepared and passed to the UNGA in July 1972, with a request for comments. The matter was sent in turn to the Sixth Committee of the UN, where the Canadian delegate, David Miller, expressed the views of many:

> Failure to conclude a convention might have adverse effects on the whole fabric of the diplomatic system and on international relations as a whole. If diplomats

had to be lodged in fortresses or were exposed to increasing danger, then freedom of opinion and their value to both the receiving and sending state would be so depreciated that in some cases they might be withdrawn.[63]

It was an appeal both to principle and to self-interest, and one which found considerable sympathy among other states. On 14 December the following year the UNGA adopted by consensus Resolution 3166 (XXVIII), which introduced a Convention on the Protection and Punishment of Crimes Against Internationally Protected Persons, Including Diplomatic Agents. Given its sensitive subject matter and the usually deliberate nature of the UN, the Convention was drawn up and opened for signature in a remarkably short time. It entered into force on 20 February 1977, after being ratified by 22 countries and only four years and three months from its initial inclusion as an agenda item.[64]

The UN Convention, also known as the New York Convention, 'establishes a legal mechanism to ensure compliance with international norms to protect persons who under international law are regarded as being entitled to special protection because of their current activities'.[65] As such, it introduced the concept of the 'internationally protected person' into international legal jurisprudence. It also specified the duty of contracting states to establish certain acts against such persons as common crimes, drawing on both the 'extradite or prosecute' formula adopted in the OAS Convention and provisions of previous legal instruments such as the Vienna Convention on Diplomatic Relations. The UN Convention also contained a number of provisions requiring states party to it to join in cooperative efforts towards the prevention and suppression of attacks against diplomats and the punishment of any person found guilty of such an offence. Paradoxically, the New York Convention in some respects parallels the draft convention proposed by the United States in 1972 to deal with the wider terrorist problem, but makes no specific reference to terrorism as such, only crimes against internationally protected persons. Thus the Convention resolved the usual problems of definition by avoiding them completely, in the manner of earlier conventions against the hijacking of aircraft. Instead, it 'focuses on functions of prime concern to all member states regardless of ideology'.[66]

Like earlier agreements on this subject, however, the New York Convention was not without certain shortcomings. As John Murphy has shown:

> there is nothing whatsoever in the terms of the convention that precludes prosecuting authorities from deciding not to prosecute an alleged offender because of sympathy with his motives.[67]

The Convention fails too, to deal with such issues as possible sanctions against states party to terrorist attacks, different strategies which might be adopted in cases where ransom is demanded and the question of state liability for injuries received in attacks. In addition, a major ambiguity was introduced into the application of the Convention by the UNGA Resolution to which it was annexed. Paragraph four of the Resolution explicitly provided that nothing in the Convention could 'prejudice the exercise of the legitimate right to self-determination and independence ... by peoples struggling against colonialism, alien domination, foreign occupation, racial discrimination and apartheid'.[68] Observers like L. C. Green have seen this qualification as, in effect, legalising terrorist attacks against diplomats and other protected persons whenever such attacks are made in the name of these causes.[69] Yet perhaps the key weakness of the Convention lies simply in the failure of all states to ratify it. To date only some 66 states are party to it, but without universal acceptance the Convention can only have limited value. Then again, when it is remembered that Iran was already party to it when its regime 'adopted' the seizure of the US Embassy in Tehran in 1979, doubts must be thrown even on this assumption.

Despite all these shortcomings, the Convention on the Protection and Punishment of Crimes Against Internationally Protected Persons, Including Diplomatic Agents was a crucial test of the international community's attitude towards the institution of diplomacy. Abraham Sofaer has correctly pointed out that a number of Third World states expressed concern that the proposed convention would serve:

> as a pretext for colonial and racist regimes to intensify the suppression of the national liberation movements recognized in various United Nations decisions and resolutions.[70]

While this concern provoked considerable debate, the underlying importance of the need to protect diplomats and diplomatic facilities from terrorist attack was not questioned. Whatever caveats might have been entered at the time, for doctrinal or other reasons, and despite any failures of observance which have been noted since, the Convention underscored the real concern felt on the part of the entire international community over the survival of diplomacy. The Convention's rapid progress through the councils of the UN showed that 'the perception of officialdom of itself and its prerogatives is shared by both developed and developing countries'[71] and demonstrated the willingness of all states to condemn universally disruptive violence of this kind.

All the international conventions and resolutions on this subject which have appeared over the past 15 years drew on a reservoir of earlier legal instruments and in that sense might be seen as superfluous. There was after all a substantial and growing body of international law which already recognised the special position of diplomatic representatives and which *inter alia* condemned attacks on them, whether they be perpetrated by states or independent terrorist groups. Instruments such as the Charter of the United Nations (1945), the Universal Declaration of Human Rights (1948), the two International Covenants on Human Rights (1966), the Declaration of Principles of International Law Concerning Friendly Relations and Cooperation among States in Accordance with the Charter of the United Nations (1970), and not least the Vienna Conventions on Diplomatic and Consular Relations (1961 and 1963) could all be cited against terrorist attacks on diplomatic targets.[72] Yet in themselves these instruments were insufficient to cope with the growing problem. They were in some cases ambiguous about the range of persons entitled to special protection and the nature of measures that should be taken to ensure inviolability. They were also unclear about the question of sanctions against people who attacked diplomats, and failed completely to address the problems inherent in cases where an attack was made in one country by terrorists who sought sanctuary in another. Traditional international legal measures also lacked established procedures for international cooperation in preventing and punishing violations of diplomatic immunity.[73]

Not all these weaknesses have yet been rectified, but the fact that there has been such an effort to do so is indicative of the strength of commitment by all states to the continued survival of diplomatic institutions. Whether from positions of principle or, as seems more likely, a coincidence of principle and self interest, they are still seen as important and worth preserving. This was demonstrated again at UNGA 35 in 1980, when the General Assembly adopted by consensus a Resolution which deplored all violations of international law governing diplomatic and consular relations, strongly condemned acts of violence against diplomats and diplomatic facilities and urged all states:

> to take all necessary measures with a view to ensuring, in conformity with their international obligations, the protection, security and safety of diplomatic and consular missions and their representatives in territory under their jurisdiction, including practicable measures to prohibit in their territories illegal activities of persons, groups and organisations that encourage, instigate, organise or engage in the perpetration of acts against the security and safety of such missions and representatives.[74]

This Resolution has been reaffirmed by the entire membership of the UNGA each year since. 1985 provided further evidence of the growing willingness of the international community to condemn such violence. In December that year the UNGA passed an unprecedented Resolution which unequivocally condemned as criminal 'all acts, methods and practices of terrorism whenever and by whomever committed'.[75] Diplomats and diplomatic facilities may be under increasing attack, and states may be party to some of those attacks, but paradoxically the institution of diplomacy quite clearly is not threatened. A greater danger would appear to arise from the overreaction of some states to these attacks.

NOTES

1. Murphy, in Evans and Murphy, p.297.
2. *Public Report of the Vice President's Task Force on Combatting Terrorism* (Washington, 1986), p.7.
3. G. P. Shultz, 'Power and Diplomacy in the 1980s', Secretary Shultz's address before the Trilateral Commission, 3 April 1984. *Department of State Bulletin* 84:2086 (May 1984), p.13. See also B.M. Jenkins, *Combatting Terrorism Becomes a War*, Rand Paper P-6988 (Rand Corporation, Santa Monica, 1984), p.3.
4. Jenkins, *op.cit.*
5. G. P. Shultz, 'Terrorism and the Modern World', Address by the Secretary of State before the Park Avenue Synagogue, New York, 25 October 1984 (State Department Press Release 242).
6. In March 1985 Lebanese operatives trained by the CIA, reportedly acting without American authorisation, hired others in Lebanon to detonate a car bomb outside the Beirut headquarters of militant Shi'ite leader Shaykh Mohammed Hussein Fadlallah, who was believed to be behind attacks on a number of US installations. More than 80 people were killed and 200 were wounded in the explosion. Fadlallah escaped injury.
7. The invasion had in fact been in the planning stages since Menachem Begin came to power and was made more likely by the appointment of Ariel Sharon as Defence Minister. See Amos Perlmutter, 'Begin's Rhetoric and Sharon's Tactics', *Foreign Affairs* 61:1 (Fall, 1982), pp.73–75.
8. C. Dobson and R. Payne, *Terror!, The West Fights Back* (Macmillan, London, 1982), p.169, and C. Dobson and R. Payne, *The Weapons of Terror: International Terrorism at Work* (Macmillan, London, 1979), pp.140–141. France gave ETA terrorists refugee status until January 1979.
9. Stephen Clissold, *Croat Separatism: Nationalism, Dissidence and Terrorism*, Conflict Studies 103 (Institute for the Study of Conflict, London, 1979), p.14 and Jenkins, *New Modes of Conflict*, p.13.
10. Quoted from a press conference given in September 1971, in Baumann, p.109.
11. Karkashian, in Herz, p.6 (emphasis retained).
12. This is the conclusion, for example, in Jenkins, *Embassies Under Siege*, and Jenkins *et al, Numbered Lives*, p.32. A study by the Carnegie Endowment for International Peace also found that a primary motive for international hostage incidents was publicity. See Murphy, in Evans and Murphy, p.297 and F. J. Hacker, 'A Case Study of Hostage Negotiation', in Herz, p.4.
13. Crenshaw, 'The International Consequences of Terrorism'.
14. *ibid.*
15. Yehuda Ofer, *Operation Thunder: The Entebbe Raid* (Penguin, Harmondsworth, 1976), pp.55–58.
16. R. H. Kupperman, 'Today's Terrorism and Tomorrow's Terrorism', paper presented at 'Research on Terrorism: An International Academic Conference', University of Aberdeen, 15–17 April 1986.
17. See Robert Jervis, 'Deterrence and Perception', *International Security* 7:3 (Winter 1982/1983), and Crenshaw, 'The International Consequences of Terrorism'.
18. In October 1986, for example, tear gas was used by members of the FRG Embassy in Tehran to disperse an angry crowd of demonstrators which had invaded the mission compound (watched by 200 Iranian police who did nothing to stop them).
19. In December 1984, for example, *Newsweek* reported that the National Research Council of the US National Academy of Sciences was developing a new kind of architecture for diplomatic buildings that was visually appealing yet secure against terrorist attack.

'Embassies Under Siege', *Newsweek*, 11 December 1984, p.146. See also R. I. Spiers, 'Legislative Proposals Regarding Diplomatic Security', Testimony before the Subcommittee on International Operations of the House Foreign Affairs Committee on 13 November 1985, *Department of State Bulletin* 86:2106 (January 1986), p.48.

20. Wilson Dizzard, 'Shots Heard Around the World', *Washington Post Magazine*, 6 January 1984, p.8.

21. Stechel, p.213.

22. Wilson, p.61. See also C.A. Madison, 'Coping With Violence Abroad', *Foreign Service Journal* (July/August 1985), p.24.

23. Wilkinson is quoted in 'Violent Tactics', *Wall Street Journal*, 21 April 1983. See also Brian Jenkins, *The Lessons of Beirut: Testimony Before the Long Commission*, Rand Note N–2114–RC (Rand Corporation, Santa Monica, 1984), p.5.

24. Statement of Secretary of State George Shultz, before the Subcommittee on Commerce, Justice, State, the Judiciary and Related Agencies of the Committee on Appropriations, US Senate, 3 April 1985.

25. 'House OKs funds to tighten embassy security', *Atlanta Journal*, 13 August 1986 and 'The Expensive Upgrading of Security at US Missions', *New York City Tribune*, 19 August 1986.

26. As explained by Abraham Ribicoff, these interests included 'oil supply, military coordination, intelligence exchange, and other relationships of both economic and geopolitical significance'. See A. A. Ribicoff, 'Lessons and Conclusions', in Christopher *et al*, p.393.

27. Jenkins, *Diplomats on the Front Line*, p.7 and J.F. Murphy, 'Report on Conference on International Terrorism: Protection of Diplomatic Premises and Personnel, Bellagio, Italy, 8–12 March 1982', *Terrorism: An International Journal* 6:3 (1983), p.483.

28. 'The Way to Fight Terror, as Learned in Argentina', *International Herald Tribune*, 19 February 1987.

29. US House of Representatives Appropriation Committee: *Hearings*, Budget Explanation: State Department FY 1984. New York has the largest diplomatic community of any city in the world, with some 10 000 accredited diplomatic personnel and 25 000 dependents. There are also some 6 000 diplomats in Washington, with around 13 000 dependents. If the 1 500 or so consuls and honorary consuls in the country are added, the US Government is responsible for the protection of a diplomatic community comprising approximately 56 000 people.

30. See Boyce, p.198 and p.213.

31. Robert B. Oakley, 'Terrorism: Overview and Developments', Address by Ambassador Robert B. Oakley, Director, Office for Counter-Terrorism and Emergency Planning, before the Issues Management Association, Chicago, Illinois, 13 September 1985, *Current Policy* 744, n.d.

32. See Dobson and Payne, *Terror!*. In his account of the development of the US's own counter-terrorist unit, Charles Beckwith described how members of Delta Force travelled around the world, carrying diplomatic bags and inspecting US embassies. See C. A. Beckwith and D. Knox, *Delta Force* (Arms and Armour Press, London, 1984), pp.170–171.

33. See *The Sunday Times'* Insight team's *Seige! Prince's Gate, London, April 30–May 5 1980* (Hamlyn, London, 1980).

34. The success of operations against hijacked aircraft at Entebbe in July 1976 and Mogadishu in October 1977 must be weighed against the debacles at Larnaca airport in February 1978 and Valetta airport in November 1985.

35. The limitations on such units are brought out by Brian Jenkins in *The Lessons of Beirut*. See also Crenshaw, 'The International Consequences of Terrorism'.

36. This was the US attempt to rescue the American diplomats held hostage in Tehran. As made clear by Charles Beckwith and others since, not all the problems arose from

external circumstances. Many were caused by the poor planning and execution of the mission itself.

37. Bass and Jenkins, p.6.
38. *Diplomatic Privileges and Immunities: Government Report on Review of the Vienna Convention on Diplomatic Relations and Reply to "The Abuse of Diplomatic Immunities and Privileges", The First Report from the Foreign Affairs Committee in the Session 1984-1985*, Cmd.9497 (HMSO, London, 1985).
39. *op.cit.* p.7.
40. The detailed findings of the Parliamentary Committee have been published in *The Abuse of Diplomatic Immunities and Privileges: Report with an Annex; together with the Proceedings of the Committee; Minutes of Evidence taken on 20 June, and 2 and 18 July in the last Session of Parliament; and Appendices*, First Report from the Foreign Affairs Committee, House of Commons, Session 1984–85 (HMSO, London, 1984).
41. Jenkins, *The Lessons of Beirut*, p.4.
42. Murphy, in Evans and Murphy, p.290. On 27 October 1986 *US News and World Report* revealed that the Reagan Administration planned to rebuild the US Embassy in Beirut at a cost of US $7.4 million.
43. *Terrorism and Security: The Challenge for Public Diplomacy*, A Report of the United States Advisory Commission on Public Diplomacy (December 1985), p.13.
44. Since 1979 US courts have refused to extradite four alleged IRA terrorists on the ground that an uprising exists in Northern Ireland, thus making crimes in furtherance of the revolt 'political'. To overcome this problem the Reagan Administration signed a Supplementary Extradition Treaty with Britain, but the proposed agreement encountered fierce opposition in the US Senate. See A.D. Sofaer, 'The US-U.K. Supplementary Extradition Treaty', *Terrorism: An International Journal* 8:4 (1986), pp.334-335.
45. Murphy, in Bassiouni, p.297.
46. Murphy, in Evans and Murphy, p.300.
47. Quoted in Baumann, p.152.
48. *ibid.* See also Juliet Lodge, 'The European Community and Terrorism: Establishing the Principle of Extradite or Try', in J. Lodge (ed), *Terrorism: A Challenge to the State* (Martin Robinson, Oxford, 1981), pp.164–194.
49. Reproduced in R.A. Friedlander (ed), *Terrorism: Documents of International and Local Control*, (Oceania Publications, Dobbs Ferry, 1979), Vol.3, p.563.
50. Quoted in Frank Brenchley, *Diplomatic Immunities and State-sponsored Terrorism*, Conflict Studies 164 (Institute for the Study of Conflict, London, 1984), p.2.
51. Declaration of the European Conference of Ministers Responsible for Combatting Terrorism (sections 5–6) and Resolution Number Three, Concerning Cooperation in Measures to Counter Terrorism Involving Abuse of Diplomatic or Consular Privileges and Immunities, and Terrorism Directed at Diplomatic or Consular Representatives, (1986).
52. Quoted in 'International Terrorism: The European Response', Foreign and Commonwealth Office, *Background Brief* (June 1986).
53. Statement on the Taking of Diplomatic Hostages, Ottawa, 22 June 1980.
54. Quoted in Brenchley, p.2.
55. Malta and Eire did not sign the European Convention, the former because it was enjoying a short-lived flirtation with Libya, the latter for constitutional reasons. Eire duly agreed to sign in February 1986, but the Convention must be passed by the Dail (Parliament) in Dublin before ratification. Malta has still not endorsed the Convention in any way.
56. Amos Yoder, 'United Nations Resolutions Against International Terrorism', *Terrorism: An International Journal* 6:4 (1983), p.509.
57. G. P. Shultz, 'Terrorism: The Problem and the Challenges', Statement by the Secretary of State before the House Committee on Foreign Affairs, Washington, 13 June 1984. *Current Policy* 586 (13 June 1984).

58. The British, French, West German and Swedish Embassies in Tehran all refused to shelter the six US Embassy staff who escaped capture by Iranian militants in 1979. Canada alone agreed to do so.

59. *United Nations Yearbook, Vol.26, 1972* (UN, New York, 1975), p.639 and p.648.

60. For example, Menachem Begin, former leader of the Zionist terrorist organisation *Irgun Zvei Leumi*, became Prime Minister of Israel in 1977 and was later awarded the Nobel Peace Prize. Regis Debray, confidant of Fidel Castro and author of *Revolution in the Revolution?* later became a Special Adviser and Envoy of President Mitterand of France.

61. *United Nations Yearbook, Vol.26, 1972*, p.648.

62. The League of Nations adopted a Convention on the Prevention and Punishment of Terrorism on 16 November 1937, but it was only ratified by one country (India, in 1941). The Convention never entered into force.

63. Quoted in Hamer, p.772.

64. See H. F. Shamwell, 'Implementing the Convention on the Prevention and Punishment of Crimes Against Internationally Protected Persons, Including Diplomatic Agents', *Terrorism: An International Journal* 6:4 (1983), p.531.

65. Amos Yoder, 'The Effectiveness of UN Action Against International Terrorism: Conclusions and Comments', *Terrorism: An International Journal* 6:4 (1983), p.589.

66. Murphy, in Evans and Murphy, p.317.

67. *op.cit.* p.309.

68. Resolution 3166 (XXVIII) of 14 December 1973, in *United Nations Treaty Series*, Vol.1035 (1977) (United Nations, New York, 1984), pp.238-239.

69. See L. C. Green, 'The Legalisation of Terrorism', in Y. Alexander, D. Carlton and P. Wilkinson (eds), *Terrorism: Theory and Practice* (Westview Press, Boulder, 1979).

70. A. D. Sofaer, 'Terrorism and the Law', *Foreign Affairs* 64:5 (Summer 1986), pp.917-918.

71. F. Saddy, 'International Terrorism, Human Rights and World Order', *Terrorism: An International Journal* 5:4 (1982).

72. Some of these documents contain the same ambiguities as the New York Convention itself. The UN Declaration of Principles of International Law, for example, decries support for terrorism but enjoins states to support movements against racism and other forms of oppression.

73. See Murphy, in Evans and Murphy, pp.295-296.

74. 'United Nations General Assembly: Resolution on the Consideration of Effective Measures to Enhance the Protection, Security and Safety of Diplomatic and Consular Missions and Representatives' (December 1980), in *United Nations Yearbook, Vol.34, 1980* (UN, New York, 1983), pp.1148-1150.

75. UNGA Resolution 40/61 of 9 December 1985, Fortieth Session, 1985/1986. UN Document A/Res/40/61.

5

THE CHALLENGE TO DIPLOMACY

All government, indeed every human benefit and enjoyment, every virtue, and every prudent act, is founded on compromise and barter.

Edmund Burke
Speech on conciliation with America (1775)

Since terrorist attacks on diplomats and diplomatic facilities first reached serious proportions some 20 years ago, diplomacy has been described as one of the world's most dangerous professions,[1] with diplomats the 'front line fighters[2]' in 'a new kind of warfare[3]' that has placed the entire system of diplomatic representation and peaceful negotiation 'under siege'.[4] United Nations Secretary-General Kurt Waldheim was reported in 1979 as saying that the occupation of the US Embassy in Tehran was 'the most serious threat to world peace since the Cuban missile crisis'[5] 17 years earlier, and the concept of diplomatic immunity is said to have become 'an anachronism'.[6] In 1984, the Acting Secretary of State in the Reagan Administration even claimed that terrorists and their state sponsors had consciously set out to destroy diplomacy itself:

> For it is not the content of our—or any—particular diplomacy that is their target but the process—a process which seeks through negotiation to address the legitimate grievances of all parties; a process that, above all, seeks to prevent one party from imposing its will on another.[7]

While it may be true that the 'instruments of diplomacy' are the 'prime targets of terror',[8] this wider claim bears closer examination. Indeed, it could be argued that, rather than being in danger from terrorism, the institution of diplomacy has become stronger because of it.

Official American statements have cast the terrorist threat to diplomacy in almost apocalyptic terms with the United States, on behalf of the world's democracies, defending a system that promotes the peaceful settlement of

79

disputes against these 'depraved opponents of civilisation itself'.[9] Although in recent years the US has tended to focus its criticisms on radical states like Libya and Iran, this apparent threat to civilised values has repeatedly been sheeted home to the Soviet Union. Yet for all its undoubted involvement with international terrorism over the years, the Soviet Union clearly places considerable value on diplomatic processes. Far from assisting in any concerted attack on the institution of diplomacy the Soviet Union has demonstrated a concern to protect and strengthen it. A greater danger to regular diplomatic intercourse and ordered international behaviour could arise from an over-reaction to the terrorist threat. The United States policy of 'active defence', for example, has been prompted by complex domestic and international pressures, but carries with it the potential for further violence and a more serious breakdown in the international peace. Care needs to be taken that in responding to the threat of international terrorism, states do not hand to the terrorists and their sponsors a victory of their own making.

THE GLOBAL FRAMEWORK

Diplomats are now exposed to greater danger than has been faced by members of their profession since organised diplomacy began in the 16th century. From the late 1960s, when attacks on diplomatic targets were found to be a powerful weapon of publicity and political extortion, the number of terrorist incidents involving diplomats has steadily grown, increasing dramatically with the arrival of the 1980s. Diplomats and diplomatic facilities now constitute two of the most favoured targets for terrorist attack. This threat and the measures that have been taken to guard against it have severely constrained diplomatic personnel in the performance of their duties and presented governments with a complex and delicate problem for the continued conduct of world diplomacy. In addition:

> campaigns of terrorism or specific incidents of terrorism directed against targets in the foreign diplomatic...community have no doubt embarrassed several governments, weakened some of them, and perhaps contributed to the downfall of a few.[10]

Terrorist attacks on diplomatic targets have caused friction between states, disrupted their economic relations and in some cases threatened their national sovereignty and territorial integrity. The emergence of such violent independent actors on the world stage has also presented a challenge to international order by striking at 'one of the most basic presuppositions of the states system, which is that only states may legitimately employ violence against each other, and then only in accordance with prescribed rules and procedures'.[11] The nature of modern society, the motivations of terrorists and their new capabilities have given them the potential to be a real peace-keeping problem.

To assess the full impact of terrorism on diplomacy, however, events over the past 20 years must be considered in the broadest perspective. No longer do a relative handful of states make the rules and no longer do states necessarily feel bound by them.[12] Since 1945 the number of states has more than trebled, with the main increase being from four to over 50 in Africa and from nine to over 40 in Asia. These newly-constituted states share an acceptance of the concepts, developed under the European states system, of external sovereignty, territorial integrity and the legal equality of states. Yet if these have not been challenged, European approaches to other matters have. Established attitudes to questions of legitimacy and self-determination, social, economic and political rights have increasingly come to be questioned. To this mixture has been added the yeast of powerful religious and ideological movements. With the loosening of controls and growth of global politics has also come the appearance of diverse non-state actors with increased capacities to affect the international system. As pressures for change have mounted, and have failed to find outlets in established negotiating groups, so solutions have been sought outside them. Many traditional restraints have been set aside and institutions which were formerly considered inviolate have come to be seen as 'legitimate' targets for criticism and manipulation. Increases in terrorist attacks on diplomatic personnel and premises, and growing abuses of diplomatic conventions, have many causes but need to be considered first in the light of these developments and the low consensus which currently prevails in many areas of world affairs. To a degree, it can be argued that such attacks are as much the symptoms of current international uncertainties as they are the causes of them.

It also needs to be remembered that, despite some dire predictions, no international terrorist group has yet managed to proceed beyond certain tactical successes to achieve its wider strategic objectives. The PLO has perhaps come closest but although it has secured a broad international commitment to a separate Palestinian state it does not seem very much closer to achieving one. No government with a genuinely popular support base has tolerated terrorism for long. Events over the past few years have shown that international terrorism, particularly if state-sponsored, can influence the foreign policies of states and disrupt important international political processes, but few major concessions have been made as a direct result of pressure from international terrorist groups. With the possible exception of Uruguay between 1969–1972, the only governments which have fallen through terrorist action have been colonial regimes in circumstances where special conditions have prevailed. Indeed, as Andrew Mack has suggested, terrorist actions have tended to strengthen the state vis-a-vis civil society.[13] Paul Wilkinson put the problem into perspective when he wrote that:

> it is manifestly improbable that tiny bands of francs-tireurs, however desperate, could seriously threaten an international order dominated by super powers with their vast military strength and global capabilities... The most they can hope to achieve is the sowing of disruption and alarm, or the temporary interruption or exacerbation of diplomatic relations between states.[14]

Terrorists have been able to attract a good deal of attention, obtain a number of minor concessions from states and force a number of changes to the day-to-day operations of international society. As Lenin, Mao Tse-tung, Guevara and some other early revolutionaries foresaw, however, they have been unable to translate the consequences of terrorism into concrete political gains or markedly affect society's vital functions. These functions include interstate exchanges through diplomatic intermediaries.

It is salutary too to look at the casualties that have resulted from attacks on diplomats and diplomatic facilities. Surveys conducted by the Rand Corporation in 1977 and 1981, of embassy seizures and international hostage incidents, suggest that in fact the number of deaths at the hands of terrorists (in the incidents surveyed at least) have been relatively small. Most people killed or injured were hurt either resisting the initial seizure or as a result of rescue operations by security forces.[15] Despite the high proportion of attacks directed against diplomatic targets less than 13 per cent of all casualties from international terrorist incidents between 1968 and 1985 were diplomatic or consular personnel.[16] With the most recent casualties included, the total number of diplomatic and consular officers killed or wounded since 1968 is still unlikely to exceed 500 killed and 1500 injured for the entire period. Tragic though these figures are, in any objective analysis of the terrorist phenomenon they must be balanced against the total number of diplomats serving throughout the world during the same period who suffered no attack, making that number seem much smaller. The fact that two ambassadors at least were killed during civil wars is a reminder that diplomacy has always had its risks, even before terrorists posed a danger.

In recent years terrorist attacks have become more deadly, resulting in a higher rate of casualties, but terrorism is and will remain primarily symbolic violence—violence for effect—with political consequences that invariably exceed the actual amount of death and destruction caused. Fewer than 20 per cent of all attacks on diplomats before 1982 resulted in casualties. Most terrorist groups 'want a lot of people watching and a lot of people listening, and not a lot of people dead'.[17] The exalted status of the diplomat in the eyes of the public, the dramatic nature of the attacks, political rhetoric, unreliable statistics and the sensationalist news media coverage usually given to such events have all combined to give a somewhat misleading impression of the scale of terrorist attacks on diplomats and their facilities. This is not to underestimate the threat, which is quite real, simply to put it into its proper context. Indeed, in contrast to statements by members of the Reagan Administration elsewhere, the Office of the Ambassador-at-Large for Counter-Terrorism in the US State Department has in recent years been attempting to place the terrorist threat in just this perspective.[18]

DIPLOMATS OR DIPLOMACY

Paradoxically, while the number and deadliness of attacks against diplomatic targets is increasing, the institution of diplomacy is becoming more secure. Terrorist attacks upon diplomats and diplomatic facilities, whether carried out by independent groups or as an extension of state policies, have almost without exception been aimed in the first instance at states—most often the sending state, but also the receiving state, or both. At times, attacks have been indirectly aimed at other states but diplomatic targets have invariably been chosen by terrorists because they are state symbols, representing the governments, policies or political systems of states. Only very rarely, if at all, have they been attacked because they represented the diplomatic system *as such*. Indeed, the only terrorist organisations which have claimed to oppose world systems of this kind have been anarchist-nihilistic organisations like the Baader-Meinhof Group (later the Red Army Faction) in West Germany—to which all politics was 'shit'[19]—and the Japanese United Red Army, which seems inspired by a vague notion of world revolution through indiscriminate violence. These groups have not often attacked diplomatic targets, though, and when they have their demands have usually been (like other groups) for the release of prisoners and monetary ransom. This was seen, for example, in the attack on the FRG Embassy in Stockholm by the 'Holger Meins Kommando' of the RAF in April 1975 and the URA seizure of the French Embassy in The Hague the year before. At no stage have such groups claimed that they were striking a symbolic blow at diplomacy, or even the diplomatic services of particular states. In October 1986, when the RAF assassinated Gerold von Braunmuehl, Head of the Political Department in the FRG Foreign Ministry, it was made clear that he had been singled out because of his membership of the European Community's Political Committee (which discussed NATO matters), not because of his diplomatic position. On at least two occasions terrorist groups have demanded that certain states break off diplomatic relations with another country, something which implies at least implicit recognition of the system and codes which govern diplomatic intercourse. Diplomatic targets have always served as a means to a variety of tactical ends, never as ends in themselves.

Another reason why the institution of diplomacy is still secure, even if its practitioners and premises are not, is that terrorists are usually alive to the role that diplomacy can play in the realisation of both their tactical and strategic goals. The kidnapping of diplomats and the seizure of diplomatic facilities in one sense represents a flat rejection of the diplomatic option of peaceful negotiations and mutually satisfactory compromises, yet such attacks are not quite the 'zero sum game' that Paul Wilkinson has suggested.[20] As events in Lebanon clearly show, they give the terrorists a bargaining position in which they achieve diplomatic leverage infinitely greater than would otherwise be available to them. Like states wielding power in a more conventional negotiation the terrorists become party to a 'coercive value exchange'[21] in which the diplomatic representatives of other countries are usually involved. States sponsoring terrorist groups utilise the same principles at a national level, in conducting their own 'coercive diplomacy'. Terrorist groups no longer seem anxious to woo international opinion in the manner of guerrilla forces in the past, but they have been quick to realise that even a negative impact can mobilise opinion and win them certain concessions. 'While terrorists attack the basic rules of international order, they depend on international pressure to achieve their political goals'.[22] This has been most apparent in the case of various Middle Eastern extremist organisations, such as the PLO.

The example of the PLO points to yet another paradox, which is that many terrorist groups, including those which most often attack diplomatic targets, seem to recognise and seek the legitimacy that diplomatic status represents. This can be achieved either as a terrorist organisation, or as a state. The PLO has managed the former and enjoys formal Observer status at the United Nations, membership of several important international organisations and full representation at a number of major conferences. In addition, the PLO maintains its own 'diplomatic service' with offices in over 100 countries, where they are accorded full or near-full diplomatic privileges. At least one member of NATO grants the PLO full diplomatic recognition.[23] Since 1973 the world has been treated to the irony of the ostensibly moderate, and now 'respectable', factions of the PLO led by Yassir Arafat seeking 'diplomatic' solutions to the Palestinian question and denouncing the 'reckless and irresponsible' acts of international terrorism carried out by other Palestinian groups. This strongly suggests that the main Palestinian factions at least wish to gain power within the current international system without undermining its basic foundations.

The other avenue through which terrorists can win diplomatic status is by having successfully achieved statehood. In some cases this aim is held largely because the easiest way to instigate desired changes in a state or world of states is to seize control of such a unit.[24] In other cases a state of their own is the ultimate aim of many terrorist groups, particularly those with ethnic, religious or other separatist ideologies. There are now a number of states in existence which achieved their independence with the help of terrorist campaigns, and then moved quickly to establish formal diplomatic establishments and arrangements. Some acknowledged terrorist leaders and sympathisers have achieved international respectability and even prominence in world negotiating groups. It is perhaps not stretching this argument too far to see in the so-called 'anti-diplomatic corps' of terrorist representatives which existed in Algeria in the early 1970s a recognition by such groups that some kind of diplomatic intercourse will always be necessary.[25]

The greatest danger terrorism poses for diplomacy lies perhaps in the blatant disregard for diplomatic norms shown by some states and their use of agitational terror as an extension of their foreign policies. Such behaviour has the potential seriously to undermine not only the established conventions through which states regulate their contacts with each other, but the whole rule of law on which such ordered contacts are based. Once again, however, these developments in themselves are not new and while a few mavericks like Libya and Iran have shocked the world with their public repudiation of customary standards even they have not rejected diplomacy outright. Iran's unprecedented abrogation of its responsibilities towards the US mission in Tehran was universally condemned, including by all members of the Security Council and by a number of states which might in other circumstances have been expected to sympathise with the revolutionaries. Yet the Iranians continued to operate their diplomatic missions abroad and to accept all the usual courtesies from receiving governments. They also 'carefully respected the immunities of other embassies and of the diplomatic emissaries who negotiated the eventual release of the hostages'.[26] In 1979 Libya loudly rejected conventional diplomatic forms, much as the Soviet Union had done in 1918, and has since demonstrated its contempt for all standards of diplomatic, and civilised, behaviour by the shooting of a policewoman in London, from protected premises. Despite its record of gross violations in some states, however, Libya seems prepared to abide by customary rules in others and there are signs that its experiment with People's Bureaux is crumbling away. Syria too has shown no intention to challenge the diplomatic system *per se*, despite its systematic abuses of diplomatic conventions. Indeed, since the expulsion of its mission from Britain in 1986, Syria has taken pains to emphasize its respect for diplomatic norms.

As states which supported terrorism in one form or another have themselves come under terrorist attack, they have usually been quick to reaffirm the value of traditional norms of international conduct. The seizure by the Black September Organisation of the Saudi Arabian Embassy in Khartoum in 1973, for example, prompted a rapid reassessment of Sudanese attitudes towards terrorism and the financial support Saudi Arabia was giving to the Palestinians. Sudanese President Mohammed Gafar el-Nimeiry described the killing of the three Western diplomats as 'a criminal, rash action devoid of revolutionary spirit and bravery' which 'could in no way benefit the Palestinian people'.[27] All Palestinian activity in Sudan was banned the following week. More recently, states like France which, while not actually condoning terrorism, had taken a rather permissive view of terrorist activities against other states, have responded more quickly and firmly when their own sovereignty has been impugned. As the scope of terrorism has become wider even some of the more radical states have begun to take a less sympathetic view of certain types of terrorist operation. In particular, since the massive increase in attacks against diplomats and diplomatic facilities in the early 1980s:

> a growing number of States have seriously questioned whether the pursuit of anti-colonialism and self-determination really necessitates the abandoning of traditional standards of State behaviour [such as diplomatic inviolability and the responsibility of host governments for the safety of foreigners]. The consensus among States seems to have moved towards rejection of those forms of political expression which violate such basic trust.[28]

This consensus is demonstrated most clearly by the support given in the United Nations and other international organisations to measures aimed at safeguarding internationally protected persons, notably diplomats.

While discussions on terrorism in international fora have revealed deep and apparently irreconcilable divisions over the nature of the phenomenon and the responses that states should make to it, they have also revealed a remarkable community of shared values and interests regarding the need to protect diplomats and diplomatic facilities from terrorist attack. No real dissent has been registered on this fundamental issue in all the times it has been raised over the past 20 years. While questions of broad principle have figured prominently in most public speeches on the subject, such wide agreement would only be possible if all states recognised that the continued functioning of diplomacy served their own vital interests and that, as noted in the 1961 Vienna Convention on Diplomatic Relations, such functions could only be carried out if certain privileges and immunities were respected. All states appear to have accepted that they are equally vulnerable to such terrorist violence. International legal measures such as the New York Convention will probably always lack effective sanctions and be subject to abuse but it is sufficient for the purposes of this study to note that states have demonstrated so clearly their willingness to develop a more elaborate body of international law on the subject of terrorist attacks against diplomatic personnel and premises. With each additional instrument the importance of diplomacy is underscored and the likelihood diminished that it will ever come under serious threat.

Indeed, it could even be argued that the institution of diplomacy thrives on discord. Throughout history it has emerged from periods of heightened international competition stronger than before. The Peace of Westphalia in 1648 was negotiated at the end of the Thirty Years War, the Congress of Vienna in 1815 took place during the Napoleonic Wars which convulsed the Old World and the 1961 Vienna Conference on Diplomatic Relations was held at a time of considerable East-West tension. Yet each saw significant additions to the code of international diplomatic practice. It is possible that the 1973 New York Convention will eventually come to be seen as this generation's response to the threat to diplomacy in a post-colonial era of revolution and socio-economic discontent. These international meetings and the legal instruments which flowed from them are all illustrative of the enduring concern felt by states, particularly in times of danger, to preserve an institution vital to them all. For as long as states remain wedded to their own interests in a world system, diplomacy will be needed. As R. B. Mowat has written, it 'meets the great secular need of mankind, the need for peoples to make arrangements with each other'.[29]

States cannot afford to be sanguine about the problems posed by international terrorism but, as Michael Palliser has warned, terrorist attacks on diplomats and diplomatic facilities should not be allowed to induce the belief 'that a code of practice which has developed over the centuries, and which for the most part works well, is in imminent danger of collapse'.[30] Clearly, it is not. By its very nature diplomacy has been able to adapt itself to changing world conditions, accommodating new requirements and meeting fresh challenges. In some respects there has been a decline in the role played by traditional diplomacy in international politics since it reached its apogee in 19th century Europe, but the institution continues to flourish. Those revolutionary regimes which initially rejected conventional diplomatic processes, such as Russia and Libya, quickly found that they could not dispense with them and still live in a plural and ordered society of states. Even if resident embassies should lose their importance or are transformed in character, states will continue to negotiate solutions to their problems in a structured fashion, just as they did before the emergence of resident embassies and professional diplomatic services over 400 years ago.

International society is now highly mobile, with power distributed among a number of centres. Even the smallest state can quickly assume global significance. Technological developments have made the nuclear balance more fragile and all states are vulnerable to an unprecedented degree. Safety can no longer be seen to lie in alliances or military strength. In such a situation not even the most powerful country can afford to ignore certain principles of statecraft. In addition, both state and non-state actors are still growing in number and becoming more interdependent. World politics is becoming increasingly complex and no state can isolate itself without harm to its own interests. This places a high premium on diplomatic contacts and skills. As suggested by Martin Wight, the diplomatic system remains of fundamental importance and in the current international environment must continue to play a vital role. Periods of low consensus, as now, only serve to emphasise that conflicts of interest are a major preoccupation of diplomats and, short of war, can only strengthen their traditional role.

Naturally, there is cause for concern in the blatant disregard for diplomatic norms and peaceful options by some states—old and new—and the use of diplomacy to excite differences rather than to settle them. Yet there has never been a golden age when diplomats were entirely free from danger, whether it be from individuals, groups or governments. In addition, questions of power and prestige have almost always figured in international negotiations and the institution of diplomacy is not going to be unduly threatened if the unspoken fear behind an agreement is one of a terrorist bomb rather than the despatch of a gunboat or the launch of a nuclear missile. Diplomacy has never been pure and while continued efforts must be made to prevent abuses of the diplomatic system it should come as no surprise if they should still occur. There will continue to be challenges to the conventions of diplomacy and terrorist attacks against diplomatic targets are likely to increase before they diminish, but diplomacy will survive as it has always done, insured against collapse by the recognition of all states that it continues to play a vital role in their affairs. Even if its component parts are threatened, the institution itself will remain secure, protected by established states and coveted by its attackers.

If these arguments are accepted, then it can be claimed that while diplomats and diplomatic facilities are facing increasing dangers from international terrorism, the *institution* of diplomacy is not. Both the terrorists and the states which support them recognise the continuing value of diplomacy and have made plain their feeling that it should be preserved. This is a fine distinction and one that offers little comfort to the officials, their families and the governments placed at risk. It is an important distinction, however, for from it flows an estimation of the scope and true nature of the threat posed to the international system of diplomacy by terrorism and the measures states can take to respond to it. It is an important distinction too for the perspective it offers on the United States Government's view that much of the world's current terrorist problems spring ultimately from the Soviet Union's desire to 'weaken liberal democracy and undermine world stability'.[31] For if, as the US claims, international terrorists are attacking the institution of diplomacy—'the process'—and the terrorists are controlled (however indirectly) from Moscow, then it follows that the US is accusing the Soviet Union of attempting to undermine the institution of diplomacy. Yet, for all the Soviet Union's diverse connections with international terrorism over the past 20 years, this does not appear to be the case.

THE SOVIET UNION AND DIPLOMACY

While the Soviet Union has shown little hesitation in using terrorist groups (and certain sponsoring states) to weaken the capacities and resolve of the West, particularly in areas of strategic significance like the Middle East, it has consistently displayed an ambivalence towards certain kinds of terrorist operations. It has had to balance its interests in supporting anti-Western forces with opposition to terrorist activities and policies to which the Soviet Union is itself vulnerable, such as attacks on diplomats and diplomatic facilities. It is true that there have been relatively few terrorist incidents reported in Eastern bloc countries, but this can be explained to a large degree by the nature of totalitarian regimes which make terrorist operations of any kind extremely difficult to plan and execute. The kidnapping of four Soviet diplomats in Lebanon in September 1985 (and the murder of one of them) served as a reminder that, after the United States, Turkey, Yugoslavia and France, Cuba and the USSR are the victims of the greatest number of terrorist attacks against diplomatic targets. In some countries, such as Peru, the Soviet mission shares the brunt of terrorist attacks with that of the United States.

For a variety of reasons, many stemming from its own weaknesses, the Soviet Union places considerable importance on its diplomatic processes and thus shares with other states an interest in seeing diplomats and diplomatic facilities receive greater protection. As early as 1972 the then Soviet Foreign Minister, Andrei Gromyko, told the United Nations General Assembly that:

> On the basis of positions of principle, the Soviet Union opposes acts of terrorism which disrupt the diplomatic activities of states and their representatives, transport communications between them and the normal course of international contact and meetings, and it opposes acts of violence which serve no purpose and cause loss of human life.[32]

The leader of the Soviet delegation, Jacov Malik, also emphasised this point when he told the same session of the UN that the Soviet Union was opposed to terrorism, 'particularly violent acts committed against heads of state and diplomats in foreign countries'.[33] As W.S. Thompson has correctly observed, these are precisely those functions of inter-state relations in which the USSR has as much at stake as any other country.[34]

For all their dissembling and posturing on other matters relating to international terrorism, these and similar statements made more recently do not seem to be simply rhetoric on the part of the Soviet Union and its allies. They were among the first states to become party to the UN Convention on the Protection and Punishment of Crimes Against Internationally Protected Persons, Including Diplomatic Agents, a step yet to be taken by a number of the United States' NATO and ANZUS allies. France, Belgium and the Netherlands, for example, have yet to become parties to the Convention and New Zealand only decided to do so in 1985, after the bombing of the Greenpeace vessel *Rainbow Warrior* by French secret agents. There is evidence too, to suggest that on occasion the Soviet Union has attempted to restrain terrorist groups over which it exercises some influence and at times it has supported counter-terrorist measures in international fora which have been opposed by its terrorist clients.

In the 17th and 18th centuries rivalries between the European powers provided an environment within which the Barbary pirates could flourish. By the 19th century, however, the major powers saw the pirates as a common enemy and joined forces to put an end to their activities. It is too early to point to a similar consensus among the superpowers against international terrorism, but there has been a number of significant examples of East-West cooperation in this field. The 1973 Cuba-USA Memorandum of Understanding on the Hijacking of Aircraft and Vessels and Other Offenses is a remarkable example of how two states with widely varying attitudes on other matters can cooperate when they perceive shared interests. The Soviet Union shared a similar agreement with the Shah's Iran and has since given practical assistance to the FRG on matters relating to the hijacking of aircraft. Even Bulgaria, which according to some theories has been guilty of supporting terrorism in recent years, assisted in the capture of a number of international terrorists and their extradition to the FRG for trial in 1978. There were rumours in early 1986 that Moscow and Washington were exploring the possibility of a bilateral agreement on cooperation against terrorism and in November that year it was announced that the United Kingdom and the Soviet Union would be holding official talks to investigate the scope for increased cooperation in counter-terrorism measures. The same year, the Soviet delegate to the Geneva Conference on Disarmament called for the International Atomic Energy Agency to develop reliable measures to deter nuclear terrorism. All these examples suggest that the Soviet Union recognises its own vulnerabilities and, when it suits it to do so, can be selective in its support for terrorist violence.

This cooperation with the West has not stemmed from any altruism or allegiance to the sanctity of traditional diplomacy. Indeed, there is no place for international commerce, interstate diplomacy or even sovereign states themselves in the world order ultimately envisaged by orthodox Marxist ideologues. It is recognised, however, that all three are unlikely to disappear in the foreseeable future and the interests of the Soviet Union and its allies currently lie in accepting these realities and utilising them for their own benefit. Given the Soviet Union's investment in the global system at present, any attack which seriously threatens it is likely to be to the detriment of the Soviet Union as much as, if not more than, other states. As Adam

Watson has noted in a wider context, both the superpowers have so far recognised, explicitly or implicitly, that:

> the preservation and effective functioning of their system and of international society must be given priority whenever the point is reached where it appears to be seriously threatened.[35]

The Soviet Union does not appear ready yet to sacrifice the advantages it gains through its influence with terrorist groups and their state sponsors, but it does seem anxious to preserve the vital elements of this system, including formal diplomatic conventions.

THE DANGER OF OVER-REACTION

From its statements over the past five years the Reagan Administration appears to feel that the USSR has abandoned any interests it may have had in the existing world system and chosen instead to undermine it through terrorist surrogates. In a news conference given shortly after taking office as Secretary of State, Alexander Haig stated that it was the Soviet Union, through its policies of training, funding and equipping international terrorists, that bore primary responsibility for the wave of terrorism confronting the United States.[36] As noted since by Michael Stohl, Mr Haig was supported in this position by key members of the Reagan Administration such as National Security Adviser Richard Allen and Secretary of Defense Caspar Weinberger.[37] While a number of other states have since been added to the US's list of terrorist sponsors, and at times been given greater prominence, the Administration has maintained its criticism of Soviet policies. In terms that US officials have long applied to communism itself, terrorism is described as a 'contagious disease' that will ultimately destroy 'civilisation itself'.[38] Terror and counter-terror have been cast in terms of an epic struggle between anarchy and civilisation, totalitarianism and democracy, extremism and moderation, violence and diplomacy.[39] Such an approach has consequences which reach well beyond the spheres of terrorism and state responses to it.

By overlooking the West's own support for terrorism now and in the past, and by failing to see the contemporary problem in a wider perspective, the Reagan Administration seems to view the current terrorist threat as something newer and more threatening to world order than is in fact the case. This is not to underestimate the dangers posed by terrorism today, but to argue against an over-reaction which could be more destabilising than the problem which it is hoped to solve. Recent US Government statements remove the terrorism problem from the political arena by stressing its essential criminality, but at the same time place it firmly on the political agenda by treating it as a matter for global concern. International consideration of the terrorist problem is necessary and, as demonstrated by the New York Convention on the protection of diplomats, occasionally successful in focussing attention on areas of universal concern. By presenting the terrorist problem as a major factor in the East-West struggle, however, the Reagan Administration has locked this complex and highly sensitive issue into the wider competition between the superpowers. As noted earlier, attempts by the US and the USSR to legitimise their own policies and delegitimise those of their opponents inevitably become of paramount concern. The deeper causes of terrorist violence and the measures necessary to prevent it become increasingly obscured. Terrorist attacks all over the world are perceived by the US as Soviet tests of its resolve and in order to maintain its reputation for strength, preserve its international prestige and keep its credibility with its allies the US has felt obliged to make a strong response. Unable to achieve any major political successes in the fight against terrorism, however, the Reagan Administration has turned increasingly to military options.

In an address before the Park Avenue Synagogue in October 1984, US Secretary of State George Shultz said that:

> the essence of our response is simple to state: violence and aggression must be met with firm resistance... there is no question about our ability to use force where and when it is needed to counter terrorism. Our nation has forces prepared for action—from small teams able to operate virtually undetected, to the full weight of our conventional military might.[40]

On another occasion Mr Shultz referred to international terrorism and spoke of the US's readiness to 'resort to arms on behalf of democracy against repressive regimes and movements'.[41] Strong statements such as these are doubtless designed in part to reassure the American public and signal to foreign governments the United States' strength and resolve in the face of continued terrorist provocation. They also reflect the Reagan Administration's impatience with the more considered responses of its allies and the lengthy, often inconclusive deliberations of multilateral institutions on this subject. Throughout history the United States has been an action-oriented society with an abiding belief in the attainability of solutions in the shorter term, achieved through the concentration of its enormous resources and its remarkable imagination and energy. This philosophy has brought it many notable successes, but the problem of international terrorism is one that does not lend itself to such an approach.

Despite all the evidence to the contrary, there still seems to be a conviction in some circles in Washington that terrorism can be 'stamped out'[42] by an equal or greater application of force. Such a view suggests either a profound misunderstanding of the nature of terrorist violence or an excessive confidence in the abilities of the US, or both. It also suggests a reluctance to allow that terrorism can be reduced, to a certain degree at least, by careful attention to its sources. The US Vice President's Task Force on Combatting Terrorism apparently considered the 'root causes' of terrorism but saw their resolution as essentially a foreign policy problem.[43] For its part, the State Department has recognised the need to examine the unresolved political and social grievances at the root of much terrorist violence, but this approach does not seem to be supported by some senior Administration officials.[44] Increased protection against attacks, international cooperation and the means to respond to particular incidents are all important, but none address the objective causes of terrorism, many of which tend to be found in ideological and religious convictions, political, social and economic discontent. As has been demonstrated in numerous unconventional conflicts since 1945, a number of which included American participation, unless these issues are also considered little progress can be made towards a lasting and peaceful solution.

Gaps between declaratory policy and operational policy are not unusual but, taken to its logical conclusion, the Reagan Administration's notion of 'active defence' against terrorism could constitute a threat to international order and world peace at least as great as that posed by terrorism itself. There may be times when the arguments for a more forceful response will be convincing, and diplomatic options are not ruled out *per se*, but efforts to explore peaceful solutions to the terrorist problem are usually given much less emphasis in official US statements than direct action. Some of the military responses canvassed might be manageable, but others would, in Paul Wilkinson's words, 'only succeed in substituting the greater evil of full-scale war...for the lesser evil of terrorism'.[45] This prospect haunted the violent confrontations between the United States and Libya in 1986 and gave rise to considerable international concern, including among the United States' friends and allies. As Carlos Marighela instructed his proteges they should do in 1969, the terrorists have succeeded in turning a political problem into a military one, except that in this case it is not the armed forces of a single developing country that is involved, but the full conventional military might of the world's greatest superpower, operating on a global scale.[46]

It is difficult to see how military responses of the kind outlined by Mr Shultz can really be effective, either in punishing terrorists or in preventing future attacks. While at first sight it might appear that there are a number of ways force can be used productively, in fact 'military options in response to terrorism are few'.[47] Repeated Israeli reprisals against Arab states and the Palestinians have not only failed to prevent further attacks from being mounted but have helped breed a new generation of terrorists anxious to claim their own retribution. After the invasion of Lebanon, for example, the number of terrorist incidents in Israel declined but the number of attacks against Israeli and Jewish targets elsewhere sharply increased.[48] In addition, a strong case can be made that Israeli actions have contributed significantly to the growing popular and diplomatic support now being shown for the Palestinian cause. French bombing raids against Shi'ite militia bases in November 1983 failed to prevent further attacks against French peacekeeping troops in Lebanon. There is also evidence to suggest that the shelling of Shi'ite 'targets' in Lebanon by the battleship *USS New Jersey* in 1983 and 1984 led indirectly to the hijacking of the TWA aircraft to Beirut in June 1985. Although there have been claims that the American bombing raids on Libya served as an effective object lesson to the world's terrorists, the results have been quite ambiguous. The State Department's own statistics show no appreciable difference in the incidence of Libyan terrorism in the months before and after the raids[49] and, despite a distinct hiatus in obvious Libyan terrorist activity in late 1986 and early 1987, this could be attributed to several causes. Falling oil revenues and Libya's drawn-out war with Chad, for example, have helped reduce Colonel Qaddafi's appetite for terrorist operations. There is no prospect that Libya will forsake the terrorist option as a result of the 1986 bombing raids.

Policies such as those approved by President Reagan in 1984 and implemented since seem to reflect domestic electoral pressures and the need for the United States to preserve its position as a global power, as much as any objective assessment of terrorist issues. By concentrating upon defensive measures against terrorist acts and offensive measures against terrorist groups, or states, the US appears to have underestimated the real complexity of international terrorism and given insufficient weight to the deeper reasons for its appearance and apparent effectiveness. There is now a danger that such policies may serve to exacerbate the problem and make long term peaceful solutions harder to find. They risk hardening the terrorists' resolve and demonstrating to them their ability to preoccupy a world power and set the agenda for international policy discussions. They also expose differences among the Western allies and win for the terrorists and their sponsors expressions of support from states which in other circumstances might have quietly encouraged initiatives against them. Such policies, and certain measures taken by other states, also raise a number of serious moral, legal and political questions, and narrow the gap between the terrorists and the states themselves.

In a speech at the National Defense University in Washington in January 1986 Secretary of State George Shultz stated that:

> We believe in the rule of law. This nation has long been a champion of international law, the peaceful settlement of disputes, and the UN Charter as a code of conduct for the world community.[50]

Yet by some of its responses to the terrorist problem to date, the Reagan Administration has raised serious concerns that in certain circumstances it is prepared to bend or even flout that law. In the same Washington speech, for example, Mr Shultz claimed that the self-defence provisions of the UN Charter permitted the US to attack terrorists on foreign soil and to use armed force against states that trained, supported or harboured terrorists. As subsequently used to justify the US bombing raids on Libya, this argument in fact constituted a significant reinterpretation of the meaning of self-defence. The definition of armed aggression against a state was extended to cover its citizens abroad, a concept common enough in the colonial era but one which has much less currency now. It was strongly argued in April 1986, for example, that the US had distorted the meaning of self-defence under the Charter and ignored those parts of it (and other UN instruments) which forbade the use of force as a measure of retaliation by an injured state. Also offered at the time were other more subtle and complex legal points against military action of this kind, stemming from such considerations as 'necessity' and 'proportionality'. Mr Shultz had earlier stated that 'The law is a weapon on our side, and it is up to us to use it to its maximum extent'.[51] The US needed to establish some kind of legal basis for its bombing raids against Libya, but tendentious arguments can in certain respects be more damaging than none at all. Major changes in established practice at times of policy significance can be self-defeating, as they raise a number of fundamental questions not only about a state's actions but also its whole attitude towards the international legal system. As demonstrated again in June 1986, when the International Court of Justice handed down its judgement on the case of *Nicaragua vs USA*, considerable care needs to be exercised in deciding to use force against what is perceived to be a delinquent state.[52]

Just as assassinations, kidnappings, torture and bombings by counter-terrorist forces have already done on a smaller scale, there is a danger that the kind of policies being pursued by the Reagan Administration could help undermine the very codes of behaviour and international legal institutions that it claims to defend. This would have consequences reaching far beyond any terrorist campaign. International law is already a fragile institution. It relies on the voluntary compliance of states, in particular the observance of certain principles and procedures by the most influential states in world affairs, namely the superpowers. As the world's leading democratic state, with perhaps the longest record of uninterrupted observance of international law, the US carries a heavy responsibility for the continued workings of those conventions and legal mechanisms which regulate and encourage peaceful contacts between states. Should the US debase or even abandon these norms and resort to the kind of cynical *realpolitik* exercised by the terrorists and their state sponsors, then the entire structure of ordered international society—including diplomacy as it is now known—will be put at risk. Should that happen, the terrorists would be handed a greater victory than any they could achieve by violent means. In this sense David Fromkin is correct when he says that terrorism 'achieves its goals not through its acts but through responses to its acts'.[53]

There is a real dilemma for the United States here. Terrorists are not vulnerable to moral force or to international legal pressure in the manner of established states and can thus violate accepted norms of behaviour in ways that governments like that of the US cannot. As Grant Wardlaw has written:

> restraint within the bounds of law and morality may limit our action as democratic states, but it is the rule of law and morality that distinguish us from the terrorists.[54]

To overstep such bounds, even in the name of the country's (or the West's) vital interests, exposes it to the censure of the international community and charges of inconsistency at best, hypocrisy at worst. The likelihood of securing wide agreement on counter-terrorist measures is diminished and serious questions are raised over foreign policy initiatives in other fields. If considered guilty of such behaviour, the United States in particular would lose any claim it might have had to moral leadership in the fight against political violence of this kind. Granted that any counter-terrorist policy is extremely difficult and the US in particular faces pressures from many different quarters, but it must take full account of legal and ethical considerations. This is in the interests of the United States as much as any other country. Considering this problem in 1985, US Senator Daniel Moynihan wrote, 'a country has the right to do what it has the right to do—not what it thinks serves its interests'.[55] The two are not incompatible, but such asymmetries as exist are exploited to the full by terrorists and their sponsors. Unless the disadvantages of this situation are accepted and the crucial distinction between states and terrorists is clearly preserved, the entire rule of law is undermined and the international order based upon it is gravely threatened.

FUTURE CHALLENGES

While their methods cannot be condoned, some terrorists have legitimate grievances and goals that are attainable in the long term. Others act out of a sense of moral grievance which, however misconceived, is nevertheless sincerely felt. As states like Britain and Italy have shown, it is possible through a combination of social and political reform, combined with concerted police action within the law, significantly to reduce the terrorist threat. It is most unlikely, however, that states will ever be able to eliminate all sources of discontent, many of which have already been examined by national governments, regional organisations and the United Nations and found to be intractable. Also, as Raymond Aron has said, 'he is not conquered who does not admit defeat'[56] and there will always be irreconcilable elements prepared to resort to violence as a means of promoting their grievances, real or imagined. It must be recognised too that the distinctions between psychopaths, idealists, independent groups and state-sponsored groups are becoming increasingly blurred, as are the forces motivating them. To a degree, terrorism has become institutionalised, an integral part of the international system that is 'simultaneously combatted, tolerated and exploited'[57] by states, in much the same way that piracy was in earlier times. As Brian Jenkins has noted:

> Beneath the rhetoric of moral outrage is a labyrinth of secret wars, deals, direct action, and deliberate inaction.[58]

Emphasis is given to particular aspects of the terrorist problem as it suits a state's perceived national needs at the time. In such an environment there is no likelihood that terrorism will ever completely disappear.

This is not to suggest that the quest for answers to the problem of international terrorist violence should be abandoned, simply that any solution is likely to be imperfect and a long time coming. The various policy options open to Western democratic states and the difficulties involved in their implementation have been canvassed numerous times elsewhere and do not need to be repeated here.[59] It is imperative, however, that there be a more sophisticated analysis of terrorist violence in all its forms and less hysteria on the part of both governments and the news media of the kind that hinders both an objective understanding of the problem and effective measures against it. While serious, international terrorism is not the only problem facing the world, nor the most pressing. Also, dramatic gestures and theatrical rhetoric are much less likely to be successful in reducing the level of terrorist violence than carefully considered measures, implemented and pursued without fanfare over an extended period. These must include improved national preventive and reactive capabilities, but also what the British Foreign Secretary has described as 'the hard slog of patient, painstaking and persistent efforts to tighten international cooperation'.[60] In these and other areas, diplomacy can play a significant role.

The conduct of international relations has changed in recent years and direct contacts between officials at the more specialised, functional level have become more frequent, but formal diplomatic exchanges still constitute the primary mode of communication between governments. Also, because of the profound effects it can have on relations between countries, as well as international society as a whole, international terrorism falls squarely within the legitimate concerns of Foreign Ministries. Indeed, given their traditional role as the officials with primary responsibility for the management of their country's external affairs, a good case can be made that Foreign Ministers (and by extension their diplomatic services) are in the best position to coordinate not only a state's broad foreign policy positions on this problem but also its international cooperative arrangements to counter it. This was recognised by the Reagan Administration, for example, in the President's National Security Directive Number 30 (NSD 30), which designated the State Department the 'lead agency' in combatting terrorism outside the United States. Under this arrangement, efforts are made to ensure that all American diplomatic, intelligence, military, police and other efforts against terrorism are coordinated, and conform with the Administration's overall foreign policy approach to this problem. As demonstrated all too clearly by the Iran arms scandal, this arrangement does not always work in practice, but the theory is sound and could usefully be copied by other governments.

The efforts of diplomatic representatives, both in bilateral negotiations and multilateral fora, do not only contribute to cooperative arrangements and conventions against specific forms of terrorist violence. They also assist in the creation of an international climate of opinion in which resort to terrorism, particularly by states, is considered unacceptable behaviour and subject to certain sanctions. Progress in such an intangible matter will always be slow but already there has been a noticeable movement in this regard as different governments have sought to demonstrate that it is in the interests of all states that terrorism be stopped. Yet there still needs to be a more imaginative and determined diplomatic effort. The continuing reliance of all states on the international system suggests that it may be possible to exert greater concerted pressure on those members of it which support or conduct terrorist operations. Even states like Libya and Iran may be persuaded to modify their behaviour if they felt the costs were too high. Certainly greater use could be made of the provisions of the Vienna Convention on Diplomatic Relations, to enforce adherence to customary norms and respond to abuses. In addition, it is often in diplomatic fora that attention can be concentrated most effectively on the political and socio-economic problems which, as Sir Geoffrey Howe has noted, 'so often lie at the root of terrorist violence'.[61] For here rests another, different kind of challenge to diplomacy, that of finding through peaceful and legal means durable solutions to the tensions which help create the political and psychological environment in which terrorism can flourish.

For such efforts to work, a serious effort must be made to rebuild the confidence of both state and non-state actors alike in diplomatic processes as the best means fairly and sympathetically to manage international change. Unless it can be demonstrated that the system works for all, then increasingly solutions to various problems will be sought outside it. Either that or, like the PLO groups will seek to gain access to international councils by unconventional means. Having achieved such an aim, they further weaken diplomatic processes by encouraging others through their example to attempt the same. Such a cycle can only be prevented by convincing evidence that mutually acceptable solutions to complex problems can be found within the international system and without recourse to violence. In this the role of the superpowers will be crucial, for unless they show a greater willingness themselves to place faith in peaceful negotiations and abide by the conventions of international behaviour, it is unrealistic to expect others to do so.

It will also be necessary for all states to make a greater effort to abide, and be seen to abide, by the provisions of the Vienna Convention on Diplomatic Relations. Governments are faced with a great many difficulties in conducting their external affairs but resort to misuse of the diplomatic system can in the long run only prove counter-productive. This will require greater political will, on the part of many governments, than has been seen to date. A serious effort will also be required from diplomats themselves, to ensure that their behaviour conforms with the standards expected. As the preamble to the Vienna Convention clearly states:

> the purpose of such privileges and immunities is not to benefit individuals but to ensure the efficient performance of the functions of diplomatic missions as representing States.[62]

Quite apart from any immediate consequences, abuses of diplomatic privileges and immunities only encourage further abuses and undermine the confidence of both governments and the public alike in the integrity of all diplomatic processes.[63] The currency of diplomatic intercourse and conduct becomes debased and crucial questions are left unresolved. Nor must the fear of further terrorist violence be permitted to erode the fundamental principles upon which the Convention is based. A weakening of its provisions as part of protective security measures may have some immediate appeal, but would ultimately work to the benefit of the terrorists. For in this, as in so many other areas of the effort against terrorism, calm resolution, a refusal to make precipitous policy changes, and adherence to the rule of law constitute the best defences against those to whom any disruption of international society would count as a major victory.

NOTES

1. Wilkinson, 'After Tehran', p.5.
2. Richard Clutterbuck, *Living With Terrorism,* (Faber, London, 1975), p.33.
3. Jenkins, *Embassies Under Siege*, p.146.

4. Michael Palliser, 'Diplomacy Today', in Hedley Bull and Adam Watson (eds), *The Expansion of International Society* (Clarendon Press, Oxford, 1984), p.372.

5. Kurt Waldheim made this comment at the UN on 25 November 1979, during his request for an urgent meeting of the Security Council to discuss the US-Iran crisis. Quoted in C.C. Aston, *Political Hostage Taking in Western Europe*, Conflict Studies 157 (Institute for the Study of Conflict, London, 1984), p.1.

6. Bell, *A Time of Terror*, p.64.

7. Dam, 'Terrorism in the Middle East', p.2.

8. *ibid*. See also Sayre, 'International Terrorism: A Long Twilight Struggle', p.2.

9. Shultz, 'Terrorism and the Modern World'.

10. B. M. Jenkins, 'International Terrorism: A New Mode of Conflict', in D. Carlton and C. Schaerf (eds), *International Terrorism and World Security* (Croom Helm, London, 1975), p.25.

11. Hedley Bull, 'Civil Violence and International Order', in *Civil Violence and the International System*, Part 2, Adelphi Paper 83 (International Institute for Strategic Studies, London, 1971), p.31.

12. B. M. Jenkins, 'When the Yellow Ribbons Fade', *Newsweek*, 9 February 1981, p.19.

13. Andrew Mack, 'The Utility of Terrorism', *Australian and New Zealand Journal of Criminology* (December 1981), p.199.

14. Wilkinson, *Terrorism and the Liberal State*, p.212.

15. Jenkins *et al, Numbered Lives*, p.2.

16. The United States, which has suffered the most attacks on diplomats and diplomatic facilities, has lost only 28 officers killed between 1973-1985. This is not, however, to discount such a number. The US has lost more diplomats killed since 1968 than have been killed in the previous 180 years. See *The Public Report of The Vice President's Task Force*, p.4.

17. Jenkins, in Carlton and Schaerf, p.15.

18. Michael Stohl, 'Terrorism, States and State Terrorism: The Reagan Administration in the Middle East', Paper prepared for the Center for Contemporary Arab Studies— Georgetown University Seminar 'Terrorism and the Middle East: Context and Interpretations', 11 September 1986.

19. Jillian Becker, *Hitler's Children* (Granada, London, 1978), p.90.

20. Wilkinson, *Terrorism and the Liberal State*, p.194.

21. Aston, p.5.

22. Jenkins, in Carlton and Schaerf, p.24.

23. This country is Greece. The *Canberra Times* reported on 24 March 1986 that Spain had granted the PLO full diplomatic recognition and that the PLO representative office in Madrid was to be elevated to the status of a diplomatic mission with the same rights as other embassies.

24. Bell, in Keohane and Nye, p.167.

25. Geoffrey McDermott, *The New Diplomacy and its Apparatus* (Plume Press, London, 1973), p.67.

26. Watson, p.140.

27. Quoted in Bloomfield and Fitzgerald, p.22.

28. Grant Wardlaw, 'Terrorism: How Big a Threat to Peace?', *The Age*, 18 April 1984. See also Crenshaw, 'The International Consequences of Terrorism'.

29. R. B. Mowat, *Diplomacy and Peace* (Williams and Norgate, London, 1935), p.199.

30. Palliser, in Bull and Watson, p.352.

31. Shultz, 'Terrorism: The Challenge to the Democracies'.

32. Quoted by Thompson, p.1285.

33. Quoted by Robert Freedman, 'Soviet Policy Toward International Terrorism', in Yonah Alexander (ed), *International Terrorism: National, Regional and Global Perspectives*

(Praeger, New York, 1976), pp.131–132.
34. Thompson, p.1285.
35. Watson, p.203.
36. ʻSecretary Haig's News Conference of January 28', *Department of State Bulletin* 81:2047 (February 1981), Special Section, p.J.
37. Stohl, 'States, Terrorism, and State Terrorism'.
38. Shultz, 'Terrorism and the Modern World'.
39. See for example Dam, 'Terrorism in the Middle East', p.2. This point is made at greater length in Schlesinger, Murdock and Elliott, p.1.
40. Shultz, 'Terrorism and the Modern World'.
41. Shultz, 'Terrorism: The Challenge to the Democracies'.
42. Shultz, 'Terrorism and the Modern World'.
43. *Public Report of the Vice President's Task Force*, p.10.
44. See, for example, press briefing given by Vice President Bush and Admiral Holloway on the Report of the Vice President's Task Force on Combatting Terrorism, 6 March 1986.
45. Paul Wilkinson, 'State-sponsored international terrorism: the problems of response', *The World Today* (July 1984), p.298.
46. Marighela, 'Problems and Principles of Strategy', in *For the Liberation of Brazil*, p.46.
47. Jenkins, *The Lessons of Beirut*, p.12.
48. B. M. Jenkins, *Some Reflections on Recent Trends in Terrorism*, Rand Paper P-6897 (Rand Corporation, Santa Monica, 1983), p.3. See also Bruce Hoffman, 'The Plight of the Phoenix: The PLO Since Lebanon', *Conflict Quarterly* (Spring 1985), pp.5–14.
49. 'Chronology of Libyan Support for Terrorism', *Backgrounder* (State Department, Washington) 21 August 1986. Even if these figures are incorrect, any apparent decline in Libyan terrorism could simply be the result of greater efforts to conceal such activities, or reflect the long time required to plan counter-attacks.
50. G. P. Shultz, 'Low Intensity Warfare: The Challenge of Ambiguity', *Current Policy* 783 (15 January 1986), p.3.
51. *ibid.*
52. See Adam Roberts, 'Terrorism and International Order', in Lawrence Freedman *et al, Terrorism and International Order* (Royal Institute for International Affairs, London, 1986), p.23.
53. Fromkin, p.692.
54. Wardlaw, 'State Responses to International Terrorism'.
55. Keynote address reprinted in 'Conference Report—Terrorism: Future Threats and Responses', *Terrorism: An International Journal* 7:4 (1985).
56. Aron, p.25.
57. Jenkins, *New Modes of Conflict*, p.14.
58. B. M. Jenkins, 'New Modes of Conflict', *Orbis* 28:1 (1984), p.24.
59. See for example Christopher Hill, 'The Political Dilemmas for Western Governments' in Freedman *et al*, and Grant Wardlaw, 'Policy dilemmas in responding to international terrorism', *Australian Quarterly* 58:3 (Spring 1986).
60. Sir Geoffrey Howe, quoted in 'EEC ministers to hold meeting on terrorism', *Australian Financial Review*, 17 September 1986.
61. *ibid.*
62. See Brownlie, p.213.
63. Efforts to promote a more balanced and objective public perception of diplomatic processes have not been assisted by sensationalist accounts of abuses such as Chuck Ashman and Pamela Trescott, *Outrage! The Abuse of Diplomatic Immunity* (W.H. Allen, London, 1986).

PART TWO

The Australian Perspective

6

THE THREAT TO DIPLOMATS AND DIPLOMATIC FACILITIES IN AUSTRALIA

Toleration of terrorism in this country is over. Whatever we import from the rest of the world we do not need that. This Government is determined that terrorism in Australia will be resolutely stamped out.

Senator Lionel Murphy
(Attorney-General of Australia)
The Senate, 27 March 1973

With some notable exceptions, Australia has remained free of the terrorist violence which has troubled other countries over the past 20 years. Almost half of those attacks which have occurred, however, have been directed against diplomats or diplomatic facilities and much of the risk of another major terrorist incident in Australia attaches to the presence in the country of a sizeable diplomatic community. This has long been a major source of concern to Australia's security and law enforcement agencies and seems likely to remain so. While the current level of threat is not high, no country is immune from terrorist attack and it would seem only prudent that the responsible authorities in Australia use the time now available to them to prepare for such violence, instituting appropriate measures where required and ensuring that sufficient resources are available for the country's protective security machinery to function effectively. Australia's federal structure and current economic difficulties place a premium on the efficiency and cooperation of all sectors of government, acting within clear policy guidelines.

THE THREAT BEFORE 1978

Generally speaking, there is no tradition of political violence in Australia. Outbreaks have been rare and, where they have occurred, short-lived. There has only been one successful political assassination in Australia's history and only two unsuccessful attempts against prominent figures.[1] In the 87 years since Federation there have been only six occasions on which State governments have felt compelled to seek help from the Commonwealth Government[2] to quell domestic violence or to maintain law and order. Only once has the problem been considered sufficiently serious to warrant Federal involvement, and that was after an apparent terrorist incident in New South Wales in 1978[3]. The country's independence and geographical isolation for long served to insulate it from many of the divisive forces found in other parts of the world and Australia's largely homogeneous population shared a basic consensus on most social and political issues. With few exceptions, the legitimacy of State and Federal governments has not been seriously questioned.[4] This may be due in part to a degree of political complacency but still, as Sir Colin Woods has noted, 'the stability of social, political and legal systems has undoubtedly served to confound extremism'.[5]

Since the 1960s, this situation has been changing. Modern transport and telecommunications have substantially eroded Australia's isolation and, through its post World War II immigration program, the country now contains a number of powerful minority groups 'which reflect all the bitterness found in those areas of the world where terrorist operations are active and most violent'.[6] The basic framework of Australian society and government has still not been seriously challenged but to an increasing degree certain sectors of the population have responded to developments overseas with political violence of various kinds. In the *Report* of his 1979 Protective Security Review, Mr Justice R. M. Hope cited 265 instances of politically motivated violence in Australia between 1963 and 1977.[7] More than one third were directly related to protests against the Vietnam War and could more correctly be classified as political vandalism, but of the remainder most cases related to acts of violence by members of ethnic or emigre groups in Australia acting out the rivalries and political differences of their homelands. The targets of these attacks were often rival members of the same community, or members of other ethnic or emigre groups. On a number of occasions, however, they included the official premises and personnel of the foreign governments they opposed.

During the 15 years preceding Mr Justice Hope's Review, there were 12 major attacks recorded against diplomats and diplomatic facilities in Australia. In January 1967 a bomb was planted in the Yugoslav Consulate-General in Sydney. In August 1968 an unsuccessful attempt was made by an unknown person or group to destroy the United States Consulate-General in Melbourne with petrol bombs. In November the same year and again in June 1969 the Yugoslav Consulate-General in Sydney suffered further bomb attacks. In October 1970 the Yugoslav Consulate-General in Melbourne was also subject to a bomb attack. In January 1971 two Bulgarian dissidents threw a bomb into the grounds of the Soviet Embassy in Canberra. An armed assault was made against the Yugoslav Consulate in Perth in February 1972. In September that year five Black September letter bombs, addressed to Israeli diplomats in Canberra and Sydney, were detected by the Australian postal authorities. Two more letter bombs, addressed to Israeli officials in Sydney, were discovered the following month. Nearly six years later, in August 1977, there was a serious fire in the Indian High Commission in Canberra which was thought to have been deliberately lit. The following month the Indian Military Attache and his wife were kidnapped from their Canberra home and the Attache stabbed in the chest. The following March a gelignite bomb was discovered in the grounds of the Indian High Commissioner's official Residence.

These attacks occurred against a continuous background of minor incidents involving diplomatic and consular missions in Australia. A search of the official records has revealed few such cases prior to 1966, but a series of questions by the Leader of the Federal Opposition in 1971 and 1972 showed that, in a very low key manner, Australia was conforming to global trends. In his formal replies, the Foreign Minister told Parliament that between November 1966 and October 1972 there had been 52 separate incidents involving the missions of some 27 different countries represented in Australia.[8] Responding to a similar question from Labor Party Leader Gough Whitlam on 23 May 1978, the then Minister for Foreign Affairs, Andrew Peacock, gave details of a further 33 incidents in the period since June 1974.[9] In all cases where incidents had occurred official apologies were offered to the governments concerned and, where necessary, repairs made at official expense. These repairs had cost the Australian taxpayer more than $A50 000 for the period. These incidents were in addition to a number of more serious attacks on other representative institutions, such as national airline offices.

While those responsible for the more significant attacks on diplomats and diplomatic facilities in Australia have been caught and convicted in only a few cases, the interests they represented were usually well known. For example, while most of the Croatian groups in the country are perfectly law-abiding, there are a small number which are dedicated to the creation of a separate Croatian state, if necessary by violent means. In March 1973 the then Attorney-General, Senator Lionel Murphy, tabled documents in the Australian Parliament which he claimed established beyond any doubt that 'Croatian terrorist organisations have existed and do exist in Australia today'.[10] He identified four in particular, the Croatian Revolutionary Brotherhood (*Hrvatsko Revolucionarno Bratsvo*, or HRB), the Croatian Illegal Revolutionary Organisation (*Hrvatska Ilegalna Revolucionarna Organizacija*, or HIRO), the United Croats of West Germany (*Ujedinjeni Hrvati Njemaske*, or UHNj) and the Croat National Resistance (*Hrvatski Narodni*

Otpor, or HNO). All were said to be connected with Croatian terrorist organisations abroad.

The most active of these groups was the Croatian Revolutionary Brotherhood, which emerged in Australia during the 1950s. It was responsible for the training of six Croatians, allegedly from Australia, who were infiltrated into Yugoslavia in 1963 to conduct a guerrilla war against the Tito Government. This unsuccessful venture was repeated in 1972, when another 19 Croatians of the HRB illegally entered Yugoslavia from Austria to carry out a campaign of sabotage and terrorism in Bosnia. Six were Australian citizens and three had been residents of Australia prior to the operation. Financial and logistical support had also been provided by members of the Croatian community in Australia. In August 1972 Commonwealth Police seized documents which revealed plans for the recruitment of more volunteers and the following year they discovered a military-style camp near Wodonga, Victoria. In September 1978 Australian police surprised a group of heavily armed Croatians on their way to another training camp near Eden in southeastern New South Wales. As late as 1979 other HRB training camps were believed to exist in Australia and probably still do.

During the late 1960s or early 1970s the HRB apparently changed its name to the Croatian Illegal Revolutionary Organisation for a period, but there was no change in its tactics, which included attacks against Yugoslav officials and official premises abroad. HRB documents tabled in Parliament by Senator Murphy in 1973 openly called upon Croatians in Australia to 'wreck Yugoslav embassies and consulates and to kill Yugoslav diplomatic representatives'.[11] Croatian newspapers in Australia have also published articles, purportedly from Serbians but obviously written by Croatian extremists, calling on other members of the Yugoslav emigre community to 'bare our teeth at the Yugoslavs! Wreck Tito's embassies and consulates!'.[12] The HRB has been attributed with the murder of a number of Yugoslav diplomats in Europe and the seizure of the West German Consulate in Chicago in 1978. It was probably responsible for the attacks on Yugoslav diplomatic facilities in Melbourne in 1970 and in Perth in 1972, and was accused of plotting to assassinate Yugoslav Prime Minister Bijedic during his visit to Australia in 1973.

The UHNj and HNO also have records of attacking Yugoslav officials and official premises. A branch of the UHNj was established in Australia around June 1971. According to Peter Janke the organisation 'specialises in the assassination of Yugoslav officials and in intimidating Yugoslav emigres into supporting and financing its activities'.[13] At the time of Senator Lionel Murphy's statement to Parliament the UHNj had been associated with a number of violent attacks on Yugoslav diplomatic and consular posts. The Senator also referred in his speech to the Croat National Resistance, which was founded in Spain after the Second World War but which seems to have developed in Australia under a former *Ustasa* officer named Srecko Blaz Rover. HNO operated a terrorist wing known as *Drina* which continued to be active (mainly in West Germany) well into the 1970s. Once again, Yugoslav diplomats and diplomatic facilities were among its favourite targets.

Until the election of Prime Minister Gough Whitlam's Labor Government in December 1972, the presence of Croatian terrorist groups in Australia was officially denied. Despite repeated warnings from the Australian Security Intelligence Organisation (ASIO) and the Commonwealth Police, the Government had steadfastly maintained that:

> although there were undoubtedly individual Croatian extremists in Australia who were prepared to resort to the most violent methods in alleged furtherance of their cause, there was no credible evidence that any Croatian revolutionary terrorist organisation existed in Australia.[14]

In his statement to the Senate in 1973, Senator Murphy strongly contested such denials, claiming that 'the Liberal Attorney-General's oft-repeated assertion that there is no credible evidence of the existence in Australia of organised Croatian extremism cannot be sustained. The contrary is true and was true at the time he made such statements'.[15] The reasons for the Government's earlier inaction is unclear, but there have since been a number of suggestions that the conservative Liberal-National Country Party Government of the time tolerated, or even actively supported, local Croatian extremist groups because of their virulent anti-communism.[16]

After 1972 stronger measures were taken against Croatian terrorists in Australia and the protection given to Yugoslav officials and official premises was increased, but these steps appear to have enjoyed only limited success. The terrorist threat to Yugoslav diplomats and diplomatic facilities in Australia is no longer at the level of the 1960s and 1970s but feelings among the local emigre community remain high. On 18 March 1986, for example, after the extradition to Yugoslavia from the United States of wartime Croatian leader Ardrija Artukovic, the Croatian language newspaper *Hrvatski Tjednik* printed an article containing implicit threats against Yugoslav government officials in Australia. It is not known to what extent, if any, the Yugoslav Government has taken the protection of its missions into its own hands but the Yugoslav State Security Service (UDBa) has apparently been responsible for the deaths of at least a dozen Croatian emigre leaders in Europe over the past 15 years and the possibility that it has contributed to violence within the emigre community in Australia cannot be entirely discounted. In his book *The Secret State*, Richard Hall purports to quote an ASIO report which stated that 'the Yugoslav intelligence services maintain a larger presence in Australia than any other foreign organisation with the exception of the CIA and KGB'.[17]

The other group which has attracted most attention for its alleged terrorist attacks against diplomats and diplomatic facilities in Australia before 1979, has been the religious sect known as *Ananda Marga*, or Path of Bliss. The group first appeared in Australia in 1972 and by the end of the decade was thought to comprise some 500 members. As Clive Williams has stated, rumours that the Australian branch of the sect was involved in terrorist activity surfaced regularly after 1976, when the sect's founder and religious inspiration, 'Baba' (leader) Prahbat Sarkar, was arrested in India and convicted on conspiracy and multiple murder charges.[18] While the sect's philosophy was essentially quietistic it apparently allowed for violence and Sarkar's imprisonment was followed by numerous terrorist acts by sect members in an attempt to secure his release. Indian diplomats and diplomatic facilities were attacked or threatened in New York, Los Angeles, Ottawa, London, Stockholm, Kathmandu, Kuala Lumpur and Wellington.[19] While few members of Ananda Marga have been arrested and convicted for such crimes in Australia, it seems clear that the attacks made on Indian representatives there at the same time were related.

When the Indian High Commission was badly damaged by fire in 1977, Indian officials claimed that it was the work of the 'Universal Proutist Revolutionary Federation' (UPRF), a small inner cell of the sect which reputedly believed in 'a form of mystical violence which would cleanse the earth, and humanity would thus be reborn'.[20] The man who kidnapped Colonel Iqbal Singh, the Indian Military Attache, and Mrs Singh in September 1977 was a member of Ananda Marga. While his motives for the abduction remain unclear, the Indian High Commission claimed at the time to have received a note from the UPRF stating:

> As we are established throughout the world the next attack may take place anywhere. Officials and lackeys of the Indian High Commission, consuls, trade offices and Air India are all targets.[21]

In September 1977, the office of Air India in Melbourne also received a note from the UPRF Central Command demanding Prahbat Sarkar's release. The note went on to outline a programme of 'regular and systematic assassination of any worker in your high commissions, consulates, trade offices and Air India, throughout the world'.[22] The following month an employee of Air India was stabbed by a man who walked into the airline's Melbourne office.

Following the kidnapping of Colonel Singh and his wife, the Australian Prime Minister sent a letter to the Indian High Commissioner expressing concern over the attack and assuring him of full protection. The Minister for Administrative Services later informed the Senate that the proposed security measures would cost approximately $A3 million per year.[23] According to one New Zealand journalist, in May 1978 110 policemen were still required to guard Indian diplomatic staff in Australia, 24 hours a day.[24] Attacks on Indian diplomats and diplomatic facilities stopped after July 1978, when Prahbat Sarkar was released from prison in India, but not before Ananda Marga was widely accused of planting a bomb which exploded outside Sydney's Hilton Hotel on 13 February that year.

THE HILTON HOTEL BOMBING AND ITS RESULTS

The 1978 Hilton Hotel bomb marked a major watershed in the Australian Government's attitude towards terrorism, and in the nature of terrorist violence in the country. Needless to say, earlier attacks on diplomats and other internationally protected persons had been of grave concern to the Australian authorities and in some cases had prompted increased levels of personal protection, but it was not until after the incident in Sydney that this subject was given priority at the highest levels of government. At the time, Australia was host to eleven Asian and Pacific Heads of Government, attending a Commonwealth Heads of Government Regional Meeting (CHOGRM). None of the visiting dignitaries or members of their entourages, nor any Australian officials, were near the bomb when it exploded, in a rubbish bin by the hotel's second entrance in the early hours of the morning.[25] Yet the incident sparked a massive reaction. Citing, among other instruments, Australia's obligations under the 1973 United Nations Convention on the Prevention and Punishment of Crimes Against Internationally Protected Persons, Including Diplomatic Agents, the Governor-General formally 'called out' the Australian Defence Force to secure the route from Sydney to the CHOGRM weekend retreat at Bowral, some 100 kilometres southwest of the city. Elements of the Australian Army were also stationed at Bowral to protect the delegates while they were there. The order was only revoked on 20 February.[26]

No-one has ever claimed responsibility for the Hilton Hotel bomb, nor, despite all the claims and counter-claims that have been made since, has any person or group been accused in law of planting it. The troop call-out appears to have served political purposes as much as any practical security concerns and gave rise to considerable debate in the country over the question of military aid to the civil power in times of emergency. It has also acted as a stimulus for scholars concerned with the important civil liberties questions associated with internal security measures of this kind.[27] Some consideration was being given to improvements in Australia's counter-terrorism capabilities prior to 1978, but that 'one exploded garbage bin'[28] stands out as the catalyst for a number of far-reaching changes in the way Australia prepared for a terrorist attack and provided for the safety of internationally protected persons visiting or resident in the country.

In a statement to the House of Representatives on 23 February 1978 the then Prime Minister, Malcolm Fraser, announced a number of measures that had been, or would immediately be taken. Sir Robert Mark, the recently retired Commissioner of the London Metropolitan Police Force, was asked to advise the Australian Government on the organisation of all police forces in the Federal sphere and recommend measures for protective security and counter-terrorism. A more comprehensive review of Australia's entire protective security machinery was to be carried out by Mr Justice R.M. Hope, who only the year before had completed a detailed examination of intelligence and security matters for the Government.[29] In addition, the Australian Government proposed to form a committee, subsequently known as the Standing Advisory Committee for Commonwealth-State Cooperation on Protection Against Violence (SAC-PAV), to ensure 'the highest degree of efficient operation and cooperation on a nation-wide basis'[30] between all levels of officialdom in the country on questions of politically motivated violence. There were two other by-products of the Hilton Hotel bombing. One was the creation in July 1978 of the Australian Bomb Data Centre as 'a national and international focal point for the rapid exchange of information on the unlawful use of explosives and, in particular, improvised explosive devices'.[31] The other was the formation, within Australia's own Special Air Service Regiment (SASR), of a specialist assault team 'available if so authorised to deal with high-risk siege-hostage terrorist incidents in Australia that may be beyond the range of police capabilities'.[32]

Sir Robert Mark's report was tabled in Federal Parliament on 13 April, just one and a half months after his enquiry began. Characteristically, the report was short (28 pages) and to the point. Sir Robert felt that in surveying Australian police resources in the Federal sphere he was being asked to 'cobble an ill-fitting 19th century boot'.[33] The complex structure of government in Australia, not least the existence at the time of nine separate police forces all under different jurisdictions,[34] militated strongly against the attainment of certainty, uniformity or simplicity in the interpretation and implementation of law in the country:

> Arrangements for the governance of States which were adequate for trade, public order and the social requirements of the nineteenth century are not appropriate for dealing with serious wrong-doing which transcends State jurisdictions and affects the interests of the Commonwealth as a whole.[35]

He made a number of recommendations, but in particular urged the Federal Government to take the lead in providing common police services which could have the responsibility of co-ordinating training and providing operational support for all counter-terrorist activities in Australia. He recommended as an initial step the amalgamation of the Commonwealth Police with the Australian Capital Territory (ACT) Police, to form a new force to be known as the Australian Federal Police (AFP). Sir Robert has been accused of 'a considerable degree of political naivety'[36] in some of his recommendations, but the need for a greater coordination of national resources and more centralised control over counter-terrorist operations was recognised by the *Australian Federal Police Act*, 1979 (which created the AFP) and in Mr Justice Hope's subsequent *Protective Security Review: Report*, which strongly emphasised the need for 'cooperative federalism' in this field.

The Hope Report was tabled in Parliament in May 1979. It covered many different aspects of protective security in Australia but noted, with regard to political violence, that national terrorism of the kind encountered in other parts of the world had not developed in Australia. There were no Australian terrorist groups the objectives of which were directed against the Australian people or government. To that time international terrorism in the country had been confined to planning for attacks overseas and operations against the representatives of foreign countries in Australia. The Judge predicted that, in general terms, the terrorist threat would remain much as it had been in the years immediately preceding his *Report*, but with the possibility of increased action by local ethnic groups. In addition, there was a likelihood that action by terrorists from overseas bases would increase with time. Mr Justice Hope identified diplomatic and consular personnel and premises as a major target of international terrorists, and added:

> This unhappy distinction is likely to continue, and requires an Australian government to look closely to the security of its own personnel and premises abroad and to the security of foreign personnel and premises within Australia.[37]

Subsequent events have demonstrated the presience of the Judge's warning.

THE THREAT SINCE 1978

In his 1979 report, Mr Justice Hope revealed that:

> There have been some occasions when plans have been made, and even implemented, for terrorists to enter Australia and carry out here some act of terrorism directed against a government represented in Australia. Whether by vigilance or good fortune, these plans have come to naught.[38]

As Mr Justice Hope predicted, however, attempts by international terrorists to attack diplomats and diplomatic facilities in Australia have persisted, and since 1979 have achieved a degree of success. In December 1980 the Turkish Consul-General in Sydney, Sarik Ariyak, and his bodyguard were assassinated by members of the Justice Commandos of the Armenian Genocide (JCAG). In December 1982 the Israeli Consulate-General in Sydney was damaged by a bomb, thought to have been planted by the Iraqi-supported May 15 Arab Organisation, a cover name for the Wadi Haddad faction of the Palestine Liberation Organisation.[39] According to the *Australian Security Intelligence Organisation Annual Report 1982-83*, both attacks appear to have been made by or with the active support of extremist elements in the Armenian and Arab communities in Australia.[40] The continuing threat posed by such extremist elements was demonstrated again in November 1986, when a large car bomb badly damaged the Turkish Consulate-General in Melbourne. Responsibility for the explosion, in which one of the terrorists was killed, was claimed by the Greek-Bulgarian-Armenian Front, a cover name adopted for the attack by local Armenian extremists. In a statement issued after the incident, Australian Foreign Minister Bill Hayden said that the Government planned to review its procedures for the protection of diplomatic premises and personnel.[41]

In addition to Armenian and Palestinian extremists, the 1982–83 ASIO *Annual Report* also identified a number of other groups in the country that were considered likely to employ violent means to achieve their political objectives. Some have singled out diplomats and diplomatic facilities as targets in the past, such as certain parts of the Croatian community, while others are believed to have the potential to do so, namely 'those elements within Middle Eastern and some other community groups which, in an extension of overseas disputes, may resort to violence'.[42] Quite large numbers of Muslims, including representatives of the more extreme factions, now live in Australia. Some members of these groups have the potential to pose a threat to diplomatic missions in the country. There have also been a number of clashes between rival Lebanese groups in Australia. Security authorities were reminded of the tensions in that part of the world when Lebanese Christians occupied Lebanese diplomatic and consular premises in Canberra, Sydney and Melbourne in May 1985, to protest over the treatment of their co-religionists in Lebanon. These actions were timed to coincide with similar protests in Belgium, France and Canada.

Since the fall of Saigon in 1975 the Vietnamese community in Australia has been swollen by a large number of refugees, a proportion of which appears to be determined to pursue in Australia the political differences of their homeland. Official representatives of the Socialist Republic of Vietnam (SRV) in Australia have been violently abused, jostled and punched by opponents of the Hanoi regime. A number of Vietnamese emigres have advocated violence against SRV officials resident in Australia and Vietnamese language newspapers such as the *Bell of Saigon* have published a number of highly inflammatory editorials. In July 1985 two shots were fired at the SRV Embassy in Canberra. There have since been reports in the press that Vietnamese immigrants were purchasing arms from an Australian-based drug syndicate and conducting weapons training in the

New South Wales countryside. Even if these reports prove to be untrue, the strength of feeling displayed by some members of the Vietnamese community in Australia must be a cause for concern on the part of those responsible for the safety of SRV diplomats in the country.[43] These disturbances also have the potential to disrupt Australia's relations with the SRV. In September 1985 Vietnamese diplomats openly criticised the Australian Government for failing to take action against those responsible for attacks on Embassy staff. In January 1986 they also hinted that the family reunion program between the two countries could be affected by the activities of local groups like the Vietnam Liberation Movement and the Coordinating Committee Against Communists in Australia.

From time to time other ethnic or emigre groups have been mentioned in connection with possible terrorist violence in Australia, including attacks against diplomats and diplomatic facilities. Some are more credible than others. The journalist Richard Hall has published what he claimed was a secret ASIO document, which stated that a small number of Chilean emigres were considered 'likely to be activists or adherents of Chilean or Latin American terrorist organisations'. Others in the Chilean community were 'likely to support the use of political violence' against representatives of the Pinochet regime.[44] At present support in Australia for the Irish Republican Army is small, and largely confined to fund-raising and the dissemination of propaganda, but this may change. One local authority has suggested on a number of occasions that acts of terrorism connected with events in Northern Ireland 'will almost certainly take place in Australia this decade'.[45] Mr Justice Hope alluded to another possibility when he referred to the potential for greater unrest in Southeast Asia. In such an event political tensions in the region could be manifested in attacks against diplomatic missions in Australia, after the manner of attacks against diplomats and their facilities in the Middle East.[46] The potential for terrorist violence from such groups can easily be exaggerated, but the Australian population now contains representatives of almost every country in the world and, depending on developments overseas, there will always be the possibility that minority elements among them may turn to violence against the official representatives of the government they oppose.

While certain diplomatic missions in Australia have supported, and probably still support, intelligence activities of various kinds, Australia has been fortunate in that few missions appear to have been used to support or promote terrorist violence in the country. In March 1978 there were press reports that the time bomb found in the grounds of the Indian High Commission had been planted by Indian diplomats or intelligence officers, in an attempt to discredit Ananda Marga. Such claims have never been verified, however, and the incident is still officially considered a terrorist attack. In March 1985 the Libyan People's Bureau in Canberra called for volunteers to join the Libyan armed forces and sought contributions to an 'International Peoples' Front', the purpose of which was to fight against imperialism, Zionism, racism and 'US aggression'.[47] The Secretary of the Bureau was issued with a formal protest by the Department of Foreign Affairs, and told that the Libyan action was in breach of the *Crimes (Foreign Incursions and Recruitment) Act*, 1978. According to the *National Times* of 9 May 1986, the Australian authorities believed that all members of the Libyan People's Bureau in Canberra had to that date been *bona fide* diplomats, and the threat of Libyan sponsored terrorism in the country was considered low. From statements made at various times by the Foreign Minister and Defence Minister, however, it would appear that the Government has seriously considered the possibility of Libyan terrorism in Australia and is monitoring the situation closely.[48]

In addition to attacks carried out by, or with the active support of, extremists based in Australia, diplomats resident in the country will always face the threat of attack from international terrorist groups based overseas. As Peter Boyce has noted:

> what helps distinguish the latest form of guerilla terrorism against diplomats is that such incidents are as likely as not to occur in countries which are not themselves direct targets of guerilla violence, but merely hosts to embassies which are.[49]

Australia has long been considered a relatively safe posting for most diplomats but, ironically, this reputation may invite greater attention from international terrorists seeking easier options than the well protected Chanceries of Europe or the Middle East. While still something of a disincentive, Australia's geographical isolation is no longer such a barrier and modern communications can provide terrorists with the publicity they crave as easily from Canberra or Sydney as from Beirut, Paris or New York. In his 1979 *Report* Mr Justice Hope felt that, if Australia was perceived as a soft target, it may attract greater attention from an Arab group or the URA.[50] In addition, a number of Australia's close friends and allies are often targets for international terrorist groups and it is possible that at some stage one of their posts in Australia may be attacked, with the terrorists counting on Australia's relative inexperience and concern for its allies to help them win various concessions. On 17 November 1986 the Special Minister of State told the Executive Council of Australian Jewry that:

> While there may not be a direct threat to Australia at present from international groups, we have close historical and political ties with a number of nations ... which are under high threat, and which have substantial diplomatic, commercial or other interests in this country ... There are 66 countries represented in Australia by diplomatic and/or consular missions, of which 50 per cent are assessed as at risk of violence to some degree.[51]

While not all these threats derive from terrorist violence, some do and the risk of an unforeseen attack against diplomats and diplomatic facilities in the country will always remain a concern to the authorities responsible for their protection.

COUNTER-TERRORIST MEASURES

The 'call out' of the Australian Defence Force in 1978 'exposed gaps, inadequacies and uncertainties in the legal and constitutional powers of the Commonwealth and State enforcement agencies, and in the powers of members of the Defence Force to cope with security emergencies whether created by terrorist activities or otherwise'.[52] There has never been any dispute, however, that the Australian Government has both the right and the obligation to protect diplomats and diplomatic facilities in the country, under both international law and its own domestic legislation. Indeed, over the past 15 years the three most important international legal instruments concerning the safety and treatment of diplomats and diplomatic facilities have been incorporated into Commonwealth law. In 1967 Federal Parliament passed the *Diplomatic Privileges and Immunities Act*, which gave the 1961 Vienna Convention on Diplomatic Relations the force of law in Australia and further bound the Government to abide by its 'special duty' to take all appropriate steps to protect diplomats and their premises. The 1963 Vienna Convention on Consular Relations was in large part also made Australian law by the *Consular Privileges and Immunities Act*, 1972[53]. When Australia signed the United Nations Convention on the Prevention and Punishment of Crimes Against Internationally Protected Persons, Including Diplomatic Agents in December 1974, it accepted the enlarged obligations to protect diplomatic and consular representatives contained in that instrument, and incorporated its provisions into law by the *Crimes (Internationally Protected Persons) Act*, 1976. In May 1980 the *Diplomatic Privileges and Immunities Amendment Act*, 1980 was passed, to include certain international organisations within the scope of the 1967 law.

Australian domestic legislation is also clear about the Government's responsibilities and the scope permitted for action to counter terrorist attacks and other kinds of threats to the diplomatic community. The external affairs power in section 51(xxix) of the Australian Constitution 'undoubtedly invests the Commonwealth with the power to investigate and deal with terrorism directed against...diplomatic and consular premises and persons'.[54] In addition, the *Public Order (Protection of Persons and Property) Act*, passed by Parliament in 1971, was intended to:

assist in giving effect, on the part of Australia, to the special duty imposed by international law on a state that receives a diplomatic or special mission, or consents to the establishment of a consular post, to take appropriate steps to protect the premises of the mission or post against intrusion or damage, to prevent any attack on the persons, freedom or dignity of the personnel of the mission or post and to prevent disturbance of the peace, or impairment of the dignity, of the mission or post.[55]

When the *Crimes (Internationally Protected Persons) Act* was passed in 1976 amendments were made to both the *Extradition (Foreign States) Act* and the *Extradition (Commonwealth Countries) Act* to give full effect to the provisions of the New York Convention regarding the classification of attacks on internationally protected persons as common crimes, not attracting political status.[56] A further step was taken to protect the dignity of diplomatic missions in Australia (and, in part at least, answer Yugoslav complaints about a self-styled 'Croatian Embassy' in Canberra) in 1978, when Parliament passed the *Diplomatic and Consular Missions Act, 1978,* preventing the improper use of diplomatic and consular signs and titles. The problem of terrorists being recruited and trained in Australia for operations against governments abroad led to the *Crimes (Foreign Incursions and Recruitment) Act, 1978.* In addition, a number of Australian States have their own emergency legislation which would permit them to respond to a terrorist incident.

As explained at length in Mr Justice Hope's *Protective Security Review: Report*, Australia has sought, within this legal framework (and other laws relating to different kinds of violent crimes) to guard against terrorist attacks and cope with those which might occur through a three stage defence system. This system stresses in turn intelligence, preventive action and crisis management.

The vital role of intelligence in combatting terrorism is widely acknowledged and in Australia has been confirmed by three official enquiries over the past ten years. Reporting again as a Royal Commissioner in 1985, Mr Justice Hope repeated his 1979 *Protective Security Review: Report,* in which he noted the importance of intelligence 'in nipping a terrorist incident in the bud, in identifying potential terrorist targets and periods of threat, and in the successful management of a terrorist crisis'.[57] As recommended in that earlier report, sole responsibility for the production of national security assessments now resides with ASIO, which under the *Australian Security Intelligence Organisation Act, 1979* collects, collates and evaluates intelligence material relating to terrorism in all its forms. ASIO gives advice oñ these matters to the Federal Government and State police, including regular reports on related protective security questions.[58] Under the ASIO Act offenses under the *Crimes (Internationally Protected Persons) Act, 1976* (and thus the New York Convention) are specifically designated matters for ASIO's concern. ASIO also 'pays attention to the use or intended use of terrorism in Australia by foreign governments to achieve State objectives'.[59] Despite considerable adverse publicity in recent years and criticism of the Organisation from Mr Justice Hope (both in 1977 and 1985), there have been few serious suggestions that Australia's counter-terrorist intelligence role should be taken away from ASIO. Indeed, the 1985 Royal Commission on Australia's Security and Intelligence Agencies noted that ASIO had recently expanded its activities in this area.[60]

Australia's second line of defence against terrorism lies in preventive action. This includes a wide range of measures, most important of which are controls on the entry to Australia of persons known or suspected of involvement with terrorism, denial of the means to conduct terrorist operations and the protection of potential targets. In the first area Australia enjoys a number of advantages. It has few points of entry from abroad and has traditionally followed a restrictive immigration policy. It is sufficiently distant from other countries to discourage clandestine landings and is not contiguous to another state which might offer terrorists sanctuary. Controls within Australia, however, are more difficult. The wide freedoms enjoyed by Australians permit terrorists easy movement and ready access to logistical support. Arms and explosives, chemical and biological agents of many kinds are all readily available. To date the authorities have concentrated on denying terrorists materials that are most attractive to them, such as military weapons and other specialised munitions but, judging from the number of reported thefts from military stores, they have not been entirely successful.[61] The same problems are encountered in the protection of potential targets. The cost of guarding all 'vital points' would be prohibitive in peacetime and even if attention was confined to diplomats and diplomatic facilities (including all consular agents and posts) the resources required for their full time protection would be enormous. Hence the importance of intelligence and other forms of preventive action, and the third line of defence identified by Mr Justice Hope, that of crisis management.

ORGANISATIONAL RESPONSES

Counter-terrorist measures in Australia require special coordination because of the country's federal system of government. Details of these measures were not given in the unclassified version of the *Protective Security Review: Report*, but the basic structure of Australia's counter-terrorist machinery was. Responsibility for co-ordinating counter-terrorism planning and responses on a national level is vested with the Standing Advisory Committee for Commonwealth-State Cooperation on Protection Against Violence. SAC-PAV consists of senior representatives of all governments and police forces in Australia, and four Commonwealth departments and agencies, including the Defence Force and AFP. It usually meets twice a year, in different State capitals, to ensure 'nationwide readiness and cooperation between relevant Commonwealth, State and Territory government departments, police forces and, when appropriate, the Defence Force, for the protection of Australia from terrorism'.[62] It is supported by five specialised working groups which examine detailed planning and operating procedures, equipment, communications, training and legal aspects of counter-terrorist precautionary measures and response capabilities.[63] The Committee's Executive Chairman, and continuing executive support, are provided by the Protective Services Coordination Centre (PSCC) in Canberra.

The PSCC was formed in 1976 within the then Department of Administrative Services, absorbing a number of functions performed until that time by elements in the Department of the Special Minister of State, Department of Administrative Services and the Attorney-General's Department.[64] PSCC's charter was 'to plan, coordinate and initiate protective security arrangements for people holding high office visiting or present in Australia, and to coordinate counter-terrorist measures'.[65] Its role was considerably strengthened after the 1978 Hilton Hotel bombing and Mr Justice Hope's subsequent review of protective security, which emphasised the need for greater cooperation and coordination in this field. PSCC also chairs and provides executive support for the Special Inter-Departmental Committee on Protection Against Violence (SIDC-PAV), which consists of representatives of all relevant Federal Government departments and agencies, the AFP and Defence Force. SIDC-PAV provides advice to the Government on the coordination of policy and contingency planning in relation to terrorism and other forms of politically motivated violence. It receives monthly reports from ASIO on current and potential threats, including those faced by diplomatic missions. A permanent subcommittee of SIDC-PAV, designated the Special Incidents Task Force (also chaired by PSCC), meets as required to consider particular issues that might arise, such as special visa cases and the need to provide increased protection for diplomatic personnel and premises that suddenly come under threat.

Through the different members of SIDC-PAV, the Protective Services Coordination Centre has access not only to a wide range of information about possible terrorist activities in Australia, but also to data and assessments about developments abroad. As Clive Williams in particular has explained, there are close connections between Australia's intelligence, security and law enforcement agencies and those of other countries. While considered by some Australians to have sinister connotations, these connections contribute significantly to the country's counter-terrorist capabilities. Interpol, for example, was for a long time forbidden by its charter to become involved in political activities but its interests inevitably cover many aspects of terrorist violence. The Australian Bomb Data Centre has established formal links with similar organisations in the United States,

United Kingdom, Canada, New Zealand, Federal Republic of Germany, Israel, Spain, West Indies, Papua New Guinea and Hong Kong.[66] In addition, the Australian Secret Intelligence Service (ASIS) reportedly enjoys good working relationships with its sister organisations in the US, Britain and elsewhere, as does ASIO with MI5, FBI and other such organisations. The strategic 1947 UKUSA agreement 'acknowledges that the UK, USA, Canada, New Zealand and Australia have common national concerns, which include exchange of intelligence on terrorism'.[67] Australia is also a member of the seven-nation Quantico Group of Western states (including the FRG, France and Sweden), which meets annually to discuss security issues. Australia's armed forces share many training programs and exercises with the forces of friendly countries and, through its relationships with the US and UK, Australia probably has access to information about international terrorism held by NATO and the European Community.

The PSCC is also responsible for advising on and improving the effectiveness of the protection offered to the representatives of foreign governments resident in Australia. Since its creation in 1976 the PSCC has conducted numerous training courses for State and Federal police officers and government officials. It has also facilitated exchanges between members of Australian enforcement agencies and those of other security forces in friendly countries. Steps have been taken to improve and coordinate the equipment used by various State, Territory and Federal police counter-terrorist units and several large-scale exercises have been held to test their capabilities. Since 1982 the PSCC and Department of Foreign Affairs have conducted regular security briefings for all Heads of diplomatic missions in Canberra and similar services have been provided to the Consular Corps in Darwin and the State capitals.

In recent years considerable attention has been focussed on the safety of diplomatic personnel and premises in Canberra where, as Sir Robert Mark pointed out in 1978, there are 'special problems'.[68] In addition to being the seat of government, there are nearly 70 Embassies and High Commissions in the national capital,[69] yet the ACT boasts little operational police capacity. The PSCC has joined with the AFP in seeking to implement a number of measures which it is felt will enhance the ability of local agencies to protect the diplomatic community from terrorist attack. Despite some frustrating delays caused by bureaucratic inertia, territorial jealousies and lack of resources, they are making progress towards the erection of security barriers around high risk missions, the relocation of scattered diplomatic premises into enclaves where they can more easily be protected and other such precautions. While the limitations of static guard posts are well recognised, a number are still maintained outside certain missions believed to face particular threats, such as the Turkish, Israeli and United States Embassies. Other missions are subject to regular checks by dedicated

AFP patrols. In his *Report to the Minister*, Sir Robert Mark recommended the installation of 'hot lines' between diplomatic and consular facilities and their local police headquarters, in the manner of the direct links installed in the United Kingdom in 1974. Whether or not the Government accepted this recommendation, however, is not known.[70] In addition, the Australian Government has encouraged resident diplomatic and consular missions (within certain prescribed limits) to take physical and other measures to protect themselves.

It is difficult to calculate the costs to Australia of providing this protection. In his replies to Mr Whitlam's questions in 1971 and 1972, the Foreign Minister stated that the overall cost of guarding missions in Canberra between 1966 and June 1972 was over $A510 000. The Minister did not have figures for the cost of protecting consular officials in all the States, but he did disclose that the Victorian Police Force had incurred costs of $A39781 between 1967 and May 1971. The Commonwealth Police had also expended $A9860 in the 1970–71 financial year, on protecting the Yugoslav Consul-General in Melbourne.[71] Updating this information in May 1978, Mr Peacock disclosed that it had cost the Australian Government approximately $A3 600 000 to protect diplomatic and consular posts in the country over the previous six years.[72] Given the relatively small size of the Australian economy and the many hidden costs not included in these figures, it is a considerable burden to carry. Should the terrorist threat continue to grow, these costs can only increase.

In the event of a terrorist attack upon a diplomat or diplomatic facility in Australia (including consular posts) immediate operational responsibilty would lie with the appropriate police force, but the national response (as required) would be coordinated by the Protective Services Coordination Centre in Canberra. A National Anti-Terrorist Plan was drawn up in 1973 and has been renewed and upgraded regularly since. It has been endorsed by all six State governments, the Government of the Northern Territory and the Federal Government. It is not an operational plan but establishes the organisational framework and procedures for the joint management of an incident involving two or more of these governments, as would occur, for example, if terrorists seized a consular post in one of the State capitals. PSCC would activate its national Crisis Policy Centre which would then maintain contact with, and offer advice to, State Crisis Centres and through them, if required, Police Operations Centres. In the case of an attack on a diplomatic mission in the ACT, the PSCC would make direct contact with the AFP Operations Centre. The PSCC would also coordinate contacts with the relevant foreign governments (through the Department of Foreign Affairs), members of the Federal Cabinet and other bodies such as the Attorney-General's Department and Defence Force.

THE CURRENT POSITION

In December 1985, six years after the *Report* of Mr Justice Hope helped establish these arrangements, the Government initiated a comprehensive review of Australia's counter-terrorist capabilities, and the administrative and financial arrangements which supported them. The review was conducted by Roger Holdich, a former Australian ambassador and Deputy Secretary in the Department of the Special Minister of State. In a statement on 17 October 1986 the Special Minister of State, Michael Young, reported on the review's findings. He told Parliament that:

> the present assessment is that there is currently no evidence to indicate that Australia is a chosen target of any international terrorist group.[73]

It was recognised that Australia had close ties with a number of nations which were under high terrorist threat. These states had substantial interests in the country, including diplomatic personnel and premises, which could be seen as attractive targets for terrorist groups. The threat of terrorist attacks against these and other targets in Australia, however, was assessed by ASIO as 'low now and in the foreseeable future'.[74] The Government acknowledged that:

> the source and the nature of the threat can change rapidly, but it accepts the advice that the current low level of threat against targets in Australia and the likely international emphasis on bombings and assassinations can generally be expected to persist for a period.[75]

Accordingly, priority would be given to preventive and contingency measures against these forms of terrorist attacks.

In general terms, the Holdich Review concluded that, since the formation of the SAC-PAV in 1979, an effective national counter-terrorist capability had been established in Australia. The basic findings of Mr Justice Hope were confirmed, with renewed emphasis on the need for timely and accurate intelligence, and effective measures to prevent the entry of terrorists to Australia. A number of adjustments to existing protective and reactive measures were recommended. The Review also examined Commonwealth-State arrangements for the protection of holders of high office in Australia and dignitaries who may be visiting Australia:

> It pointed to the need for agreement on minimum standards of protection in response to different levels of threat. This will be pursued in the SAC-PAV forum.[76]

It was revealed that since 1980–1981 the Commonwealth had spent about $A10 million on equipment, ammunition and training through SAC-PAV. Annual costs for counter-terrorism aspects of ASIO, the Defence Force, the AFP and the Department of the Special Minister of State (which includes the PSCC) amounted to approximately $A30 million.

Although it was never officially announced until Mr Young's statement to Parliament, the Australian Government had long endorsed a 'hard line' policy against making significant concessions to terrorist demands. The National Anti-Terrorist Plan is reported to specify some circumstances in which negotiations with terrorists would be countenanced, but official policy is firmly against any 'diplomatic solutions' to terrorist incidents. In his 1979 *Protective Security Review: Report*, for example, Mr Justice Hope stated:

> Australia has a long standing position of opposition to terrorism in all its manifestations...It is in the interests of all countries that they be seen to be adopting a hard line policy.[77]

These sentiments were echoed in October 1981, when the Australian representative in the Sixth Committee of the United Nations in New York spoke on the question of 'Effective Measures to Enhance the Protection, Security and Safety of Diplomatic and Consular Missions and Representatives'. On that occasion Australia's spokesman condemned attacks on diplomatic and consular personnel and said that Australia was resolved 'to stand firm in the face of terrorist blackmail'.[78] This position was formally announced for the first time in October 1986, when the Special Minister of State told Parliament that:

> A major element of Australia's response to incidents of terrorism is a policy of no concessions, other than tactical ones, to terrorist demands. That policy has been considered and re-endorsed by the Government as a result of the review.[79]

Fortunately, there has never been a need for this policy to be tested.

Both State and Federal police forces have small armed units specially trained in offensive tactics but, in the event of an armed assault against a terrorist-held aircraft, building or installation, these units would probably not be used. Sir Robert Mark's view that 'the close quarter battle is a task for the most sophisticated soldiery, not for police' has been accepted by the Australian Government. In such a situation, it would call upon Australia's own Special Air Service Regiment. In the words of the Defence Minister, the Government:

> maintains a highly skilled counter-terrorist force within the SASR to have the option of resolving terrorist situations by force, while protecting innocent life, should resolution be beyond the capacities of the police.[80]

An idea of the priority given to this counter-terrorist capacity can be gauged by the Government's decision in April 1986 to spend $A22 million on new training facilities for the SASR in Western Australia. The new facilities include indoor and outdoor close quarter battle ranges, mock-ups of aircraft and urban environments, and sniper training areas. In Australia as elsewhere it is envisaged (publicly at least) that the SASR team would only be used as a last resort, and would use the minimum amount of force necessary to save lives.

While all these measures can be taken to prevent a terrorist attack on diplomats and diplomatic facilities in Australia, and to handle it should one occur, the possibility of such an incident will always remain. The same asymmetry between terrorist groups and government forces exists in Australia as in other parts of the world and it will never be possible for all potential targets in the country to be guarded. Even if political sensitivities sometimes prevent it saying so, the Australian Government accepts that there is no such thing as absolute protection and there will always be areas which remain vulnerable. There is now a strong legal and administrative framework in place to meet a terrorist attack against diplomats and diplomatic facilities in Australia but resources available to State and Federal security forces are limited. These services cannot be expected to do more than stretch their funds and manpower to cover those targets which appear to attract the highest risks. As the 1983–84 ASIO *Report to Parliament* stated, 'the terrorist threat to Australia is dynamic'[81] and security authorities in the country will have to be sufficiently flexible and responsive to shift their scarce resources quickly to deal with new situations as they arise.

NOTES

1. D. W. Rawson, 'Political Violence in Australia', *Dissent* 22 (Autumn 1968), pp.18–27. See also M. C. Havens, 'Assassination in Australia', Supplement 1 in J. K. Kirkham, S. G. Levy and W. J. Crotty, *Assassination and Political Violence: A Report to the National Commission on the Causes and Prevention of Violence* (Praeger, New York, 1970), p.721. In 1975 letter bombs were sent to the Prime Minister and the Premier of Queensland, but there cannot have been any real expectation that these letters would be opened by their addressees.

2. Although a member, the Commonwealth of Australia is entirely distinct from the (formerly British) Commonwealth of Nations.

3. C. M. Doogan, 'Defence Powers Under the Constitution: Use of Troops in Aid of State Police Forces—Suppression of Terrorist Activities', *Journal of the Royal United Services Institute of Australia* 5:2 (October 1982), p.55.

4. The best known exception to this rule is the interim Fraser Government of 11 November 1975—13 December 1975, which was appointed by the Governor-General, Sir John Kerr, after he had dismissed from office the elected Labor Government of Prime Minister Gough Whitlam.

5. Sir Colin Woods, 'Problems of International Terrorism', *Australian Journal of Forensic Sciences* 12 (December 1979–March 1980), p.72.

6. Kerry Milte, 'Terrorism and International Order', *Australian and New Zealand Journal of Criminology* 8:2 (June 1975), p.102.

7. *Protective Security Review: Report* (hereinafter referred to as *PSR*) (Unclassified Version), Parliamentary Paper 397/1979, 15 May 1979 (Australian Government Publishing Service (hereinafter referred to as AGPS), Canberra, 1979), p.312.

8. 'Diplomatic Missions: Incidents', Question Upon Notice, House of Representatives, *Hansard*, 7 April 1971; 'Diplomatic Missions and Consular Posts', Question Upon Notice, House of Representatives, *Hansard*, 19 August 1971; and 'Diplomatic Missions and Consular Posts', Question Upon Notice, House of Representatives, *Hansard*, 25 & 26 October 1972. Although listed in *Terrorism: An International Journal* 6:2 (1982) as an attack by terrorists, the murder of the Greek Consul-General in Sydney in November 1981 was a criminal assault quite unrelated to terrorism.

9. 'Attacks on Diplomatic Premises', Question Upon Notice, House of Representatives, *Hansard*, 23 May 1978.

10. 'Croatian Terrorism', Ministerial Statement by the Attorney-General, Senator Lionel Murphy, to the Australian Senate, *Hansard*, 27 March 1973.

11. Quoted in 'Croatian Terrorism'. Clissold appears to quote the same document more fully in his monograph, p.16.

12. Quoted in 'Croatian Terrorism'.

13. Janke, p.115.

14. 'Croatian Terrorism'.

15. *ibid.* The former Attorney-General to whom Lionel Murphy referred, Senator Ivor Greenwood, later made a statement to Parliament in which he denied these charges.

16. See for example Paul Wilkinson, *Political Terrorism* (Macmillan, London, 1974), pp.150–151.

17. Richard Hall, *The Secret State: Australia's Spy Industry* (Cassell, Sydney, 1978), p.97. See also Clissold, p.14.

18. C. O. G. Williams, *Terrorism: An Australian Perspective*, (based on data available to 1 September 1980), Unpublished Master of Arts thesis, University of Melbourne, 1980, p.171.

19. The first such incident in fact occurred in 1975, when the New Zealand Security Intelligence Service reportedly discovered a plan by three sect members to plant a bomb in the Indian High Commission in Wellington.

20. Max Teichmann, 'Terror Australis', *Australian Penthouse* 2:8 (May 1981), p.41. It must be said that no hard evidence has ever been produced to show any connection between Ananda Marga and the UPRF. The sect claimed that the UPRF was created by the Indian Central Bureau of Investigation to discredit them. See Tom Molomby, *Spies, Bombs and the Path of Bliss* (Potoroo Press, Sydney, 1986), p.18.

21. Quoted in Molomby, p.20.

22. Quoted in Molomby, pp.20–21. See also Peter Samuel, 'Ananda Marga the big worry', *The Bulletin*, 31 October 1978, pp.28–29.

23. Molomby, p.20.

24. Michael Parker, *The S.I.S.* (Dunmore Press, Palmerston North, 1979), pp.184–185.

25. Two dustmen were killed in the explosion and a policeman later died as a result of wounds received in the blast.

26. See A. R. Blackshield, 'The Siege of Bowral—The Legal issues', *Pacific Defence Reporter* (March 1978), pp.6–10, and Doogan, pp.55–60.

27. Grounds for such concerns have been found, for example, in the findings of Mr Justice Hope's 1977 Royal Commission on Intelligence and Security, and the Report (presented in December the same year) of Mr Acting Justice White into the South Australian Police Special Branch. For details of the latter, see Stewart Cockburn, *The Salisbury Affair* (Sun Books, Melbourne, 1979).

28. Blackshield, p.6.

29. This earlier study also covered certain aspects of protective security arrangements. See

Royal Commission on Intelligence and Security (hereinafter referred to as *RCIS*), (AGPS, Canberra, 1977), Fourth Report, Vol.1, pp.59–66.

30. Statement by the Prime Minister on Protective Security and Counter Terrorism to the House of Representatives on 23 February 1978, reprinted as Appendix 1 in *PSR*, p.251.

31. *Australian Federal Police Annual Report 1983–84* (AGPS, Canberra, 1984), p.26.

32. 'Establishment of a Specialist Counter-Terrorist Reaction Force', Department of Defence Press Release 127/79, 3 July 1979.

33. *Report to the Minister for Administrative Services on the Organisation of Police Resources in the Commonwealth Area and Other Related Matters* (AGPS, Canberra, 1978), p.3.

34. These were the police forces of the six States, the Northern Territory Police, the Australian Capital Territory Police and the Commonwealth Police.

35. *Report to the Minister*, p.2.

36. David Biles, 'Terrorism as a Social Issue in Australia', Paper presented to the American Connection II Seminar, Sydney Hilton Hotel, 3 May 1978.

37. *PSR*, p.24.

38. *op.cit.*, p.23.

39. See for example 'Sydney bombing linked with Iraqi-backed PLO body', *Australian*, 11 April 1983.

40. The *Australian Security Intelligence Organisation Annual Report 1982–83* (AGPS, Canberra, 1984) states that 'Violence-prone elements in the pro-Palestinian community are considered to have been responsible for the December 1982 bombings of the Israeli Consulate-General and Hakoah Club in Sydney' (p.17). It is not made clear whether these elements were thought to have been members of an international terrorist group or not.

41. 'Explosion at Turkish Consulate-General, Melbourne', Minister of Foreign Affairs News Release M186, 23 November 1986.

42. *ASIO Annual Report 1982–83*, pp.16-17.

43. See for example 'Vietnamese Bring Their Politics to Australia', *National Times*, 20–26 May 1979, and 'Indochina Forum Axed Amid Fears of Violence', *Sydney Morning Herald*, 28 June 1985.

44. Hall, p.99 and pp.243-245.

45. Grant Wardlaw, 'The Mounting Threat of Terror', *Pacific Defence Reporter* 9:2 (June 1983), p.14.

46. *PSR*, p.25. See also Williams, p.173.

47. 'Libyan Peoples' Bureau', Minister for Foreign Affairs News Release M43, 5 March 1986.

48. Interview with Bill Hayden, 'Today' television show, 17 April 1986 and 'Libyan terrorist scare prompts security review', *National Times*, 9 May 1986. Since this book went to press, the Libyan People's Bureau in Canberra has been instructed to close and all Libyan officials expelled from Australia. Significantly, the decision was justified primarily on the basis of Libya's 'increasingly disruptive activities' in the South Pacific region. While referring to Libya's 'record of subversion and terrorism elsewhere in the world', and its contribution to 'dissension and confrontation' among communities in Australia, the Australian Government made no reference to Libyan terrorist activity within Australia itself. See Media Release by the Prime Minister, 19 May 1987. Commenting on 20 May 1987, the *Canberra Times* reported that 'the decision to expel the Libyan bureau comes as a surprise because Australia's intelligence gathering agencies have no evidence of any Libyan activity in the South Pacific region being initiated or co-ordinated out of Canberra. In fact, the Kuala Lumpur bureau is believed to be the conduit for the limited amount of funds and training which Libya has provided to nationals in some South Pacific countries'.

49. Boyce, p.213.
50. *PSR*, pp. 23–24.
51. Speech to the Annual Conference of the Executive Council of Australian Jewry by the Special Minister of State, Michael Young, 11 November 1986.
52. 'Legal and Constitutional Problems of Protective Security Arrangements in Australia', *Australian Law Journal* 52 (June 1978), p.296. See also N. S. Reaburn, 'The Legal Implications in Counter Terrorist Operations', *Pacific Defence Reporter* 4 (April 1978), pp.34–36.
53. The provisions of the Vienna Convention on Consular Relations relating to private residences of consular officers were not included among those provisions given the force of law in Australia.
54. *RCIS*, Fourth Report, Vol.1, p.62.
55. *Public Order (Protection of Persons and Property) Act*, 1971, section 14.
56. See *RCIS*, Fourth Report, Vol.1, p.61. Also, the *Extradition (Foreign States) Act*, 1976 (section 5b) and the *Extradition (Commonwealth Countries) Act*, 1976 (section 4b).
57. Royal Commission on Australia's Security and Intelligence Agencies, *Report on the Australian Security Intelligence Organisation*, December 1984 (AGPS, Canberra, 1985), p.87. See also PSR, p.37.
58. *Report on ASIO*, p.89 and pp.112–113. In 1980 the SAC-PAV requested that ASIO train tactical intelligence units of State and Territory police forces in counter-terrorist aspects of intelligence work, as part of Australia's National Anti-Terrorist Plan. *ASIO Annual Report 1982–83*, p.25.
59. *Australian Security Intelligence Organisation: Report to Parliament 1983–84* (AGPS, Canberra, 1985), p.17.
60. Royal Commission on Australia's Security and Intelligence Agencies, *General Report*, December 1984 (AGPS, Canberra, 1985), p.12.
61. On 7 March 1985, for example, *The Age* reported that four men had been able legally to collect more than $A40 000 worth of arms and ammunition to smuggle to New Caledonia for use against Kanak activists. A smaller cache, also bought in Australia, was discovered on board a ship in Auckland in December 1985. (This ship was also bound for New Caledonia). There have been a large number of thefts from military stores in Australia, in which various types of automatic weapons and explosives have been taken. Only a small proportion appears to have been recovered.
62. *Report on ASIO*, p.113.
63. *Department of Administrative Services Annual Report 1981–82* (AGPS, Canberra, 1982), p.54. See also T. H. Mooney, 'Australia's Approach to Counter Terrorism', Address by the Assistant Secretary, Counter Terrorism Branch, Protective Services Coordination Centre, Department of Administrative Services, Canberra. Appendix 11 to Annex D, *Report of the Proceedings of a Study on the Protection of the Australian Public from Ionising Radiation* (Australian Counter Disaster College, Mt. Macedon, 1983), p.176.
64. As early as 1973 there appears to have been a 'Special Interdepartmental Committee on Counter Terrorism', consisting of representatives of the Department of the Prime Minister and Cabinet, Attorney-General's Department, Department of Foreign Affairs, ASIO, the AFP and other government agencies as required. See 'Secret Study of Terror Tactics', *Canberra Times*, 5 July 1974.
65. *PSR*, p.249.
66. *Australian Federal Police Annual Report 1985–86*, (AGPS, Canberra, 1986), pp.79–80.
67. Williams, p.147.
68. *Report to the Minister*, p.24.
69. At the beginning of 1985 there were 68 resident Embassies and High Commissions in Canberra (including the Apostolic Nunciature of the Holy See, the Libyan People's

Bureau and the Delegation of the European Communities). In addition, there were over 275 Consulates-General, Consulates, Commercial and Cultural Offices scattered throughout Australia's six States and the Northern Territory. While only a small proportion of the latter were staffed by foreign officials attracting privileged status, they nevertheless represented a significant addition to the country's 'diplomatic' community. See the *Diplomatic List* and the *Consular, Trade and Other Official Representatives List*, published at irregular intervals by the Department of Foreign Affairs, Canberra.

70. *Report to the Minister*, p.12.
71. 'Diplomatic Missions and Consular Posts' (19 August 1971) and 'Diplomatic Missions and Consular Posts' (25 & 26 October 1972).
72. 'Attacks on Diplomatic Premises' (23 May 1978).
73. 'Counter Terrorism in Australia', Ministerial Statement by the Special Minister of State, House of Representatives, *Hansard*, 17 October 1986.
74. *ibid.*
75. *ibid.*
76. *ibid.*
77. *PSR*, p.113.
78. Copy of speech provided by the Department of Foreign Affairs under Freedom of Information request F85026 of 15 April 1985.
79. 'Counter Terrorism in Australia'.
80. 'Boost to Army Counter-Terrorist Facilities in W.A.', Press Release by the Minister for Defence, 16 April 1986.
81. *ASIO Report to Parliament*, p.17.

7

TERRORISM AND AUSTRALIAN DIPLOMACY

I believe that relatively small countries can exert great influence in international affairs as long as they do not over inflate their estimation of their capacity to exert that influence.

Senator John Button
(Leader of the Government in the Senate)
The Senate, 17 April 1986

The increased frequency of terrorist incidents in recent years and their impact on the international environment have contributed to a growing demand in Australia for articles and comments about the global terrorist problem and its implications for the world order. The local news media has been quick to publicise developments in this field, particularly where there appear to be domestic implications. In all the attention that has been given to these matters to date, however, little has been accorded to the Australian Government's approach to international terrorism as a foreign policy issue. It seems to be taken for granted that the Government condemns such violence and is doing what it can to help end it. This happens to be true, but these responses are not simply expressions of moral outrage, or the result of sudden decisions by Ministers burdened with responsibilities in this field. Rather, they reflect a longstanding opposition to terrorism in all its forms, wherever it may occur, and a concern for Australia to contribute where it can to cooperative measures designed to combat this threat.

Since international terrorism first assumed major proportions in the late 1960s, there have been three changes of government in Australia,[1] but no significant changes in the Australian Government's attitude towards this problem. The variations in foreign policy which have been seen in other fields, through different party philosophies or changing national and international circumstances, have been largely absent in regard to terrorist issues. Both sides in Parliament have taken the opportunity to capitalise on the occasional discomfort of their opponents and there have been one or two major clashes, such as occurred over the issue of Croatian terrorism in 1973, but successive Australian Governments seem to have shared perceptions of the threat from international terrorism and the ways in which it should be overcome. Indeed, by surveying Australia's foreign policy responses to terrorist issues over the past 15 years it is clear that, in most crucial areas, the approaches of different Australian Governments to these matters have been remarkably consistent.

THE REACTION TO EVENTS IN 1972

International terrorism did not become a major foreign policy concern of the Australian Government until 1972, when attacks assumed more significant proportions and the subject began to receive prominence on the agenda of major negotiating groups. In particular, Australians were shocked by the terrorist attacks that year at Israel's Lod Airport and the Munich Olympic Games, which resulted in 36 people killed and 76 wounded.[2] Three months after the latter incident Australians saw the problem brought closer to home when Palestinian extremists seized the Israeli Embassy in Bangkok. When United Nations Secretary-General Kurt Waldheim placed the terrorist problem on the UN agenda that year Australia was quick to respond. Addressing the General Assembly on 27 September 1972 the then Minister for Foreign Affairs, Nigel Bowen, devoted a significant proportion of his speech to the problem of international terrorism. He welcomed the initiative of the Secretary-General in raising the issue and emphasised the need for consideration of terrorism in the UN to be followed by practical and effective measures to combat the problem. Referring to a number of incidents perpetrated by Croatian and Palestinian terrorists in Australia earlier that year, the Minister stated that his Government 'regards all acts of that kind as utterly abhorrent to our way of life' and called for urgent action 'to defeat the indiscriminate threat of terrorism'.[3] Looking to the longer term, he raised the possibility of an international convention, drafted by the International Law Commission, 'aimed at outlawing acts of violence and intimidation which arise essentially from local conflicts but which are in effect directed primarily at innocent people and uninvolved governments'.[4]

After the election of the Whitlam Government in December 1972, attention in Australia tended to focus more on the terrorist problem in Australia rather than that growing abroad. This was largely due to the domestic political controversy which erupted in March 1973 over the extent of Croatian terrorism in the country. After the 1963 armed incursion into Yugoslavia, the then Australian Minister for External Affairs, Garfield Barwick, expressed concern over the foreign policy implications of Croatian terrorist activities and warned the Attorney-General that they may 'embarass our relations with other governments'.[5] Following the HRB's 1972 expedition the Tito Government presented a strongly-worded Aide Memoire to Canberra, alleging that a number of Croatian terrorist organisations existed in Australia and had benefited from Australian Government support. A 'bland interim reply'[6] was given to the Yugoslav Government on 20 October, simply stating that the matter was being investigated. When the McMahon Government appeared not to take its protest seriously, and further bomb attacks against official Yugoslav premises occurred in Sydney (in which 15 people were injured), Yugoslavia even threatened to break off diplomatic relations with Australia unless stronger measures were taken to curb the activities of Croatian terrorist groups in the country. The Whitlam Government's response to these concerns and the furore which followed ensured that developments overseas were largely overshadowed by local issues.[7]

While preoccupied with these and other domestic problems, the Whitlam Government continued to speak out strongly in the international arena against terrorist violence. It also joined with other countries in cooperative measures designed to counter this threat. At the Twenty-Eighth Regular Session of the United Nations General Assembly between September-December 1973 the US proposal for an international convention against terrorism quickly succumbed to sterile debate, but the Australian delegation played an active role in negotiations on the draft convention to protect diplomats from terrorist attack. The eventual adoption by consensus of the New York Convention was one of the main achievements of the session. When it signed the Convention in December 1974 Australia was among the first countries to do so.

After December 1975 the Fraser Government maintained these concerns. In his speech to the United Nations General Assembly in September 1976 the new Australian Foreign Minister, Andrew Peacock, reflected longstanding Australian policy when he said of terrorism:

> Regardless of the justification which its proponents advance for it, it remains a completely unacceptable form of political pressure. It is unacceptable because it is barbarous and haphazard. It undermines the general fabric of lawful and decent behaviour. Those who pursue it deliberately and flagrantly violate the right to life, liberty and protection from injury of those who are made the innocent victims of their pressures. We condemn terrorism and will join in efforts to eliminate it.[8]

Australia continued to play an active role in United Nations debates on terrorism. In 1977 it was one of the early co-sponsors of a Resolution on the Safety of International Civil Aviation which condemned aircraft hijacking and appealed to states which had not become parties to the relevant international conventions to do so.[9] In the Sixth (Legal) Committee of the General Assembly Australia supported the Federal Republic of Germany's proposal for a draft Convention Against the Taking of Hostages and co-sponsored the Resolution establishing an Ad Hoc Committee to examine the matter.

By 1978 Australia was a party to all the major treaties which dealt with terrorist violence. These included the 1963 Tokyo Convention on Offences and Certain Other Acts Committed on Board Aircraft, the 1970 Hague Convention for the Suppression of Unlawful Seizure of Aircraft, the 1971 Montreal Convention for the Suppression of Unlawful Acts Against the Safety of Civil Aviation, and the 1973 New York Convention. All had been incorporated into domestic legislation.[10] Australia had also supported the International Atomic Energy Agency's proposal for a convention requiring states to take strong action against any crime, including terrorist activity, involving nuclear materials or facilities. At the regional level, Australia had joined with other Commonwealth countries at the Commonwealth Heads of Government Regional Meeting in Sydney in February 1978, in agreeing 'to explore ways in which their respective countries could enlarge collaboration, both regionally and internationally, in combatting terrorism'.[11] An Ad Hoc Working Group was established under the Chairmanship of Singapore to pursue such efforts.[12]

Another significant step was taken by Australia after the seven Summit countries, meeting in Bonn in July 1978, issued a formal Declaration on Terrorism. With the Hilton Hotel bombing still fresh in the public mind, Prime Minister Malcolm Fraser made a statement to Parliament in which he said that Australia welcomed 'this further constructive initiative to enhance the international cooperative efforts required to combat the menacing crime of hijacking'. He continued:

> The Australian Government strongly supports this constructive action against the threat of terrorism and agrees completely with the objectives of the Declaration... Australia has a long-standing position of opposition to terrorism in all its manifestations...Australian support of the Bonn Declaration means that we consider ourselves committed to its objectives.[13]

The Australian Government subsequently advised the FRG Government, as the representative of the Summit Seven, that Australia supported the Declaration and would cooperate in the attainment of its objectives. This committed Australia to intensify its efforts to combat international terrorism, in particular to take action against countries which gave sanctuary to aircraft hijackers, even to the extent of severing civil aviation links with such a country.

THE HAWKE GOVERNMENT'S RESPONSE

When it came to power in March 1983, the Hawke Labor Government inherited the counter-terrorist policies and administrative machinery of its predecessor. The latter has since been re-examined. In addition to the

Holdich Review of Australia's domestic counter-terrorist capabilities announced in December 1985, the Department of Foreign Affairs was also requested to examine the way in which terrorism was considered as a foreign policy issue. As a result, in April 1986 the Department established a Counter Terrorism Policy Section within its International Security and Policy Planning Branch. The new section was charged with the coordination of Australia's broader foreign policy responses to international terrorist issues. It thus complemented and enhanced the work of the Diplomatic Security Section, and the specialist geographical and functional areas of the Department which already managed a wide range of diverse responsibilites touching on the terrorist problem. These two reviews did not, however, betoken any change in the direction of Australia's foreign policy against terrorism. To the contrary, the Hawke Government quickly reiterated Australia's strong condemnation of terrorist violence. At its 1986 National Conference in Hobart the Australian Labor Party amended its platform to include a specific clause opposing 'all acts of terrorism as a means of pursuing political objectives', the first Australian political party to do so.[14] Representatives of the Hawke Government have also spoken out strongly against terrorism and, in some instances, have taken a prominent position on terrorist issues in international fora.

The Government's increased attention to the problem of international terrorism arose from a number of developments, both in Australia and overseas. The greater frequency and deadliness of international terrorist attacks since the beginning of the 1980s, the increasing use of terrorist tactics by established states like Libya, Syria and Iran, and the weight given to terrorist issues by the Reagan Administration, have all brought terrorism to the forefront of global politics. The American bombing of Libya in April 1986 raised serious questions over the use of force as a means of reducing the threat from terrorist violence. As an increasingly active member of the international community, and a traditional ally of the United States, Australia has been called upon to take a public stand on a number of complex terrorist issues. There has also been a growing public awareness in Australia of the scope and potential of the terrorist problem, to which the Government has needed to respond. Because of the country's isolation from major world centres, Australians tend to be particularly sensitive to any threat to international air services. Of concern to many now is the danger of becoming involved in a terrorist incident while travelling overseas.

There have been a number of suggestions in recent years that Australians are identified with popular terrorist targets like Americans or Israelis, or are seen in some other way as representing policies inimical to certain terrorist groups. In June 1985, for example, Australia's links with the United States were strongly criticised by the 'Peace Conquerers', one of the seven groups which claimed responsibility for a bomb explosion at Frankfurt Airport in which three people were killed and 42 others were injured. An Australian school teacher and his family, who were on the TWA jet hijacked the same month by Shi'ite terrorists, later told news reporters that the gunmen had shown no love for Australia, which was considered to be a friend of Israel.[15] Although publicly refuted by Government spokesmen, reports persist that Australians were also viewed in a bad light by the terrorists who seized the cruise ship *Achille Lauro* in October 1985.[16] The hijackers of an Egypt Air passenger plane in November apparently placed Australians high on a list of nationalities deserving harsh treatment, after Americans and Israelis and before Canadians and French citizens. Early in 1986 Foreign Minister Bill Hayden acknowledged that Australians had received some unwelcome attention from Middle Eastern terrorists but was quick to correct inaccurate news reports suggesting that Australians were specifically being singled out as terrorist targets.[17] According to a set of 'Hints for Australian Travellers' produced by the Department of Foreign Affairs in May 1986, and distributed widely to travel agents and airline offices, there is no definitive evidence that Australians abroad are at particular risk from terrorist attack.[18]

Between June 1985 and July 1986 some 275 000 Australians travelled abroad.[19] Statistically, the chances of one of them becoming involved in a terrorist incident overseas were small. This is still the case. There is always the possibility, however, that Australians overseas may become incidental victims, simply by being in the wrong place at the wrong time. In June 1985 there was the case of the Australian family caught up in the hijacking of TWA Flight 847. Two of those killed in the Frankfurt Airport bombing that month were Australian children. Also in June 1985, two Australian tourists were slightly injured when a bomb exploded in the foyer of their Kathmandu hotel. Three Nepalis were killed in the incident. In November 1985 a young Australian woman died when Egyptian commandos stormed the Egypt Air Boeing 737 which had been hijacked to Malta. Another Australian passenger on the plane received slight injuries. Three Australians narrowly escaped injury in May 1986 when a bomb planted on an Air Lanka Tristar exploded prematurely at Colombo Airport. Twenty-two others were killed and another 41 injured. These incidents all help confirm Mr Hayden's statement to Parliament in November 1985, that 'we are not immune from this global problem which jeopardises not only individual lives and liberties but the civilised conduct of relations between states'.[20]

AUSTRALIA'S SIX POINT POLICY

There has been no formal, comprehensive statement on the foreign policy aspects of international terrorism made by the Hawke Government since it first assumed office more than four years ago, but a number of Ministers and other senior Government representatives have referred to the subject on numerous occasions, in speeches, press releases and in Parliament. By surveying these scattered references it is possible to identify six broad themes which run consistently through the Government's public comments on the terrorist problem. In brief, they are an unequivocal condemnation of terrorism, a 'hard line' policy against terrorist demands, a commitment to international cooperation as the most effective means of combatting the problem, an emphasis on peaceful and legal counter-measures, a continuing belief in the role of multilateral institutions like the UN and a concern to give appropriate weight to the 'root causes' of extremist discontent. These policy themes are noteworthy not only for what they reveal of the Hawke Government's approach to terrorist issues, but also for the fact that they so closely match the approaches to this problem taken by earlier Australian Governments.

Condemnation of Terrorism

Since 1983 different members of the Hawke Government have stated on numerous occasions, in Parliament and elsewhere, their firm belief that 'terrorism and violence are unacceptable means by which to pursue political objectives'.[21] Terrorism has been characterised as a destructive force more likely to harden attitudes and exacerbate differences between peoples than to achieve any political objectives. Australian representatives have also made it clear to whom they feel the term 'terrorist' should apply, directly confronting the moral and political confusion so often associated with debates on this issue. In an address to the Australian-Lebanese Chamber of Commerce in Sydney on 24 October 1985, for example, Foreign Minister Bill Hayden said:

> It is often argued that it is not possible to distinguish between a terrorist and a freedom fighter—that the use of one particular label is a purely subjective assessment depending on one's support for or opposition to a particular cause. However, there is a distinction. It is questionable to describe as a terrorist those who seek the overthrow of a cruel and repugnant regime through the use of force when all other efforts to achieve peaceful change have failed. But violence can never be justified if there are alternatives. Nor can the threat of violence against innocent civilians ever be condoned. Such actions are those of the terrorist.[22]

The Government endorsed a strong condemnation of terrorism issued by the ASEAN countries in July 1985 and Mr Hawke was among those Commonwealth Heads of Government meeting in Nassau in October that year who together 'condemned all terrorist activities whether perpetrated by individuals, groups or states, and resolved to counter them by every means available'.[23]

The Nassau Communique also 'acknowledged the duty of Governments to refrain from acts of, and encouragement to, terrorism in the territories of other states'[24] and Australia has been quick to condemn states known to be engaging in or sponsoring terrorism. In July 1985, for example, after French secret service agents sank the *Rainbow Warrior* in Auckland harbour, Prime Minister Bob Hawke condemned the action as a 'cold-blooded, premeditated act of international terrorism' and expressed Australia's support for the New Zealand Government's efforts to have those responsible brought to justice.[25] Australia has vigorously condemned Libya for its involvement in and support for international terrorism and has called for the Qaddafi regime to disavow terrorist violence as an instrument of Libyan foreign policy. In October 1986 the Australian Foreign Minister expressed his grave concern over Syria's involvement in the attempted bombing of an El Al airliner at Heathrow Airport.

Australia's attitude was also made clear on 6 May 1986 after the seven Summit countries, meeting in Tokyo, issued a new Declaration on Terrorism, including a further call for an end to abuses of diplomatic privilege. Questioned about the Government's attitude to this Declaration, Mr Hayden told the House of Representatives that:

> the specific measures agreed upon by the Summit Seven in Tokyo are matters which Australia has already implemented or taken steps to implement.[26]

Australia already had strict controls on the export of arms and munitions, already monitored the movement of known or suspected terrorists and was in the process of reviewing and extending its extradition arrangements with other countries. Strict visa and immigration controls were already in place. In listing these and other measures, Mr Hayden said that 'the fact that we are well ahead in anticipation of the decisions of the Tokyo Summit . . . is a convincing demonstration' of Australia's firm rejection of terrorism as a means of pursuing political objectives.[27]

'Hard Line' Policy

The 'hard line' policy against making significant concessions to terrorists which was endorsed by the Labor Government, and formally enunciated by the Special Minister of State in October 1986, has also been demonstrated in the international arena. In June 1985, for example, the Prime Minister told an Australian Broadcasting Corporation (ABC) radio reporter that he agreed with the principle behind the United States' policy of not treating with terrorists. Mr Hawke continued:

> I believe that if you have a situation where you allow terrorism and the tactic of terrorism to become legitimised in international relationships then you are proceeding down a very dangerous path.[28]

This approach was also affirmed by the Foreign Minister. In a statement on the TWA hijacking incident later the same month, Mr Hayden said:

> Governments are now all too frequently forced by terrorists to make crucial decisions involving the lives of their citizens held captive or threatened by terrorists. To give way to terrorist demands, however, only encourages further acts of terrorism and undermines the fabric of international relations. The use of terrorism against innocent civilians must not be permitted to become an accepted norm in international relations and negotiations.[29]

At the 1985 Commonwealth Heads of Government Meeting (CHOGM) Australia once again undertook to resist the demands of terrorists. Australia's main concern over the secret US arms sales to Iran in 1985-1986 was that they might 'be interpreted by those with a propensity for terrorism, or potentially with such a propensity as an indication that terrorism can be rewarded, that hostage taking can bring its profit'.[30]

International Cooperation

Following on from this basic position, Australia has placed considerable emphasis on increased international cooperation as the most effective means for members of the world community to counter terrorism. In his 28 June 1985 news release on 'International Terrorism', for example, Mr Hayden was reflecting longstanding Australian policy when he said that:

> the Australian Government called on all nations to work to combat the spread of terrorism and to take whatever action was necessary to discourage and to counter terrorist acts. It would only be through concentrated international cooperation that terrorism would be combatted[31].

The need for a joint approach to the terrorist problem was again stressed in the Nassau Communique and has been reiterated in subsequent Australian statements on the issue. It is also reflected in practice at the working level. As noted already, Australia enjoys close working relations in the counter-terrorism field with its friends and allies. These exchanges are in addition to those conducted by Australia's diplomatic representatives abroad who, in consultation with specialist departments and agencies, are in continual contact with members of other governments on security issues, including aspects of the terrorist problem. Until a review of its overseas representation in 1986, ASIO also maintained 14 Liaison Officers overseas, usually on secondment to the Department of Foreign Affairs or the Department of Immigration and Ethnic Affairs.[32] In November 1984 ASIO also organised the first Pacific Regional Conference on International Terrorism, at which several problems common to the region were identified.

A new dimension was added to this international cooperation in January 1986, with the announcement that Federal Cabinet had authorised the Prime

Minister to advise President Reagan of the Australian Government's desire to work with Western and other governments for a concerted international approach to dealing with international terrorism. In a news release issued on 20 January Mr Hayden stated that Cabinet had also authorised him 'to consult other governments and report back to Ministers on measures to promote a sustained long-term effort to defeat the threat of international terrorism'.[33] Contrary to assertions made at different times by the Leader of the National Party and the Shadow Foreign Minister, it is clear that these consultations are now taking place.[34] On 8 September 1986, for example, after terrorist incidents in Karachi and Istanbul, the Prime Minister revealed that:

> The Government made approaches earlier this year to a number of governments, including our traditional allies and a number within our region, seeking avenues for increased co-operation in the fight against international terrorism. Those approaches have been positively received.[35]

The Australian Government's concern to cooperate against terrorism was also cited in November 1986, when Australia agreed to represent British interests in Syria, after the United Kingdom broke off diplomatic relations with the Assad regime. At the time, Mr Hayden revealed that 'sensitive discussions' on this matter had also been held with the United States, Canada and members of the European Community.

Peaceful and Legal Counter-Measures

A fourth theme running consistently through the Australian Government's statements on terrorist matters is that emphasising the peaceful resolution of disputes and reliance on international legal norms as the basis for responses by states toward this problem. Australia's approach to external policy has long rested primarily on a non-military appraisal of power politics, been averse to options of military intervention and, conversely, has actively sought and emphasised the preferred alternatives of political contest and diplomatic dialogue. Such an approach also reflects traditional Australian Labor Party philosophy, which includes a firm commitment to 'finding peaceful solutions to all international disputes'.[36] In keeping with the Government's 'hard line' against terrorism, this approach does not extend to treating with terrorists themselves but it strongly influences Australia's approach to these questions in multilateral fora and its responses to the counter-terrorist policies of other states. In his address to the Australian-Lebanese Chamber of Commerce in October 1985 the Minister for Foreign Affairs put this commitment to legal processes into a practical perspective when he said:

> ...every legal effort should be employed to apprehend and bring to justice those responsible for acts of terrorism. It is to be hoped that the capture, prosecution

and punishment of those responsible for terrorist attacks will act as a deterrent to other would be terrorists. It should also encourage Governments to seek to exercise the due process of law in punishing such people rather than resorting to armed retaliation which serves only to expand the cycle of violence.[37]

This statement is reminiscent of the address given to the UN by Nigel Bowen in 1972, when the then Foreign Minister told the General Assembly that Australia condemned not only terrorism but also 'those acts of violent retaliation, understandable as they may be, which in themselves carry the seeds of escalation into further terrorism'.[38]

Australia has spoken out strongly against states claiming to fight terrorism, if the actions of those states were considered to be in violation of international law. In October 1985 it condemned Israel for its bombing raid on a Palestinian base in Tunisia and called on Israel to respect the norms of international law. Speaking in the UN Security Council the Australian delegate succinctly expressed his Government's position when he said:

> Australia condemns all acts of terrorism and violence, wherever and whenever they take place. On this occasion, Israel has engaged in an act of violence which has resulted in the death of innocent civilians and which is clearly a breach of international law and the United Nations Charter. Whether or not the Palestine Liberation Organisation [PLO] has carried out acts of terrorism against Israel is not really the point at issue. The point is that even if we were to accept Israel's version of events, two wrongs do not make a right.[39]

As it had also done in 1973, Australia strongly criticised Israel in February 1986 for its interception of a civilian airplane thought to be carrying terrorists. On the latter occasion Mr Hayden stated that he 'could understand the motive of Israel in seeking to act against international terrorism, but that did not justify this interception of a civil aircraft in international air space'.[40]

Such sentiments were relatively muted, however, when United States Navy jet fighters forced down an Egypt Air Boeing 737 carrying the terrorists responsible for the seizure of the Italian cruise ship *Achille Lauro* and the death of an elderly American passenger. Although it was not clear that the United States had acted within the bounds of international law, the Acting Prime Minister, Lionel Bowen, stated under Opposition pressure in Parliament on 16 October 1985 that Australia supported the American action. A carefully worded message sent to President Reagan the same day, however, avoided any explicit expressions of approval. Apparently reflecting the more cautious approach recommended by the Department of Foreign Affairs, the message stated that the Australian Government:

> agrees with, and has complete sympathy with, the declaration of the Government of the United States of America that terrorists should be proceeded against according to the established legal processes and that all countries in the inter-

national community should meet their proper obligations in this process. Australia will certainly meet its responsibilities in this respect and we have conveyed this commitment to your Government. The Government of Australia understands the concerns of the Government of the United States of America to make these terrorists subject to legal accountability.[41]

Explaining this apparent difference in Australian standards, as applied to the Americans and the Israelis, the Foreign Minister later told Parliament that 'It is not possible to state in a general way how or when the interception of a civil aircraft in international air space may be justified. Much will always depend on the prevailing circumstances at the time'.[42]

There have been other occasions when Australia has expressed guarded approval of military action against terrorists or states known to be sponsoring terrorism. After Israel rescued the passengers and crew of the Air France Airbus hijacked to Entebbe in July 1976, for example, Senator Reginald Withers (speaking on behalf of the Minister of Foreign Affairs) told Parliament that:

> The Australian Government consistently has affirmed its unequivocal condemnation of terrorism and its desire to see effective measures taken against terrorism and force, particularly when these involve innocent civilians. The Government therefore deplores the hijacking of the Air France aircraft, which led to the situation at Entebbe in July, and regrets that this situation deteriorated to such an extent that it caused the Israeli Government to conclude that it had to intervene militarily. The failure of multilateral efforts in the United Nations and elsewhere to get effective international action against terrorism clearly leaves in certain circumstances little alternative to unilateral action, and that was the situation faced by the Israeli Government. Australia is very ready at all times to help seek international agreement on effective means to counter terrorist activities.[43]

This statement in many respects foreshadowed the response made by the Prime Minister after the United States bombing raids on Libya in April 1986. Clearly, military responses against terrorist groups or their state sponsors will continue to be launched by some countries and there are bound to be times when, for one reason or another, Australia will be reluctant openly to speak out against them. On such occasions it can be expected that Opposition Parliamentarians will attempt to score political points by noting apparent inconsistencies and demanding stronger and more specific statements from official spokesmen. The Australian Government of the day, however, whether it be Coalition or Labor, is equally likely to respond in general terms, repeating its condemnation of terrorist and other violence, and calling for a greater reliance on peaceful, legal means of settling disputes, exercised through appropriate international institutions.

The importance Australia places on international legal efforts to combat terrorism is perhaps most clearly seen in the area of multilateral agreements. The draft Resolution on terrorism which Australia co-sponsored at the

Twenty Seventh Regular Session of the UN General Assembly in 1972 would have authorised the ILC to prepare draft Articles for a convention on measures to prevent international terrorism, for presentation to the General Assembly the following year. As it happened, this draft Resolution was not put to the vote, having been pre-empted by a less strongly-worded 'non-aligned' Resolution. The Australian delegation expressed its disappointment at the failure of the UN to proceed with a convention but reaffirmed its support for such instruments, in the UN and elsewhere, as important contributions towards the effective reduction of terrorist violence.

Since the adoption of the Tokyo, Hague and Montreal Conventions on air safety and the 1973 New York Convention on crimes against internationally protected persons, a number of other international instruments have been negotiated to cover offenses which may be regarded as acts of terrorism. These include the 1979 International Convention Against the Taking of Hostages and the 1980 Vienna Convention on the Physical Protection of Nuclear Material. Australia is a signatory to the latter instrument and has begun action formally to ratify it. This will be possible when the Nuclear Non-Proliferation Safeguards Bill (introduced into Parliament in 1986) becomes law. Curiously, given its earlier support for it in Committee, Australia is not yet a signatory to the 1979 Hostages Convention. It hopes to accede to it in due course but, once again, this is likely to require new domestic legislation. Once this process is completed Australia will be party to all international conventions against terrorist acts.[44] Australia has also, in Mr Hayden's words, 'repeatedly called for the more effective implementation of international legal measures against terrorist acts'.[45]

Role of Multilateral Institutions

The fifth theme running consistently through official Australian statements on terrorist issues flows directly from the third and fourth, that is the important role played by multilateral institutions such as the United Nations, the International Civil Aviation Organisation (ICAO) and the International Maritime Organisation (IMO). Both Liberal/Country Party and Labor Party Governments have turned to these bodies to achieve broad-based cooperative measures against international violence, including terrorism. On 6 May 1986, for example, the Foreign Minister told Parliament that Australians 'strongly support the role of the United Nations, in helping combat terrorism'.[46] In the Sixth Committee in particular, Australian delegates have made significant contributions to UN debates on terrorist issues. The Australian statement on terrorism at the Fortieth UN General Assembly in 1985, for example, attracted widespread attention. It 'noted that there were strict prohibitions in the law of armed conflict against the use of terrorist methods in international and non-international armed conflicts'.[47]

Drawing on the 1949 Geneva Conventions for the Protection of War Victims and the two 1977 Additional Protocols, the Australian delegate argued that principles applicable internationally in peacetime and in certain ill-defined areas (where the applicability of laws of armed conflict were in doubt) could not be less rigorous than those applying in cases of open armed conflict. The statement was 'an attempt to refute the highly political stances of some delegations designed to suggest that existing law does not apply to violent acts committed for purposes of national liberation struggles against racist regimes and so on'.[48]

The two Additional Protocols provide an interesting example of the complex political and legal questions faced by the Australian Government in dealing with international terrorism. Both Protocols are the result of the Geneva Diplomatic Conference on the Reaffirmation of International Humanitarian Law Applicable in Armed Conflict, which met under the auspices of the Red Cross between 1974–1977. A number of radical groups, including the PLO, attended the Conference as Observers. Protocol I revises and supplements the 1949 Conventions with regard to the protection of the victims of international armed conflict. Article 1(4) also makes the laws of war applicable to 'armed conflicts in which peoples are fighting against colonial domination and alien occupation and against racist regimes in the exercise of their right of self determination'.[49] The proponents of Protocol I have claimed that, while it may now permit the PLO and other such groups to claim the protection of the laws of war, it also becomes incumbent upon them to observe these rules. Other states, notably the US, have claimed that terrorist groups have now been given 'legal legitimacy' by Protocol I and have refused to ratify it.[50] Australia signed Protocol I on 7 December 1978 but reserved the right to make comments on ratification. In March 1986 the Government announced it would take this step but appears to be in no hurry to do so. Should other signatories, like the UK or Canada, move to ratification, however, then Australia may feel able to do so in 'good company', despite the strong feelings of the United States on this matter.

As a member of the Security Council (and President for a month) Australia was also in a position to play an active part in the consideration of a number of significant terrorist issues which arose during the 1985 UN session. Following the *Achille Lauro* seizure, for example, the Council unanimously agreed with a Presidential Statement which condemned the hijacking and 'terrorism in all its forms, wherever and by whomsoever committed'.[51] After a number of kidnappings, including the abduction of an Australian couple from Pakistan to Afghanistan, Australia co-sponsored Security Council Resolution 579, which condemned unequivocally all acts of hostage-taking and abduction. It called upon all states to take measures to secure the safe release of hostages and to facilitate the prevention, prosecution and punishment of all acts of hostage-taking and abduction. The day after its unanimous adoption by the Council, Mr Hayden stated that Australia had co-sponsored the Resolution 'as an indication of the strength of the Government's concern over this issue'.[52]

Australia has also supported action against international terrorism in specialised multilateral agencies like ICAO and the IMO. This support has been expressed on numerous occasions, including at the Nassau CHOGM. On that occasion Commonwealth Heads of Government agreed 'to strengthen their adherence to the relevant legal instruments including those adopted under the auspices of the International Civil Aviation Organisation...'.[53] The Australian representative at the ICAO Council meeting in Montreal on 3 July 1985 was reflecting this attitude when he stated that:

> His country felt confident that ICAO could play a significant and perhaps major role in strengthening the provisions on aviation security to the extent that such acts of terrorism would be kept to a minimum and hopefully abolished.[54]

Australia has since co-sponsored a Canadian initiative in the ICAO designed to help prevent terrorist attacks at international airports. In the wake of the *Achille Lauro* seizure in October 1985 Australia also co-sponsored an IMO resolution drafted by the United States which called upon all governments, port authorities, shipowners, shipmasters and others to take steps to review and, as necessary, strengthen port and onboard security. Australia also participated in the drafting of the final Resolution at the IMO Assembly in November 1985 and joined in its unanimous acceptance in September 1986.

The Root Causes of Terrorism

In keeping with this emphasis on the peaceful and legal resolution of political disputes through international negotiating groups, successive Australian governments have called for states and multilateral organisations to look beyond purely preventive and reactionary counter-terrorist measures to a greater appreciation of the 'root causes' of extremist discontent. In his speech to the UN General Assembly in 1972 former Foreign Minister Nigel Bowen called for 'a stringent combination of domestic and internationally agreed penalties' against those guilty of terrorist acts. He added, however, that:

> My Government understands fully the kinds of frustration, grievance, and despair that can lead particular groups and individuals to embark on desperate enterprises designed to hold persons, often innocent persons, and even governments to ransom.[55]

The unsuccessful draft Resolution which Australia co-sponsored in the UN that year would have also established an Ad Hoc Committee to study the underlying causes of terrorism.

The Australian Labor Party has taken this issue further and since 1983 has called for a more serious commitment to the elimination of factors which, in many instances, have contributed to the rise of international terrorism. In his address to the Australian-Lebanese Chamber of Commerce, for example, the Foreign Minister unequivocally condemned terrorist violence but acknowledged that sometimes there may be legitimate cause for grievance:

> It is of course necessary to seek to solve as well as prevent the problem of terrorism. The primary objective must be the removal of the causes of terrorism.[56]

Again, on 2 May 1986, in an address on human rights issues to a seminar of the Catholic Commission for Justice and Peace, Mr Hayden repeated this theme:

> I understand, of course, that terrorism is not born in a vacuum. Such terrible indiscriminate behaviour must be formed by terrible causes. I appreciate also that the causes of terrorism have to be faced before terrorism itself can be eradicated.[57]

Such an approach has not always met with a warm reception. Israel, for example, has criticised it as 'a total non-starter'. In a formal statement issued by the Israeli Embassy in Canberra on 16 May 1986, terrorism in the Middle East was described as 'part of the traditional violence endemic to the region' and 'the real root cause' of such violence identified as Palestinian intransigence.[58] These comments were no doubt made with official Australian views in mind.

The Hawke Government believes it is pursuing a 'very even-handed' policy towards the Middle East. It 'respects', but sees certain shortcomings in, Israel's position. It also recognises the 'justifiable claims' of the Palestinian people and accepts that the PLO has a role to play if there is to be any peaceful and durable conclusion to the problems of the region.[59] (This role, however, depends on acceptance by the PLO of Israel's right to exist). As a means of keeping the Government fully informed on developments in the Middle East, Australian diplomatic representatives abroad, including ambassadors, have been authorised to maintain informal contacts with PLO representatives and in November 1985 Mr Hayden met the PLO representative at the United Nations. The Foreign Minister is also on record as stating that:

> a fundamental cause of tension, conflict and terrorism in, and arising from the Middle East, occurs because of the failure to bring about a resolution of the Middle East problem and in particular the Palestinian issue.[60]

In the light of this approach, the Australian Government has been at a loss to explain the unwelcome attention apparently given to Australians by Middle Eastern terrorists in a number of incidents in 1985. Suggestions that the terrorists were responding to Mr Hawke's reputed emotional ties to Israel have been dismissed. Nor has there been any perception that Australia has been identified as a particular target by Colonel Qaddafi, despite the Hawke Government's strong condemnation of Libyan terrorism.

AUSTRALIA AND LIBYAN TERRORISM

The six themes which consistently run through Australian foreign policy statements on international terrorism can all be seen in the Hawke Government's responses to Libyan terrorism, in particular its reaction to the bombing of a West Berlin discotheque in April 1986 and the American bombing raids on Tripoli and Benghazi which followed. Australia had been monitoring Libyan activities for some time prior to 1986, including its possible involvement in a number of international terrorist incidents and increasing Libyan interest in the South Pacific. As a sign of the disfavour with which Australia viewed the policies of the Qaddafi regime, a number of formal protests had been made and official restraints introduced to limit the bilateral relationship. The sale of arms and warlike stores to Libya was banned, Libyans wishing to come to Australia were carefully screened and a limit was placed on the staffing of the Libyan People's Bureau in Canberra.

These measures were extended in January 1986, after the Prime Minister received a letter from President Reagan outlining American responses to terrorist attacks at Rome and Vienna Airports on 27 December 1985. Presented with 'fairly convincing evidence' of direct Libyan involvement in these two incidents,[61] Federal Cabinet announced that the level of official Libyan representation in Australia was to be further reduced from seven to five and, pending an official review, no new places were to be made available in Australia for Libyan students. In addition, the Australian Trade Commission was directed not to provide finance and insurance facilities for new Australian business with Libya, apart from contracts in the food and agriculture sectors. These measures were taken 'as part of collective international measures to demonstrate to Libya that its behaviour in support of international terrorism is totally unacceptable to the international community'.[62] Despite American calls for comprehensive economic sanctions, the Government did not agree to any further restriction on commercial activity with Libya. It said, however, that Australia would be prepared to consider trade sanctions provided they had widespread international support, and thus a greater likelihood of being effective.[63]

When the United States launched a series of bombing raids against Libya on the night of 14-15 April Mr Hawke told Parliament that the Government:

is profoundly concerned that the situation has reached the point where Libyan actions have driven the United States to regard it as essential that it take military action. Australia works persistently for a peaceful world. We are opposed to the use of violent means to resolve differences between nations...[It] deeply regrets that this conflict has taken place and urges both sides to suspend hostilities and engage in genuine efforts to bring about the peaceful resolution of their differences.[64]

Australia accepted, however, that 'there is a substantial body of evidence of Libyan involvement in and direction of international terrorism', including 'apparently compelling evidence' of direct Libyan links with the bombing of the Berlin nightclub.[65] The Australian Government called for Colonel Qaddafi to 'terminate his Government's indiscriminate export of terrorist activity against civilians and civilian targets, especially United States civilians'. Two days later, in comments to President Reagan in Washington, Mr Hawke was even more forthright in his condemnation of Libya but was equally careful not specifically to endorse the American action:

We are at one in our determination to see an end to the scourge of international terrorism and therefore condemn unequivocally Libya's role in directing, exporting and supporting such activities. The Australian Government does not accept that violence, in particular terrorism, is a solution to the complex problems of the world we share. We have referred in the Security Council to a number of possible courses open to the international community to bring about a peaceful resolution of the current situation in the Mediterranean region.[66]

Mr Hawke's final remark referred to a statement made earlier that day by the leader of Australia's delegation to the United Nations. Addressing the Security Council on 17 April, the Permanent Representative said that Australia rejected any attempts to resolve differences between states by violent measures, in particular through terrorism. This was 'a principle which has guided the Australian delegation in its approach to many of the issues which have come before this body'. He said that the Australian delegation regarded the adoption by consensus of a Resolution on measures to prevent terrorism as one of the achievements of the Fortieth General Assembly. Australia deeply regretted that this conflict had taken place and urged both sides to settle their differences peacefully. In words that echoed those of Nigel Bowen nearly fifteen years earlier, the Australian delegate added that his country stood ready:

...to work with the whole membership of this organisation to bring international terrorism to an end. If terrorism cannot be rooted out, the international community faces a dark future of increasing violence. Already, the situation has reached the point where the United States has felt compelled by Libyan actions to regard it as necessary to take military action.[67]

Again recalling earlier Australian statements on terrorist issues the delegate

called for 'mediation, negotiation, conciliation—in short, a peaceful settlement. If we do not make a stand in favour of such peaceful means,
we will be surrendering to an intensifying cycle of violence'.[68] It was a
statement that could have been made as easily under a Liberal/National
Party Coalition Government as under the ALP.

As if to emphasise the Australian Government's complete rejection of
Libya's behaviour, another member of the Australian delegation at the
UN subsequently made a statement to the General Assembly in which he
drew together the various themes pursued by the Australian Government
since the Secretary-General first raised the terrorist issue in the UN more
than fourteen years before. Speaking on 19 November 1986 he noted that,
despite all the efforts made since 1972, terrorist organisations continued
to proliferate and casualties from terrorist attacks continued to mount.
Of particular concern to Australia was the involvement of certain states,
members of the UN, 'which have seen in terrorist tactics or the employment
of terrorist surrogates a means of extending their foreign policy options
beyond the bounds of accepted behaviour'. Such a development was felt
to threaten not only individual lives and liberties but also 'the fabric of
international relations on which depends the security and well-being of
all states'.[69] In particular, Australia was determined that terrorism would
not be exported to the South Pacific, Australia's own region.

Since 1984, Australia's concerns about Libyan activity in the South Pacific
have been focussed primarily on its contacts with radical elements in New
Caledonia and Vanuatu. Colonel Qaddafi has sponsored the travel to Libya
(for unspecified 'training' and indoctrination) of several groups of militants
from the National Kanak Socialist Liberation Front (*Front de Liberation
National Kanak et Socialiste*, or FLNKS). Similar training has been provided
to members of Vanuatu's ruling Vanua'aku Party, and attempts made to
establish a Libyan People's Bureau in Port Vila. There have also been
reports that Libya has been in contact with the Free Papua Movement
(*Organisasi Papua Merdeka,* or OPM), which has as its main aim the
expulsion of Indonesia from Irian Jaya, if necessary by violent means.
Members of Australia's own Aboriginal community have also established
links with the Qaddafi regime. To date, Libya's influence in the region
is slight but it has demonstrated that, with little effort and cost to itself,
it can make considerable mischief and provoke serious concerns on the
part of countries like Australia. In the South Pacific, as elsewhere, care
will need to be taken to ensure that any responses made to Libyan activities
are proportionate to the real threat they pose, and are not self-defeating.
The newly-independent states in the region, for example, are very sensitive
to any suggestion that Australia (or any other country) is in a position
to dictate their foreign policies, and Libya would be quick to exploit any
rifts that may occur.[70]

OTHER POLICY RESPONSES

Although the growing abuse of diplomatic conventions for terrorist purposes was not specifically mentioned by the Australian representative in his November 1986 speech, it is clear from the Government's earlier responses to terrorist violence, both in the UN and other fora, that this particular problem is also a subject of considerable concern to the Australian Government. In 1979 Australia was outspoken in its support for international legal measures to end the hostage crisis in Iran and in April 1984, after WPC Fletcher was murdered by a member of the Libyan People's Bureau in London, Bill Hayden bitterly condemned the Libyan Government for its behaviour, including its abuse of diplomatic privileges. The Foreign Minister has since reiterated Australia's support for efforts by the European Community, Council of Europe and Summit Seven to curb abuses of diplomatic privilege by countries supporting or using terrorism. In November 1986, for example, Mr Hayden welcomed the Declaration and supporting Resolutions agreed upon by the Council of Europe in Strasbourg, which called for greater efforts to counter terrorism involving the abuse of diplomatic and consular privileges and immunities.[71] Commenting the same month on the Syrian Embassy's involvement in the attempted sabotage of an El Al airliner in the United Kingdom, Mr Hayden said:

> The implications of the matter, in terms of both the abuse of diplomatic practice and the callous indifference to the lives of aircraft passengers and crew, can only be condemned.[72]

It was a view endorsed by all members of Parliament in Canberra.

On the related question of a review of the Vienna Convention on Diplomatic Relations, the Australian Government has been much more cautious. In a statement to the House of Representatives after the 1984 Libyan shooting in London, the Foreign Minister said:

> I have noted reports that the British Government may decide to call for a review of the Vienna Convention on diplomatic relations as a result of this episode. If it should do so, Australia would be willing to join in any international consideration of the problems which the shooting incident has revealed so starkly, but no one should underestimate the complexity of the issues and the difficulty in securing international agreement to any significant revision of the Convention.[73]

This remains the Australian position, and is unlikely to change in the foreseeable future. The Government has, for example, recently restated its strong opposition to the introduction of any measures aimed at permitting the inspection of diplomatic bags, counting such action a direct contravention of Article 27 of the Convention. When Kuwait attempted to scan diplomatic bags electronically in 1984, as a precaution against terrorists, Australian diplomatic couriers then in the Middle East were instructed to return home without passing through Kuwaiti Customs. Strong representations were subsequently made to the Kuwaiti Government. It is likely that a similar position would be adopted if the French and Italian Governments went ahead with their proposals to introduce scanning measures. The Australian Government acknowledges that a number of states may abuse the freedom of the diplomatic bag but believes the interests of the international community are best served not by individual countries imposing general restrictions, but by encouraging all governments to respect the provisions of the Vienna Convention.

In this regard, it is worth noting that in recent years there has been a greater assertion by Australia of its rights as a receiving government, particularly as they relate to the administration of the Vienna Conventions. Some of the new measures taken do not bear much relation to security questions, dealing for example with the purchase and sale of motor vehicles, but the increased attention paid to these rights by the Australian Government results directly from the number of terrorist incidents overseas involving the abuse of diplomatic privileges.[74]

Perhaps the most contentious aspect of the Australian Government's foreign policy approach to international terrorism is the question of its relations with groups like the Palestine Liberation Organisation, the African National Congress (ANC) and South West Africa People's Organisation (SWAPO). All three have openly used violence, including at times terrorist tactics, to pursue their wider political objectives. All three also maintain Information Offices in Australia. The Government has been quick to point out that while the Palestine Information Office in Melbourne is operated by a Palestinian obviously sympathetic to the PLO, the Director is an Australian citizen and is not breaking Australian law. Neither he nor the Office itself is in any way accorded official recognition by the Government. Both the ANC and SWAPO Offices were established after permission was granted through the Minister for Foreign Affairs and announced by him in October 1983. As explained by Senator Gareth Evans in September 1986:

> The conditions of operation of those organisations here are that neither the representatives nor their respective offices will enjoy any status, privileges or immunities, that they will not espouse the cause of violence, that they be subject to Australian laws and that the Australian Government will provide no financial assistance to their office or their respective representatives.[75]

The Government accepts that the two organisations have to date abided by the terms of these agreements. While strictly speaking correct in terms of international law and diplomatic behaviour, this position has drawn the criticism from certain conservative political and ethnic groups that the Government has adopted double standards towards terrorist violence.[76]

Depending on developments overseas, some of these accusations may become more difficult to answer. At the moment, however, it would appear that despite some of the rhetoric heard on the issue all four major political parties accept the existence of these Offices in Australia, and senior members of them all have met organisation representatives.

AUSTRALIA'S ANTI-TERRORISM TRADITION

In surveying official Australian statements on the international terrorist problem, it is immediately apparent that there is a remarkable consistency in the approaches taken by the Hawke Government and those taken by earlier Administrations, whether they be Coalition or Labor. At times, the wording of such statements is almost identical from one Government to the next, yet there does not seem to have been any conscious attempt over the longer term to model responses to terrorism—or to particular aspects of the problem—on those of the past. Despite the similarities between them, few of the statements made on these issues by successive Government spokesmen refer directly to precedents set by earlier Administrations. Rather, they have been content simply to cite formulae such as Australia's 'long-standing position of opposition to terrorism' or the fact that Australia had 'consistently affirmed its unequivocal condemnation of terrorism'. This impression is strengthened by the infrequency of major policy statements on international terrorism, and the apparent reliance of the Government on ad hoc responses to particular terrorist incidents in order to inform others of its views on this matter. Since the 1980s there have been certain variations of emphasis or delivery, reflecting developments in the nature and dimensions of international terrorism, and in the global environment generally, but no appreciable departure from the anti-terrorist policies first announced years ago.

The consistency seen in Australian foreign policy responses to terrorism should not be considered unusual, whatever the circumstances in which it may have come about. All Australian political platforms include commitments to broad legal and ethical principles such as the peaceful settlement of disputes, and express support for cooperative measures in institutions like the United Nations. Rhetoric aside, politicians from all parties can be relied upon to take much the same attitude toward certain kinds of political violence and to express strong opposition to terrorism in particular. In addition, there is doubtless some form of institutional memory within the Department of Foreign Affairs and other areas of the Federal Public Service which militates for similar official responses in situations which have certain characteristics in common. These factors could not in themselves, however, account for the remarkable uniformity seen in government statements on this issue since the early 1970s.

The policies adopted by successive Australian Governments towards international terrorism seem to have been consistent largely because they reflect something more fundamental and enduring than any particular party line or official point of view. Responding to demands for national positions on terrorism over the years, Australia's policy makers have been inspired by the same perceived national interests that have always governed Australia's approach to certain international phenomena. Successive Governments have drawn too on the same deep-seated values, and attitudes to indiscriminate violence, which have characterised the Australian community since it first became aware of the terrorist problem. As these attitudes have remained largely unchanged so the Government policies reflecting them have done the same. Should Australians become more directly affected by terrorist violence—either at home or abroad—this situation may change, but unless and until these community values markedly alter, it is unlikely that Australia's foreign policy responses towards international terrorism will do so.

NOTES

1. These have been the Governments of William McMahon (Liberal/Country Party Coalition) March 1971–December 1972, Gough Whitlam (Australian Labor Party) December 1972–November 1975, Malcolm Fraser (L/CP Coalition) December 1975–March 1983, and Bob Hawke (ALP) March 1983–present. See also Chapter 6, note 4.
2. This figure does not include casualties among the terrorists themselves, seven of whom died in the two attacks.
3. 'Statement by the Minister for Foreign Affairs, The Hon. Nigel Bowen, in the General Debate at the United Nations General Assembly on 27 September 1972', Annex 4 of *Report of the Australian Delegation*, Twenty-Seventh Regular Session of the General Assembly of the United Nations (AGPS, Canberra, 1973), pp.43–49.
4. *ibid.*
5. Quoted in E. G. Whitlam, *The Whitlam Government, 1972–1975* (Penguin, Ringwood, 1986), p.168.
6. 'Croatian Terrorism'.
7. During a visit to Yugoslavia in August 1984, Foreign Minister Bill Hayden received a complaint from the Yugoslav Government that Australia was still not doing enough to curb Croatian emigre activities against 'the Yugoslav Communist system'. See B. G. Martin, *International Terrorism: Recent Developments and Implications for Australia*, Current Issues Brief 5 (1985–86), Legislative Research Service, Department of the Parliamentary Library, Canberra, 1986.
8. Cited in 'International Initiatives to Combat Terrorism', Department of Foreign Affairs *Backgrounder* 62 (Week ending 22 October 1976), p.6.
9. 'Terrorism: UN Hijacking Resolution', *Australian Foreign Affairs Record* 48:11 (November 1977), p.585.
10. These include the *Crimes (Aircraft) Act* 1963, *Civil Aviation (Offenders on International Aircraft) Act* 1970, *Crimes (Hijacking of Aircraft) Act* 1972, *Crimes (Protection of Aircraft) Act* 1973 and the *Crimes (Internationally Protected Persons) Act* 1976.

11. 'International Measures to Counter Terrorism', Question Upon Notice, House of Representatives, *Hansard*, 11 April 1978.
12. The Commonwealth Regional Working Group on Terrorism only met once, in Singapore, in February 1979. See *PSR*, p.20.
13. 'Bonn Declaration on Terrorism', Statement by the Prime Minister, Malcolm Fraser, House of Representatives, *Hansard*, 26 September 1978.
14. Australian Labor Party, *Platform, Resolutions and Rules* (ALP, Canberra, 1986), p.132. The clause continues '... and support efforts to achieve binding and universal international agreements which will effectively counter those practices'.
15. 'Australia on Middle East Terrorists' Hit List', Interview with Bill Henderson on Macquarie Network News, 8 January 1986. See also 'The Lingering Nightmare of Flight 847', *The Age*, 14 June 1986.
16. Speaking in Parliament on behalf of the Foreign Minister, Senator Gareth Evans stated that; 'I am told that we have investigated a claim that two Austrians were singled out among the *Achille Lauro* passengers in the belief that they were Australians. The assertion that Australian citizens travelling abroad are in some way at risk is unfounded'. 'Mr Ali Kazak', Question Without Notice, The Senate, *Hansard*, 7 November 1985.
17. Bill Hayden, Interview on Radio 2GB, 8 January 1986; and Press Conference given by Mr Hayden on 9 January 1986 in Ipswich, Queensland.
18. 'Terrorism: Hints For Australian Travellers', Department of Foreign Affairs *Backgrounder* 524 (14 May 1986), p.20.
19. 'Estimates Committee E', Senate, *Hansard*, 23 September 1986.
20. 'Australia's Foreign Policy', Statement by the Minister for Foreign Affairs, Bill Hayden, 26 November 1985.
21. *ibid.*
22. 'Address to the Australian-Lebanese Chamber of Commerce', Address by the Minister for Foreign Affairs in Sydney on 24 October 1985, Minister for Foreign Affairs News Release M176, 24 October 1985.
23. The Nassau Communique, Commonwealth Heads of Government Meeting, Nassau, 22 October 1985.
24. *ibid.*
25. 'Rainbow Warrior', Media Release by the Prime Minister, 18 September 1985.
26. 'International Terrorism', Question Without Notice, House of Representatives, *Hansard*, 6 May 1986.
27. 'Australia's Foreign Policy'.
28. Interview with the Prime Minister on 'The World Today', ABC Radio, 20 June 1985.
29. 'International Terrorism', Minister for Foreign Affairs News Release M111, 28 June 1985.
30. 'United States of America-Iran: Arms Trade', Question Without Notice, House of Representatives, *Hansard*, 26 November 1986. The speaker was the Foreign Minister.
31. 'International Terrorism', News Release M111. See also Media Release by the Prime Minister on 21 June 1985, commenting on the Frankfurt Airport bombing.
32. *Australian Security Intelligence Organisation Report to Parliament 1984-85* (AGPS, Canberra, 1985), p.19.
33. 'Australia's Relations With Libya', Minister for Foreign Affairs News Release M15, 20 January 1986.
34. 'Libya: Economic Sanctions', Question Without Notice, House of Representatives, *Hansard*, 15 April 1986. (The Country Party was renamed the National Party in 1984). See also 'Fighting Terrorism', Statement by the Shadow Foreign Minister, Andrew Peacock, 8 September 1986.
35. Media Release by the Prime Minister, 8 September 1986.
36. ALP *Platform Resolution and Rules*, p.136.

37. 'Address to the Australian-Lebanese Chamber of Commerce'.
38. Nigel Bowen, 'Statement'.
39. 'Provisional Verbatim Record of the 2611th Meeting of the Security Council', UN Document S/PV.2611, 2 October 1985.
40. 'Interception of Libyan Aircraft', Minister for Foreign Affairs News Release M24, 6 February 1986. Both in 1973 and in 1986 the matter was placed before the UN Security Council. Ironically, Australia was a member of the Council on both occasions.
41. Cited in *'Achille Lauro:* Hijack', Question Without Notice, House of Representatives, *Hansard,* 16 October 1985.
42. 'Interception of Aircraft', Question Upon Notice, House of Representatives, *Hansard,* 29 April 1986.
43. 'Raid on Entebbe Airport', Question Without Notice, The Senate, *Hansard,* 18 August 1976.
44. See G. M. L. Harrison, 'Terrorism and International Law', Paper prepared for a seminar on international law at Monash University, Melbourne, 17–18 May 1986.
45. 'International Terrorism', *Hansard.*
46. *ibid.*
47. 'United Nations Action on Terrorism', Department of Foreign Affairs *Backgrounder* 507 (15 January 1986), p.1.
48. *ibid.*
49. 'Protocol Additional to the Geneva Convention of 12 August 1949, and relating to the protection of victims of international armed conflict'(Protocol I), *United Nations Juridical Yearbook, 1977* (United Nations, New York, 1979), pp.95–142. Protocol II related to the protection of victims of non-international armed conflicts. The 1949 Conventions had not applied to unconventional conflicts at all.
50. For an exposition of the Reagan Administration's view, see Sofaer, 'Terrorism and the Law', p.912 *et seq.* By 1986, 55 states were party to Protocol I.
51. 'Note by the President of the Security Council', UN Document S/17554, 9 October 1985.
52. 'Security Council Condemnation of Hostage-Taking', Minister for Foreign Affairs News Release M210, 19 December 1985.
53. The Nassau Communique.
54. ICAO Council Minutes, Session 115/Meeting 14, 3 July 1985.
55. Nigel Bowen, 'Statement'.
56. 'Address to the Australian-Lebanese Chamber of Commerce'.
57. 'Human Rights: Vision and Reality', Address by the Minister for Foreign Affairs, News Release M69, 2 May 1986.
58. *Canberra Times,* 22 May 1986.
59. Interview on Radio 2GB, 8 January 1986.
60. 'Australia's Relations With Libya'.
61. Bill Hayden, 'Libya: Australia's Response to American Initiatives', ABC Radio 'AM', 10 January 1986.
62. 'Military Action Against Libya', Statement by the Prime Minister, House of Representatives, *Hansard,* 15 April 1986.
63. 'Australia's Relations With Libya'.
64. 'Military Action Against Libya'.
65. *ibid.*
66. White House Statement by the Prime Minister, 17 April 1986, (AAP transcript).
67. 'Security Council: Libya/United States', Department of Foreign Affairs News Release D11, 17 April 1986.
68. *ibid.*

69. 'UNGA 41: Item 142. Statement on Terrorism Delivered by Mr M. Potts on Behalf of Australia, 19 November 1986'. Department of Foreign Affairs *Backgrounder* 552, 26 November 1986, Annex A1.
70. See Chapter 6, note 48.
71. 'Australia Supports Anti-Terrorism Declaration', Minister for Foreign Affairs News Release M184, 21 November 1986.
72. 'Implications of the Hendawi Trial', Minister for Foreign Affairs News Release M177, 13 November 1986.
73. 'Libyan People's Bureau in London', Question Without Notice, House of Representatives, *Hansard*, 3 May 1984.
74. Letter from the Acting Assistant Secretary, Security and Communications Branch, Department of Foreign Affairs, 23 December 1986, in response to Freedom of Information request F86070 of 11 November 1986.
75. 'South West Africa People's Organisation and African National Congress: Information Offices', Question Without Notice, Senate, *Hansard*, 18 September 1986.
76. In a characteristic outburst on 9 September 1986 the Premier of Queensland accused Prime Minister Hawke of providing 'a real haven' for terrorists 'completely protected and fostered by the Federal Government'. See, for example, *The Age*, 10 September 1986.

8

THE THREAT TO AUSTRALIAN DIPLOMATS AND DIPLOMATIC FACILITIES ABROAD

Obviously the Department wishes to, and will, do all it reasonably can to enhance the safety of staff through a combination of improved physical security measures and, at least as important, staff awareness of risks and security precautions. But it must also be acknowledged that it is not possible to provide an absolute guarantee concerning the safety of officers and their families overseas.

'Contingency Planning'
Department of Foreign Affairs Administrative Circular (9 May 1985)

The diplomatic profession has always enjoyed a rather mixed reputation among members of the Australian public. On the one hand, diplomats seem to be widely admired for their apparently arcane skills and envied for their rather privileged and exotic lifestyle. Also, rightly or wrongly, the diplomatic profession still commands a high status in the community. At the same time, however, diplomacy has long suffered in Australia from a public image of luxury and privileged ease enjoyed by public servants at the taxpayers' expense. Consideration seems rarely given to the discomfort and dangers often faced by diplomats and their families abroad. This image is slowly changing as more and more reports appear concerning terrorist attacks against diplomats and diplomatic facilities, but many politicians and members of the news media in Australia still seem to find it more rewarding to perpetuate the myths and popular misconceptions of the Foreign Service than to present a more balanced and accurate view. This has added to the problems faced by those who wish to see increased protection for diplomats and their families, and a better understanding of the difficulties they sometimes face.

While successive Australian Governments have made considerable efforts over the past 15 years to establish the legal and administrative machinery felt necessary to protect diplomats and diplomatic facilities in Australia, and to respond to a terrorist incident in the country should one occur, much less attention has been given to the protection of Australia's own officials and official premises abroad. This difference in approach seems, in large part, to reflect an assessment that Australian diplomats and their families, and Australian diplomatic facilities, are not high priority targets for international terrorist groups. Australia is not a major power and, while a member of the Western Alliance, has tended to take an independent and somewhat cautious attitude towards many of the contentious issues that have attracted most attention from international terrorists. Yet Australian officials and their families have already encountered terrorist and other violence on overseas assignments and, as Australia adopts a higher profile in international affairs, there can be little doubt that sooner or later they will become more directly affected by the global terrorist problem.

AUSTRALIAN DIPLOMACY AND ITS DANGERS

Judged by the usual criteria of population, economy and military strength, Australia is not a large country nor a major power, yet it is widely represented overseas at an official level, both by diplomatic missions accredited to particular countries and by representatives formally attached to major international organisations such as the United Nations and OECD. In 1975, Australia maintained 81 such posts overseas. Ten years later there were 101 diplomatic and consular posts in 79 countries. Australia's representatives were also accredited on a non-resident basis to a further 60 countries.[1] These missions were staffed by 1361 Australians, from 23 Federal Government departments and statutory bodies, including (besides the Department of Foreign Affairs) the Departments of Trade and Resources, Defence, Immigration and Ethnic Affairs, the Australian Development Assistance Bureau and Australian Information Service.[2] A little more than 50 per cent of all official personnel abroad, or 778 staff members, were members of the Department of Foreign Affairs and included about 275 Foreign Affairs Officers (ie political officers or professional diplomats). There were also more than 2000 locally-engaged staff employed at Australian missions around the world.[3]

Despite its popular image in Australia, diplomacy has never been without risks for these officials and their families. Questioned in Parliament by the Leader of the Opposition in 1971 and 1972, for example, the then Minister for Foreign Affairs revealed that there had been a number of assaults against Australian diplomatic staff in the ten years since 1961.[4] In March 1983, less than one month after taking office, Foreign Minister Bill Hayden called for a report from his Department on the safety of Australian diplomatic personnel and their families abroad. When the report was provided the Minister was reportedly 'stunned' at the high incidence of violent attacks upon them.[5] The 19 page report listed more than 250 incidents over the previous five years in 61 of the 85 cities in which Australia then maintained resident diplomatic or consular posts.[6] Statistics later obtained from the Department of Foreign Affairs under the *Freedom of Information Act* show that between 1 January 1980 and 30 June 1984 there were 63 confirmed cases of assault (including a number with firearms) and 84 cases where threats were made (including 29 bomb threats).[7] In his comprehensive *Review of Australia's Overseas Representation*, published in late 1986, the Secretary of the Foreign Affairs Department listed a further 115 incidents between September 1984 and March 1986 which directly involved or threatened Australian personnel and their families.[8]

A number of these incidents appear to have been motivated by political considerations. In March 1964, at the height of the Confrontation with Indonesia, the Singapore Office of the Australian High Commission in Malaysia was badly damaged by a bomb planted outside its main entrance, on the second floor of the Hongkong and Shanghai Bank building. Although no staff of the mission were seriously injured in the explosion there were 35 casualties, including the deaths of three Singaporeans working in the banking chamber on the floor below. The Singapore Government later executed two Indonesian commandos for their part in the attack.[9] During the Vietnam War Australian diplomatic property was damaged during military operations in the Saigon area and there have been several reports of official vehicles and premises in other countries being damaged during violent demonstrations against Australia. While there is often no way of knowing, political motives could have been behind some of the bomb threats received by Australian missions in recent years.

Few, if any, of the attacks or threats recorded against Australian diplomats and diplomatic facilities appear to have been at the hands of terrorists although some, like the fake bomb left outside the Australian Embassy in Copenhagen in October 1980 by the 'Socialist Freedom Front', or the suspected parcel bomb received by the High Commission in New Delhi in October 1986, no doubt gave cause for concern at the time. Three members of the Ananda Marga sect were arrested in Bangkok in April 1978 and charged with planning to bomb the Australian Embassy and Ambassador's guest house. The attack was allegedly planned as a protest against the Australian Government's 1977 ban on entry to the country of sect members not of Australian citizenship. Although all three admitted to carrying explosives and pleaded guilty to the charges, they were released from gaol after six months. This suggests at least that the episode was not taken very seriously. Tom Molomby has claimed that:

> even Australian diplomatic representatives in Thailand, according to US diplomatic cables obtained under the Freedom of Information Act, did not believe the allegation that the three intended to bomb the Australian embassy.[10]

When questioned about the subject generally in May 1985, a spokesman for the Department of Foreign Affairs stated categorically that:

Our records do not indicate any politically motivated violence against officers and their families from international terrorist groups.[11]

This is not to say, however, that Australian officials and Australian premises have not encountered terrorist violence in other ways or that they are immune to such attacks in the future.

As international terrorist attacks against diplomatic targets increase in scope and frequency, so too will the chances of Australian officials and their families becoming incidental victims. This nearly occurred in October 1984, for example, when IRA terrorists exploded a bomb in the Grand Hotel in Brighton in an attempt to assassinate British Prime Minister Margaret Thatcher and her Cabinet. The Australian High Commissioner to the United Kingdom, Alfred Parsons, was staying in the same hotel at the time and was lucky to escape with only shock and minor injuries. In April 1985 the Australian Embassy in Lisbon was damaged by a bomb attack on the nearby premises of Air France. Fortunately, no Embassy staff were in the mission at the time. The bombing was later claimed by the French terrorist group *Action Directe*. When a missile bomb was fired at the Japanese Embassy in Jakarta the following month the projectile narrowly missed the Australian Embassy situated next door. The incident was part of a coordinated series of bomb attacks on diplomatic missions in the Indonesian capital, probably carried out by Japanese URA terrorists. Similar concerns regarding the safety of Australian officials were felt in December 1985 when a series of bombings occurred in New Caledonia, one close to the Australian Consulate-General in Noumea.[12] While strictly speaking not a terrorist attack in the sense that such incidents have been considered here, nor an attack specifically directed against an Australian, it is also worth recording that the First Secretary of the Australian Embassy in Cairo was shot and critically wounded during the assassination of President Anwar Sadat in October 1981.

There are other ways in which Australian officials and their families can become the incidental victims of terrorist attacks. There is always the possibility of an Australian diplomat or diplomatic facility being seized by a terrorist group, not specifically because they were Australian but simply as instruments in a wider competition. Such seizures can apply pressure on the receiving government and other governments, and need not have any direct connection with the particular dispute being addressed. Saudi Arabia, for example, was not a direct party to any dispute when Black September terrorists seized the Saudi Embassy in Khartoum in 1973. The kidnapping and murder of the West German Ambassador in Guatemala in 1970 was not aimed at the FRG but at the Guatemalan Government.

Often Australian diplomatic missions and residences are situated near those of other, more threatened countries, and Australians may be mistaken for other nationalities more at risk. The terrorist tactic of seizing official premises during social functions for the local diplomatic community, as occurred in Bogota in 1980, raises the possibility of Australian officials and their spouses inadvertently being caught in the net and held hostage. Such gatherings can also invite bomb attacks, as suggested by the number of bomb threats received by host missions in recent years.

Nor can attacks directly against Australians be ruled out. After the murder of the Turkish Consul-General in Sydney in 1980 British police reportedly warned members of the Australian High Commission in London that they could also be targets for Armenian terrorists.[13] More recently, the spokesmen of a number of Arab organisations have warned that Australians overseas may become terrorist targets because of the identification of Australia with the United States and widespread perceptions that Australia supports some of Israel's more controversial policies. In October 1985, for example, the unofficial PLO representative in Australia stated that the Prime Minister's alleged personal sympathies for Israel exposed Australians abroad to the risk of attack by Palestinian terrorists.[14] Similar fears were expressed in October 1986 when the Hawke Government agreed formally to protect Britain's interests in Syria, after London broke off relations with Damascus for its terrorist activities.[15] If Australia was to play a more active role in international affairs it may attract greater attention from terrorist groups. Australia's election to the United Nations Security Council on 1 January 1985 (for two years) placed it at the centre of many of the world's most volatile political, economic and social issues. As demonstrated by Libya's strong reaction to the Australian statement to the Council after the American bombing raids in April 1986, even the most carefully considered and balanced position can offend certain governments. As Grant Wardlaw has observed:

> The reality is that expressing a view on any significant matter now subjects a government to potential violence.[16]

The most obvious, and often most accessible, symbols of the Australian Government and its policies are its diplomats and diplomatic facilities.

In addition, it is always possible that, as extremist ethnic and emigre groups within Australia come to realise that attacks on the representatives of particular governments in the country are unlikely to have the desired effects, they may turn their attention more to Australian targets as a way of achieving their objectives by more indirect means. Already Croatian terrorists have attempted operations against Australian population centres as a means of bringing official pressure to bear on the Yugoslav Government and on more than one occasion terrorist groups in Europe have used such methods to try and persuade one state to break off diplomatic relations with another.[17] Should the Australian security authorities participate in certain actions against international terrorists or their state sponsors (as did Britain in April 1986), or succeed in capturing an international terrorist, then all Australian officials, their families and official premises abroad would immediately fall under a greater threat. In circumstances such as these other terrorists (or states) have been quick to seek revenge or a bargaining position from which to negotiate the prisoner's release. The seizure of the FRG Consulate in Chicago by HRB terrorists in 1978, for example, was designed to give Croatian extremists a position from which to bargain with the West German Government for the release of six Croats held in FRG prisons, and sought by the Yugoslav Government for trial in Belgrade. There are other possible scenarios.

It is easy to exaggerate these risks and obviously some can never be eliminated, or even reduced, without the essential functions of Australian diplomatic and consular posts being seriously impaired. Yet the threat is real and the potential for a sudden increase in the dangers faced by Australian officials overseas is always present. Receiving states are bound to provide adequate protection for Australian diplomatic personnel and premises, but the Australian government also carries a responsibility to protect its officials abroad. As Mr Justice Hope has said, the Commonwealth is under an obligation to:

> ensure that the service of these people on its behalf does not expose them to excessive or avoidable personal danger. Those personal dangers range from being taken hostage by terrorists to being attacked over the counter by irate clients or armed robbers.[18]

Responsibility for the protection of Australian officials and their families, and Australian diplomatic facilities overseas, lies initially with the Department of Foreign Affairs under its Secretary and, ultimately, through the Foreign Minister to the Prime Minister and Cabinet.

PROTECTIVE SECURITY MEASURES

According to its Secretary and numerous official publications, the Department of Foreign Affairs takes its responsibilities for the protection of Australian diplomats and diplomatic facilities very seriously.[19] It has claimed, for example, that it is 'committed to providing security for its missions and personnel abroad' and is constantly developing measures for their safety through the use of advanced alarm and surveillance systems, physical shields, access controls, security lighting and guard services.[20] Emergency radios and 'safe havens' have been provided for Chanceries and staff residences in many countries and officers at a number of high risk posts have access to specially armoured vehicles. Detailed contingency plans have been drawn up for use in the event of a terrorist attack. The Department recognises that there can never be absolute protection against a determined and imaginative terrorist attack, but believes that 'a terrorist is usually deterred by visible and credible security measures'.[21] Indeed, the Department of Foreign Affairs' entire protective security policy is 'largely based on this premise, and on the consequent need to design and install security measures appropriate in a given situation'.[22]

The picture painted by these official statements, however, can be misleading. In 1985 the Department wrote that:

> the Government's commitment to provide security for its missions and personnel abroad was reflected in the level of funds allocated for these purposes'.[23]

The Department's definition of 'security' is necessarily very broad and its annual security allocations also reflect perceived threats to Australians and Australian interests from espionage and purely criminal activity. Yet if these allocations are taken as a general guide to the importance the Government places on this aspect of its operations since the terrorist threat to diplomats and diplomatic facilities reached serious proportions, there is cause for concern. There is little reason to doubt that the Minister and Department of Foreign Affairs place a high priority on the protection of Australian officials and their families overseas, but it is difficult to see how the funds allocated to the Department for protective security in recent years permits the kinds of ambitious programs mentioned in its Annual Reports.

Between the 1980–81 and 1984–85 financial years the allocations given by Australian Parliament to the Department of Foreign Affairs for protective security increased some five-fold, but started from such a low base that the amount in 1984–85 still only amounted to about A\$3 million.[24] According to the Department's *Annual Report 1983–84* this was less than half the sum requested by the Department in its draft estimates for that financial year[25]. When it is remembered that this last allocation had also to include commitments formerly paid for from another area of the federal budget, the sum available to the Department for protective security in 1984–85 was further reduced to some \$A2.6 million. This was about \$A300 000 *less* than was allocated to the same area of official expenditure in 1983–84, and this in purely numerical terms only. The Department fared little better in the years that followed. In the 1985–86 financial year it received some \$A4.4 million for protective security, almost \$A2 million less than was originally sought. In 1986–87 the Department asked for \$A4.5 million and received \$A4.9 million, but this appropriation included over \$A900 000 to cover a number of items formerly administered by the Department of Local Government and Administrative Services, such as annual Chancery guarding contracts and the periodic costs of maintaining security equipment.[26]

Given the level of inflation over the past seven years, the falling value of the Australian dollar and the high cost of providing security at Australia's many diplomatic and consular posts abroad, the allocations made by Parliament to date must be considered very small. They may be sufficient to cope with the current low level of threat faced by Australian diplomats and diplomatic facilities overseas, but they are scarcely adequate to provide improved protection over the longer term, either as a precaution against a suddenly increased threat to 'Australians, or simply as a prudent measure in the face of a growing global problem. The Foreign Affairs Association (FAA), which represents many members of the Foreign Affairs Department, concedes that greater resources have been allocated to this field in recent years but believes 'an enormous amount remains to be done'. As expressed by the President of the FAA in December 1986:

> While, clearly, the allocation of scarce resources to providing extensive protection against what is currently judged a relatively low level of threat might invite criticism, there remains a strong possibility that, sooner or later, Australian officials and their families may fall victims to terrorist acts of violence and that, only belatedly, will measures be designed to cope with such incidents.[27]

In such a situation, considerable weight rests on the agencies responsible for assessing the level of threat to Australian interests abroad, and forewarning missions of any likely terrorist action.

Since its formation in April 1986, the task of compiling assessments of the threat from politically motivated violence faced by individual posts has fallen to the Department's Counter Terrorism Policy Section. The Section draws on information and comments from a wide variety of sources, both in Australia and overseas.[28] These assessments are then used by the Security and Communications Branch as the basis for its annual protective security programs. Yet here too problems remain. Since 1984-85 the bulk of the Department's protective security expenditure has been spent on improvements to Chancery premises (including the fitting out of new Chanceries). Most attention has been paid to the security of Australia's 19 (now 18) missions in the Americas, and 24 missions in Europe. In 1985-86 posts in these two regions accounted for more than half the Department's protective security expenditure for the year, followed by the Middle East where until 1986 Australia maintained 12 posts.[29] Curiously, only one per cent of the available funds was spent on Australia's South Asian posts, despite the increased levels of domestic terrorism in that region. These spending patterns, however, must be considered carefully. It is possible, for example, that expenditure levels in some areas are low because major security programs prior to 1984-85 now make further measures unnecessary. A high level of spending at a particular post or in a particular region could follow an increased threat from crime or espionage, and bear little relation to the threat from terrorism. Yet the emphasis on Chancery security in all regions suggests that highest priority is still given to the protection of official facilities, with all their sensitive documents and equipment, rather than to staff residences, which in the event of an increased terrorist threat would be most vulnerable. This may be in keeping with other national security requirements and alliance commitments, but cannot be the source of much comfort to mission staff and their families.

As the terrorist problem has become more serious in recent years so the Department of Foreign Affairs has paid greater attention to the provision of training courses and security briefings for officers and their families, usually before their departure from Australia. For obvious reasons these courses are not as lengthy or elaborate as those given by the governments of more threatened Foreign Services, but are designed primarily 'to familiarise [officers] with the terrorist problem and to help them minimise the risks to themselves and their families in the event that they should become involved in an incident'.[30] Prospective Foreign Affairs Trainees are warned of the dangers of overseas service and after their admission to the Department recruits are given a short introductory briefing on the terrorist threat to diplomats and diplomatic facilities. The Department periodically offers full courses on 'Coping With Terrorism' which last a whole day, but more often shorter, half-day briefing sessions are included in other regular training programs such as Overseas Familiarisation Courses or Head of Mission Courses. These sessions have taken several forms but usually include a film, briefings by and discussions with scholars and officials with particular expertise in the fields of counter-terrorism and post-incident management. They are also complemented by more detailed security briefings by post security officers on arrival at the overseas mission. As a matter of policy, the Department of Foreign Affairs does not instruct its staff in the use of firearms or other protective devices, such as mace sprays. Emphasis is placed instead on the need for common sense and an enhanced awareness of security threats.

In looking at the security and conditions of its officers overseas, the Department has also been conscious of the need to cater for the needs of officers' families. As pointed out to a British Parliamentary Inquiry by the UK Diplomatic Service Wives Association in May 1986:

> the wife and family of serving officers remain very visible and unprotected in their pursuance of a quasi-normal existence in a high or medium risk post. While husbands work inside a secure Mission and perhaps have the use of an armoured vehicle their families have to manage and carry out household, school and social activities in a hostile environment. The implied psychological strain of coping with such a situation puts a great burden on the family with the result that the wife and children may not accompany the Diplomatic Service officer to post.[31]

In the Australian context, the members of the Foreign Affairs Womens Association have registered many of the same concerns with the Department of Foreign Affairs and taken an active interest in measures implemented to protect officials and their families overseas. Members of the Diplomatic Security Section have been invited to address FAWA meetings and, with the help of the Department's Family Liaison Officer, spouses have been kept informed of developments in this field. The partners of officers going overseas on posting are now invited to attend those parts of Departmental training courses in which the terrorist problem is discussed.

As do most other Foreign Services, the Australian Department of Foreign Affairs faces a continual problem in striking the right balance between educating its members about the terrorist threat and making them sensitive to security requirements overseas, while at the same time not over-reacting and instilling exaggerated fears in its personnel and their families which could prove counter-productive. In the absence of a tangible threat, particularly one directed at Australia or Australians, there is still a natural tendency for officials and their families overseas to relax and feel that they cannot become terrorist victims, or even be involved in a terrorist incident. This poses a number of dangers, one being that a post will be ill-prepared to cope with any attack that may take place.

DEPARTMENTAL RESPONSE MECHANISMS

Should a terrorist attack be made against an Australian diplomatic facility overseas, or should Australian lives and interests abroad in other ways be affected by terrorist action, primary responsibility would lie with the Foreign Minister. In consultation with the Prime Minister, the Minister would usually handle the incident through the Foreign Affairs Departmental Emergency Task Force (DETF). Chaired by the Senior Assistant Secretary of the Department's Corporate Management Division, the DETF 'is designed to provide a central 'contact point' within the Department of Foreign Affairs for overseas posts in the event of an emergency and to meet problems including those arising from terrorist attacks'.[32] Following a reorganisation in late 1985, it consists of three groups, the Core Group, Policy/Action Group and Support Group. The first includes the DETF Chairman, representatives of the appropriate geographical Branch (or Branches) and the Security and Communications Branch. They are supported by the Policy/Action Group consisting, as required, of members of the Executive, Public Affairs, Consular and Personnel Branches. The Support Group draws on the resources of the Department's Communications, Technical and Management areas, again as the need arises. Members of other government departments, such as Prime Minister and Cabinet, Immigration and Ethnic Affairs and Defence may be attached to the DETF in circumstances where specialist expertise is required or other official interests are directly involved. Where events are moving very quickly, these formal divisions may be blurred to permit a more flexible and responsive structure.

As the situation dictates, the Core Group may establish itself in the Department's Crisis Centre, from where it can more easily draw on the specialised expertise of the other Groups and maintain communications with all posts which may become involved in the emergency. Under the broad guidance of a DETF 'Leader' of Deputy Secretary rank the Core Group would pass information to, and seek advice from, senior Departmental staff and the Minister. The Core Group would also consider such questions as the need for contacts with any local representatives of the host government and links with the missions of friendly governments represented in the country of the incident. The Head of the Protective Services Coordination Centre, as Chairman of the SIDC-PAV, would usually be kept closely informed of developments and, in the event of a major incident involving the portfolios of other Ministers, the national Crisis Policy Centre in Canberra may be activated.[33] In certain circumstances a special interdepartmental task force may be formed for the duration of the emergency.

In the event of a terrorist incident overseas involving its diplomats or diplomatic facilities, Australia's first response would most likely be an immediate request for the host government to assume its responsibilities as the receiving state and take all appropriate steps to ensure the protection of Australia's officials and official premises. In the event of an abduction or the seizure of a mission the host government would also be requested, if necessary, to effect the safe release of any Australians being held by the terrorists. In normal circumstances any communications between Australia's representatives and the terrorists would take place through the host government, but in certain cases there may be a need to make direct contact with the terrorists themselves. In any event, close consultations between the Australian Government and the host government would be sought in all aspects of the incident. The primary channel of communication between the DETF in Canberra and the local authorities would normally be the Australian Head of Mission on the scene. One of the mission staff would be appointed media liaison officer to respond, in consultation with the DETF in Canberra, to local media enquiries. Press enquiries in Australia would be managed in the normal way, through the Department's Public Affairs Branch and Official Spokesman. In certain special circumstances consideration may be given to the despatch of an officer from Canberra or a nearby post to assist in the resolution of the incident.[34] This would occur, for example, if an Australian mission was seized by terrorists and all its staff held hostage.

The Departmental Emergency Task Force is not only activated in response to a terrorist incident involving Australian diplomats and diplomatic facilities. Australian missions also have a responsibility to protect Australian citizens abroad and are likely quickly to become involved in, for example, the hijacking of an aircraft with Australian passengers aboard. In such circumstances the mission is responsible for keeping the DETF, and through it the Government and the public, informed of developments. During the hijacking of Egypt Air Flight 648 to Valetta, for example, the Australian High Commission in Malta kept in close contact with the DETF in Canberra, and performed an important liaison role with Maltese authorities at Valetta Airport. The mission's Consular Officer subsequently went to considerable lengths to assist the one Australian passenger who survived the seizure and the costly Egyptian rescue attempt. Similar assistance was given to the Australian family released from TWA Flight 847 in Algiers in June 1985 and the Department's consular staff were closely involved in the aftermath of the Frankfurt Airport bombing the same month, when two young Australian children were killed.[35] The Department's Consular Training Courses now include a half-day session on post-incident trauma to assist officers in carrying out these difficult duties.

When he was Prime Minister, Malcolm Fraser revealed that contingency plans had been drawn up for any 'international terrorist incident which might occur... in another country affecting Australian lives and interests'.[36] He did not make clear what the nature or scope of these plans were but it can be assumed that they followed the same general policy guidelines laid down in 1978 emphasising the Government's refusal to make significant concessions to terrorist demands. Just what would follow from such an approach is not clear. The Department of Foreign Affairs places primary responsibility for the resolution of a prolonged terrorist incident on the host government, citing the Vienna Convention and New York Convention, among other international legal instruments. There is, however, another alternative. In his statement to Parliament on the Holdich Review in October 1986, Special Minister of State Michael Young said that:

> There may be terrorist incidents arising overseas in which Australian interests would be heavily involved and in which Australia could be called upon to assist. The Government is examining the complex issues raised by such situations.[37]

In principle, such assistance could range from an offer of advice and equipment to the deployment of the SASR Tactical Assault Group (TAG). The TAG could be used, for example, to rescue Australian diplomatic staff held hostage inside one of their own missions, in a regional country which lacked the necessary means to mount such an assault. As the Minister pointed out, however, the political, legal, administrative and other issues raised by such questions are indeed extremely complex and even if they could somehow be resolved much would depend on the circumstances at the time.

Until May 1985, when a classified Administrative Circular on contingency planning arrangements was sent by the Department of Foreign Affairs to all its posts, few members of the Department or other Australian officials assigned overseas seem to have been told that the Government had formally adopted a 'hard line' policy of refusing to make significant concessions to terrorists.[38] Even then, there was a notable reluctance to inform officers' families of the policy. In June that year, when the President of the Foreign Affairs Womens Association sought details of the Department's approach to terrorist incidents, she was told that there was a policy but that she could not be informed what it was. While no doubt prompted by genuine security considerations at the time, this response was, naturally enough, one which she and other wives considered completely unsatisfactory.[39] Their concerns were heightened by the fact that under the arrangements then in force, no government compensation was payable in the event of an officer's spouse or children being killed or injured by terrorists during an overseas posting. Since Mr Young's statement to Parliament on 17 October 1986, however, any official reluctance to discuss the Government's 'no concessions' policy has disappeared.

CONDITIONS OF SERVICE

The reaction of Australia's diplomats and their families to the 'hard line' approach favoured by their Government can only be guessed at, but already there has been considerable concern expressed by staff associations and other groups like FAWA over the deteriorating security environment overseas. The customary reticence of public servants in general, and Foreign Affairs officers in particular, makes it difficult to gauge their true feelings on such matters, however, and the picture has once again been distorted by sensationalist reports in the news media. It may be true, for example, that Lima is now 'one of the world's most dangerous capitals for diplomats' but, despite reports in the press, the Australian Embassy there was not closed in 1986 because of the city's security problems. The measure was prompted very largely by budgetry considerations, as was the closure of a number of other Australian posts (in less dangerous areas) that year.[40] While there is no apparent danger from terrorism in Papua New Guinea, lack of security has also been cited (probably with greater justification) for the reluctance of many married officers to accept postings to Port Moresby. There has been little evidence to date of officers refusing to accept postings abroad because of the threat of terrorism *per se*, but it is clearly a factor which is increasingly weighing on their minds. This concern has been strengthened in recent years by changing conditions of service and the perceived inadequacy of compensation provisions for officers and their families injured or killed during the course of an overseas assignment.[41]

In October 1981, after an Australian diplomat was shot and seriously wounded in Cairo, colleagues were reported to have described compensation provisions for Australian officials and their families as 'grossly inadequate'.[42] Apart from special *ex gratia* payments the only compensation was that provided by the *Compensation (Commonwealth Government Employees) Act*. Under this law the maximum benefit was A$52 980, payable only to employees of the Government. Family members were excluded and officers were only entitled to compensation when they were formally on duty. At the prompting of staff associations, in particular the FAA, this matter was subsequently taken up by the Department of Foreign Affairs, with the aim of introducing a new compensation scheme that took account of the special hazards encountered by officers and their families overseas. With the support of the Minister, a proposal was formulated and put to Federal Cabinet. In 1984 the matter was referred in turn to a committee of officials which, inexplicably, did not include a representative from the Foreign Affairs Department. Foreign Minister Bill Hayden successfully pressed for the inclusion of his department on the committee, and expressed concern for the safety of his officers and their families. Finally, in June 1986, Federal Cabinet instituted a special scheme which addressed a number of major inadequacies that had been seen in the existing Act. For the first time, members of officers' families (including de facto spouses) became eligible for compensation in the event of injury or death on overseas postings and coverage was extended to 24 hours a day. Injuries incurred as a result of terrorist actions were specifically covered by the new provisions.[43] To the disappointment of both the Department and staff associations, however, the maximum benefit payable under the scheme remained at the same level as for service in Australia. According to the FAA President:

> Staff often feel, unfortunately, that a sensible level of compensation will only emerge when legal action is taken following a specific incident.[44]

Negotiations are continuing but even with the support of the Minister some major bureaucratic obstacles still remain.

There are many factors militating against the early resolution of these and other difficulties faced by those responsible for protecting Australian diplomats and diplomatic facilities abroad. One of the strongest is the apparent remoteness of a terrorist threat. There is thus no political or bureaucratic imperative impelling a speedy and sympathetic consideration of the problems involved. Also, as Mr Justice Hope noted in 1979, 'protective security has an image problem because it appears to be negative and unproductive'.[45] The problem is further exacerbated by the relative lack of scholarly interest in terrorist studies in Australia. With some notable exceptions, the field has been left largely to journalists and commentators whose treatment of the terrorist threat to Australia and Australians has been characterised more by sensationalism and factual inaccuracies than any sober consideration of the issues. Add to this the widespread suspicion in Australia regarding the lifestyle of diplomats and the activities of the security and intelligence agencies responsible for threat assessments and the result is an inertia and lack of resources which appear likely to be dissolved only by a serious terrorist incident directly affecting Australian interests.

NOTES

1. There were 22 posts in Asia, 11 in the Pacific, 20 in Africa and the Middle East, 29 in Europe, 8 in Central and South America and 8 in North America. *Department of Foreign Affairs Annual Report 1985–86* (AGPS, Canberra, 1986), p.7.
2. 'Profile of Australia's Overseas Representation', draft report obtained from the Department of Foreign Affairs under Freedom of Information request F85026 of 8 July 1985.
3. 'Profile of Australia's Overseas Representation'. See also Laurie Oakes, 'Foreign Affairs' staff servants to everyone', *The Bulletin*, 9 July 1985, pp.42–46.
4. 'Diplomatic Missions: Incidents' and 'Attacks on Australian Properties or Representatives'.
5. 'Diplomats face high risk, says Hayden' and 'Dangers of diplomacy', *The Age*, 25 March 1983.
6. 'Schedule of Incidents Involving Australian Officials Abroad: 1978 to date', obtained under Freedom of Information request F 86070 of 11 November 1986. See also FAWA *Newsletter* 48 (December 1983), p.1. FAWA is the Foreign Affairs Womens (formerly Wives) Association.
7. Statistics provided by the Department of Foreign Affairs under Freedom of Information request F85026 of 15 April 1985.
8. *Review of Australia's Overseas Representation* (AGPS, Canberra, 1986), pp.272–275.
9. I am indebted to David Rutter for drawing my attention to this incident. The Australian Embassy in Jakarta at the time escaped serious threat, despite its high profile as friend and, at times, protector of the beleaguered British mission.
10. Molomby, p.33.
11. Letter to the author from the Assistant Secretary, Security and Communications Branch, Department of Foreign Affairs, in reply to Freedom of Information request F85026 of 15 April 1985.
12. 'Security alert for our Noumea envoy', *Herald*, 3 December 1985.
13. 'Our Envoys Get Warning', *Herald*, 18 December 1980.
14. 'Australia Next On PLO Hit List', *Sunday Telegraph*, 13 October 1985. See also 'Mid-East Policy Puts Australians in Danger, Arab Leaders Warn,' *The Age*, 22 January 1986.
15. Under the arrangement agreed between the Australian and UK Governments, a British interests section was established in the Australian Embassy in Damascus. The Australian Ambassador acts on Britain's behalf in making formal representations to the Syrian Government.
16. Grant Wardlaw, 'The Terrorist Threat to Australia and the Region', Paper prepared for a seminar on 'International Terrorism and the Australian Experience', sponsored by the Australian Institute of Jewish Affairs and the Institute for Studies in International Terrorism, State University of New York, Melbourne, 8–9 June 1986.

17. In February 1980 six Croatians were convicted in Sydney of plotting to bomb (among other targets) the city's water supply.

18. *PSR*, p.181.

19. Letter to the author from the Secretary of the Department of Foreign Affairs, 28 October 1986.

20. *Department of Foreign Affairs Annual Report 1982* (AGPS, Canberra, 1983), p.88 and *Department of Foreign Affairs Annual Report 1983-84* (AGPS, Canberra, 1984), p.42.

21. 'Off the champagne trail: Diplomatic security abroad', *Australian Foreign Affairs Record* 54:5 (May 1983), p.168.

22. *ibid.*

23. *Department of Foreign Affairs Annual Report, 1984-85* (AGPS, Canberra, 1985), p.64.

24. Statistics provided by the Department of Foreign Affairs under Freedom of Information request F85026 of 15 April 1985.

25. *Department of Foreign Affairs Annual Report 1983-84*, p.42.

26. Details provided by the Department of Foreign Affairs under Freedom of Information request F86070 of 11 November 1986.

27. Letter to the author from the President of the Foreign Affairs Association, 9 December 1986.

28. Letter to the author from the Secretary, 28 October 1986.

29. Details provided by the Department of Foreign Affairs under Freedom of Information request F86070 of 11 November 1986. In 1986 financial constraints forced the closure of Australia's missions in Abu Dhabi, Bahrain, Kuwait and Lima. The Australian Embassy in East Berlin is due to be closed in 1987.

30. Letter to the author from the Secretary, 28 October 1986.

31. 'Copy of a Letter to the Chairman of the Committee from the Diplomatic Service Wives Association', Annex to 'Minutes of Evidence', *FCO/ODA Supply Estimates 1986-87*, Foreign Affairs Committee, House of Commons, Session 1985-86, 21 May 1986.

32. *PSR*, p.109.

33. *ibid.* See also Williams, p. 246.

34. 'Contingency Planning', Department of Foreign Affairs Administrative Circular 30/85, 9 May 1985, obtained under Freedom of Information request F86070 of 11 November 1986.

35. 'The lingering nightmare of Flight 847'. See also the Foreign Minister's reply to 'Egyptian Airliner Hijacking', Question Without Notice, House of Representatives, *Hansard*, 25 November 1985.

36. Statement to the House of Representatives on 23 February 1978, reproduced as Appendix 1 to *PSR*, p.250.

37. 'Counter Terrorism in Australia'.

38. 'Contingency Planning'.

39. Minutes of the Staff Management Advisory Committee, Subcommittee on Conditions of Service, 29 June 1985, obtained from the Department of Foreign Affairs under Freedom of Information request F86070 of 11 November 1986.

40. On a single day in February 1986 the Embassies of the United States, the Soviet Union, China, West Germany and India were all bombed by left-wing terrorists. On 18 May, bombs also exploded at the Chinese and Soviet Embassies, as well as the US Ambassador's Residence. 'Terror and Keating's Axe drive Aussies from Lima', *Australian Financial Review*, 24 September 1986. See also 'Estimates Committee E', The Senate, *Hansard*, 23 September 1986.

41. See for example 'Budget cuts may sever 100 overseas postings', *National Times*, 20 June 1986 and 'Our Third World Diplomats', *Australian*, 9 October 1986.

42. 'Security riles diplomats', *Australian*, 9 October 1981. See also 'Officials at risk overseas', *Canberra Times*, 4 April 1985.

43. 'Special Compensation for Injury in Exceptional Circumstances', Department of Foreign Affairs Administrative Circular 81/86, 15 July 1986, obtained under Freedom of Information request F86070 of 11 November 1986.

44. Letter to the author from the President of the FAA, 9 December 1986.

45. *PSR*, p.xxxi.

9

AUSTRALIA AND THE TERRORIST THREAT TO DIPLOMACY

The extent to which Australia and Australians have suffered terrorism is small when compared with what has happened in other places. But however much the absence here of the grosser tragedies that other communities have had to suffer justifies a feeling of relief, it does not justify complacency.

Mr Justice R. M. Hope
Protective Security Review: Report (1979)

There are dangers in translating the experiences of other countries and nationalities to Australia and Australians without first making careful allowances for different circumstances, but this should not blind observers to the implications for Australia of the growing global threat to diplomats and diplomatic facilities from international terrorism. As Brian Jenkins warned a group of the country's most senior officials in the counter-terrorism field in 1982,[1] Australia can expect sooner or later to become affected by terrorist violence to a greater degree than has been the case to date. While a balance must be struck between this and other government concerns, apparent savings made in certain protective security measures now may prove to be very expensive over the longer term. There are other steps too, that can be taken to provide a more coordinated Australian response to developments overseas and a more independent analysis of long term terrorist questions. In the wider diplomatic arena, Australia will need to consider its more immediate national interests in the light of the interests it shares with other countries in the preservation and effective functioning of the international system as a whole.

FUTURE PROTECTIVE SECURITY QUESTIONS

In his statement to Parliament on 17 October 1986, Special Minister of State Michael Young rightly emphasised that:

> It is important . . . that we not lose a sense of proportion and base our arrangements for counter terrorism on worst case scenarios: rather we need to make a sober and rational assessment of the threat.[2]

This advice was no doubt intended to dampen down any feelings of alarm fostered by the news media and popular literature[3] in Australia at the time. It may have also been designed to forestall any attempts at bureaucratic expansion by government departments and agencies concerned with counter-terrorist measures. Such concerns, however, should not prevent the consideration of other protective security questions where they are necessary. The 1979 Hope Review and the 1986 Holdich Review (which in many respects brought up to date consideration of the matters examined by Mr Justice Hope) were primarily concerned with domestic counter-terrorist capabilities and arrangements. While under their terms of reference they naturally examined the protection of diplomats and diplomatic facilities in Australia, neither Review gave any real consideration to Australia's overseas interests and responsibilities in this field. This is one area where further attention seems required.

As the global terrorist problem has grown in recent years, so the Department of Foreign Affairs has increased its capacities to evaluate the threat faced by Australians abroad and to take measures to protect them. Procedures for obtaining assessments of the risks at diplomatic posts have been revised and upgraded, and lines of responsibility for terrorist issues have been clarified. The Security and Communications Branch has been allocated increased funds and a number of improvements have been made in the administration of annual protective security programs. The Department's contingency planning arrangements and crisis management procedures are probably better now than they have ever been. Despite these many improvements, however, protective security matters are still subject to considerable bureaucratic pressures, notably staffing and financial constraints, all of which must affect the Department's capacity to respond to the needs of its personnel and their families overseas. If the level of terrorist threat was suddenly to rise, even if only at a particular post, the Department could still face considerable difficulties in responding quickly and effectively.

Bearing in mind that no amount of physical security can give absolute protection against a determined attack, the Australian Government needs to consider carefully the measures it is able and willing to take to protect its personnel and premises overseas. The threat to Australia is not high at present but many missions and official residences are clearly in a vulnerable position. Should the terrorist threat suddenly increase, for whatever reason, it is unlikely that there would be sufficient time to take additional measures, many of which would be expensive and require considerable lead time. This may be a risk the Government is willing to take at present, counting on the country's diplomatic efforts and modest global profile to help it avoid becoming a terrorist target. The alternatives, however, are either to provide a significantly increased level of funding to the Department of Foreign Affairs (and the staffing resources necessary to implement and maintain a substantially increased protective security program) or, following the US example, to consider closing down certain missions where an official Australian presence is not considered important enough to justify such an outlay of resources. Given the Australian Government's firm, and publicly stated, resolve not to give in to terrorist blackmail, it would find it difficult thus to alter the pattern of its official representation abroad but in certain circumstances it may have little choice. One option not available to the Government is to assign officers to posts overseas knowing that the protective security measures provided for them and their families, either by Australia or the receiving government, are inadequate.

No cause would be served by exaggerating the threat currently faced by Australian diplomats and diplomatic missions overseas but it remains the case that their position has never been subject to the kind of searching enquiry that has characterised other aspects of Australia's protective security arrangements. Given the threat from terrorist groups currently faced by such officials and offices around the world it would be timely for the Australian Government to undertake a formal examination of such matters, in the manner of its earlier reviews of domestic counter-terrorist arrangements and capabilities. The Department of Foreign Affairs has already reported to its Minister on the level of violent attacks on its officers and their families abroad and, conceivably, could be instructed to provide a more critical and wide-ranging report on its responses to the terrorist threat. It is unlikely, however, that a purely internal assessment of this question would be able to canvass all the issues thoroughly enough, be considered objective enough by the public or carry as much weight with the Government, as a more independent, official enquiry. Besides, if undertaken seriously, the scope of such an enquiry could reach well beyond purely protective security questions to include other aspects of Australia's approach to the international terrorist problem.

OTHER AREAS FOR REVIEW

One additional area that could usefully be examined by an official enquiry is the bureaucratic coordination of Australia's external counter-terrorist arrangements. Since it became a major policy concern in the early 1970s, responsibility for the handling of international terrorism has been divided between a number of government agencies and departments. Partly as a consequence, there has been a significant growth in the number and range of Australia's external links on counter-terrorist matters. Most of the country's various intelligence agencies, police forces, armed services and bureaucratic departments have developed relationships of one kind or another in this field with their counterparts overseas. In addition, politicians and officials at both the Federal and State level have travelled to other countries to examine national counter-terrorist arrangements and discuss aspects of the terrorism problem. Broadly speaking, such cooperative links and demonstrations of official interest are laudable and should be encouraged, but there is a danger that, without greater coordination, these contacts will result in considerable confusion and duplication of effort. There is currently no formal apparatus, for example, to monitor, coordinate and consider external contacts on counter-terrorist matters, the way that SIDC-PAV performs such a role with regard to the internal threat and domestic countermeasures.

At present, issues of this kind appear to be considered as occasion demands by the Security Committee of the Federal Cabinet, supported by the Secretaries Committee on Intelligence and Security. At the everyday working level the Department of the Prime Minister and Cabinet exercises a degree of oversight but different arms of government still enjoy various degrees of independence. The specialised links that Australian departments and agencies like Defence, ASIO and the AFP share with their counterparts overseas are legitimate and valuable extensions of their responsibilities for aspects of counter-terrorism in Australia. Not only must they be closely coordinated at the operational level, however, but they must also operate within, and be fully consistent with, the wider framework of Australia's foreign policy and its diplomatic efforts in other related spheres. As was clearly shown by the European Community's consultations on international terrorism in 1986, it is often difficult to divorce operational aspects of counter-terrorist policies from wider political considerations. Given the Department of Foreign Affairs' continuing responsibility for the overall management of Australia's relations with other countries, it was only logical that in January 1986 Federal Cabinet should charge it with the investigation of possible avenues of increased international cooperation in the counter-terrorism field. There does not appear to have been any decision made yet to appoint a 'lead agency' (in the manner of President Reagan's NSD 30) to coordinate all Australia's external dealings on these matters. As this issue develops, however, it may be necessary for such a formal demarcation to be made, or formal apparatus devised, to ensure the most efficient and profitable handling of all these contacts.

If the Government was to conduct a formal review of the kind suggested, consideration might also be given to the best way of centralising, or at least coordinating, analyses of international terrorist developments, and developing further Australia's own intelligence capacities in this field. This task is currently performed to varying degrees, and for different purposes, by a number of official agencies. The Department of Foreign Affairs review which resulted in the creation of the Counter Terrorism Policy Section was largely an internal response to the demands being made on the Government to develop and coordinate its broad approaches to a problem of increasing foreign policy importance. In conjunction with other Branches of the Department the Section considers and advises on aspects of the terrorist problem but lacks the resources to develop any detailed understanding of the global scene. There is no Australian counterpart, for example, to the British Foreign and Commonwealth Office's Research Department, or the US State Department's Bureau of Intelligence and Research. More detailed analyses are doubtless carried out by ASIO, but that organisation necessarily focuses on matters pertaining to its domestic security responsibilities. Even if it was permitted under its charter, ASIO is unlikely to have the resources or appreciation of wider political issues needed to conduct longer term analyses of terrorist developments around the world, of the kind required. The consideration of broad terrorist questions and related international security issues is a major task which would fit more logically into the duties of one of Australia's intelligence analysis organisations, like the Office of National Assessments (ONA). Yet for this to be done the Government would need formally to allocate such a role to ONA and clearly define its relationship on counter-terrorist issues with the many other official bodies now actively involved in this field.

The Australian Government has accepted that international cooperation is an important (if not crucial) aspect of counter-terrorism and has put considerable effort into developing the means to share information and assessments about the subject. At the same time, real benefits could be gained from an increased capacity to provide independent analyses of developments in this field. Australia's friends and allies provide much valuable material and many useful insights, but inevitably they have perceptions and interests of their own. Alliances notwithstanding, there are bound to be times when these do not coincide with Australia's, as was seen for example after the French attack on the *Rainbow Warrior* and the US bombing of Libya. In addition, there are obvious differences in traditions and styles of conflict resolution among these countries themselves which Australia needs to know about and be able to evaluate. For example, Australia's current policy approach to counter-terrorism seems in many respects to accord more with that of the United Kingdom, than the United States. In some areas, such as the coordination of State and Federal responses to terrorist incidents, Australia has had to develop procedures of its own. Only by assessing these and other matters itself will the Australian Government be able clearly to judge what counter-terrorist policies are in Australia's own best interests, and act accordingly.

AUSTRALIA'S INTERNATIONAL ROLE

A more independent and comprehensive intelligence analysis of international terrorism would not only serve Australia's more immediate security and policy concerns. It could also underpin the efforts currently being made by the Department of Foreign Affairs, both to provide a more coordinated and considered foreign policy approach to terrorist issues, and to investigate and pursue opportunities for increased cooperation in the counter-terrorism field with other states. Australian involvement in international efforts against terrorist violence will depend on a number of diverse factors, but will need in any event to be supported by a sound appreciation of the nature of the terrorist problem, in all its ever-changing complexity. This argues for a more comprehensive and coordinated intelligence effort, and a clearer appreciation of precisely what part Australia can play in global efforts to counter the problem, both in the operational and diplomatic spheres. It is clearly not enough for Australia's representatives abroad simply to reiterate their Government's condemnation of terrorist violence and register its willingness to join in international efforts to combat it. They must also be in a position to make worthwhile, original contributions to the examination of this problem and offer concrete proposals for cooperative efforts. Without them, any approaches made will be in danger of sounding like the rhetoric employed by other states less serious about taking resolute action.

At first sight, there would appear to be good arguments against Australia attempting to play any significant role in global efforts to counter terrorism, at least at the diplomatic level. Australia is not a major player on the world stage and, not having suffered from international terrorism to any significant degree, cannot claim to speak on such matters with authority. Indeed, to claim to do so could invite a rebuff from those countries more affected by terrorist violence and thus more familiar with the policy dilemmas faced by governments trying to cope with it. Australia's position suffers too, from being seen by some states as a close ally of the United States and a friend of Israel, and thus biased towards those countries' particular interests. Rightly or wrongly, these perceptions limit the influence Australia may be able to exert outside the Western Alliance on sensitive matters like international terrorism. Apart from very broad security considerations and humanitarian concerns, Australia also has no direct involvement in any of the various Middle Eastern disputes, nor are Australian interests directly engaged in many of the other problems which have given rise to terrorist violence elsewhere in the world. It might thus appear that any role Australia might attempt to play in countering international terrorism in world affairs would be doomed to be ineffectual, if not actually counter-productive. For Australia to try and take 'the high moral ground'[4] on sensitive issues like the United States bombing of Libya, for example, may reflect genuine concerns over the possibility of an escalation of the violence but risks interposing Australia between two implacable opponents, to no appreciable benefit. It could also draw unwelcome attention to Australia from terrorists and their sponsors. This last factor should not be permitted to deter the Government from its proposed course of action, but would have to be taken into account in formulating any public responses. The desire of the Australian Government to contribute to a reduction of terrorist violence must always be tempered by a sense of perspective regarding its own position and influence in world affairs.

Despite all these considerations, there is scope for Australia to play a role. Its close relationship with the United States can be turned to advantage, to press the Reagan Administration to exercise greater restraint and to adopt more far-sighted and balanced policies. Its membership of the Western Alliance notwithstanding, Australia can still claim to speak on terrorist issues as a concerned, but independent observer, as yet unencumbered by many of the complex policy considerations which surround those states currently facing terrorist problems of their own. Simply by virtue of its relatively small size and modest influence, it can speak where certain other more involved countries cannot. Its membership of the Asia-Pacific region and multilateral organisations like the Commonwealth give it access often denied to larger powers. Its attempts to implement an even-handed policy towards the Palestinian question and its preparedness to criticise other Western states on certain terrorist issues gives it some credibility in Third World circles which may be drawn on to advantage. Australia also has a long record as a country concerned with humanitarian questions and to speak out against terrorist violence would only be in keeping with this established position.

These considerations aside, Australia has every right to express its concern whenever it considers that its vital interests are being affected. As a relatively small country in many ways dependent on others for its own security and commerce, Australia has a strong interest in the maintenance not just of peace and order in the world, but also the effective and predictable func-tioning of the international system.[5] Like all such states, Australia has good reason to be concerned at any weakening of the international order, par-ticularly if it appears to herald a greater propensity by others to ignore legal avenues and resort to force to solve their problems. The emergence of state-sponsored terrorism, whether by radical Third World states like Syria or Libya, or by developed Western countries like France, endangers Australia by threatening a system on which all countries place considerable reliance and importance. Such fears must be even greater if the superpowers themselves display an inclination to pay less attention to customary norms of diplomatic behaviour. Countries like Australia can only view with concern any signs of unwillingness by such states to pay heed to the decisions of world bodies like the United Nations or the International Court of Justice.

For Australia to make its voice heard and taken seriously on international terrorist issues, it is imperative that it adopts a considered and consistent approach. To condemn some forms of terrorism and not others, or to adjust the level of its condemnation depending on the country perpetrating the violence, would leave Australia open to just those accusations levelled at some other countries, that they are not serious about combatting international terrorism but are merely serving their own short term strategic interests. Australia has suffered little from terrorism to date, and so has found it relatively easy to pursue a principled and consistent policy. It has not entirely escaped the kinds of problems encountered by other states, however, and depending on developments both in Australia and outside it, obvious contradictions in Australian policy could become more difficult to avoid. Pressures on the Government would be particularly strong if Australia itself should fall victim to a terrorist campaign of some kind. Following a consistent policy, or set of policies, will not always be easy and may require considerable political will, but is necessary if Australia is to retain its credibility and make any impact on the problem. Only then would Australia be able to command the respect and influence it needs to work with other, like-minded states in trying to curb terrorist violence, focus attention on sources of global tension, work within the international system to strengthen the role of multilateral negotiating groups, and above all to encourage a closer observance of international laws and conventions. In these ways Australia's contribution to peace and international order can be an important one.

NOTES

1. 'Terrorism on increase, says expert', *The Age*, 1 November 1982. Jenkins was addressing a Command Management Conference at the Australian Counter Disaster College at Mount Macedon, Victoria.
2. 'Counter Terrorism in Australia'.
3. Around the time of the Minister's statement, there appeared a short book by James Crown, entitled *Australia: The Terrorist Connection* (Sun Books, Melbourne, 1986). Drawing mainly on newspaper reports, Crown linked Australia's few genuine terrorist attacks with a number of violent criminal incidents and fictional scenarios, to argue for a significantly increased counter-terrorism capability.
4. Interview with Foreign Minister Bill Hayden for the '7:30 Report', ABC Television, 16 April 1986.
5. This has been a recurring theme in public statements by New Zealand representatives. See, for example, 'International Law in the Foreign Policy of a Small State', Address by the Deputy Prime Minister, Geoffrey Palmer, to the Columbia University School of Law, 26 September 1985.

APPENDICES

Appendices A–D are taken from the US State Department's *Terrorist Incidents Involving Diplomats: A Statistical Overview of International Terrorist Incidents Involving Diplomatic Personnel and Facilities from January 1968 through April 1983*, (Washington, August 1983). As with all such statistics, they need to be used with considerable care. It is not clear, for example, why Australia is included in the list of countries whose diplomats have been 'victimised' by international terrorism. Such reservations aside, however, this publication still constitutes one of the most useful compilations of data on terrorist attacks against diplomatic targets published to date. Appendix E is a list of incidents in Australia since 1970, known or presumed by the Australian Government to be terrorist in nature. Appendix F is taken from *United Nations Treaty Series*, Vol.1035 (1977) (United Nations, New York, 1984), Treaty 15410, pp.167–172.

APPENDIX A

Table 1

Terrorist Incidents Involving Foreign Diplomats January 1968–April 1983, by Type

	1968	1969	1970	1971	1972	1973	1974	1975	1976	1977	1978	1979	1980	1981	1982	1983[a]	Totals	Percent of Grand Total
Kidnapping	1	3	30	14	2	8	5	10	6	4	12	8	4	10	3	1	121	3.7
Barricade/hostage	1	0	4	1	3	7	7	9	3	5	11	9	24	28	15	9	136	4.1
Bombing	63	53	98	71	114	73	89	68	84	89	113	101	128	119	131	45	1439	43.6
Armed attack	0	4	2	3	8	4	6	7	6	6	9	10	30	21	6	4	126	3.8
Hijacking	0	0	0	0	0	0	0	0	0	0	0	2	3	2	7	1	15	0.5
Assassination[b]	2	5	10	8	3	5	5	6	14	11	11	15	29	22	21	2	169	5.1
Threat, hoax	11	10	42	36	61	68	17	15	41	28	86	61	136	128	189	60	989	29.9
Sniping	2	2	4	3	4	3	1	7	13	5	10	24	20	12	12	6	128	3.9
Other[c]	0	14	14	9	5	6	6	9	7	7	13	11	35	25	20	12	181	5.5
Total	80	79	204	145	200	174	136	131	174	155	265	241	409	367	404	140	3304	

[a] Includes incidents from January through April 1983.
[b] Includes attempted assassinations that failed.
[c] Includes shootouts, smuggling, and so forth.

Table 2
Locations of Terrorist Incidents Involving Foreign Diplomats, January 1968–April 1983, by Type

	North America	Latin America	Western Europe	Eastern Europe/ Soviet Union	Sub-Saharan Africa	Middle East	Asia	Pacific	Other	Total (percent)
Kidnapping	2	57	14	0	13	26	7	0	2	121 (3.7)
Barricade/hostage	9	58	41	2	1	21	3	0	1	136 (4.1)
Bombing	192	327	529	15	20	234	93	14	15	1439 (43.6)
Armed attack	1	38	15	0	6	54	11	0	1	126 (3.8)
Hijacking	0	2	0	3	3	4	3	0	0	15 (0.5)
Assassination[a]	13	24	59	4	5	45	15	3	1	169 (5.1)
Threat, hoax	146	236	260	34	35	163	88	22	5	989 (29.9)
Sniping	16	63	9	1	1	29	8	1	0	128 (3.9)
Other[b]	24	44	45	4	12	33	16	0	3	181 (5.5)
Total	403 (12.2)	849 (25.7)	972 (29.4)	63 (1.9)	96 (2.9)	609 (18.4)	244 (7.4)	40 (1.2)	28 (0.8)	3304

[a] Includes attempted assassinations that failed.
[b] Includes shootouts, smuggling, and so forth.

APPENDIX B

Countries Whose Diplomats Have Been Victimized by International Terrorism

This list includes the names of each country whose foreign diplomats have been victimized by international terrorism. It is based on media coverage of these events and therefore may not cover countries that do not report incidents.

Afghanistan	Guyana	Peru
Albania	Haiti	Philippines
Algeria	Honduras	Poland
Angola	India	Portugal
Argentina	Indonesia	Romania
Australia	Iran	Saudi Arabia
Austria	Iraq	Senegal
Bangladesh	Ireland	Somalia
Belgium	Israel	South Africa
Bolivia	Italy	South Korea (ROK)
Brazil	Ivory Coast	South Vietnam
Bulgaria	Jamaica	South Yemen (PDRY)
Burma	Japan	Spain
Canada	Jordan	Sri Lanka
Cape Verde	Kenya	Sudan
Chad	Kuwait	Suriname
Chile	Laos	Sweden
China	Lebanon	Switzerland
Colombia	Liberia	Syria
Congo	Libya	Tanzania
Costa Rica	Malawi	Thailand
Cuba	Malaysia	Tunisia
Cyprus	Mali	Turkey
Czechoslovakia	Mauritania	Uganda
Denmark	Mexico	United Arab Emirates
Dominican Republic	Mongolia	United Kingdom
East Germany	Morocco	United States
Ecuador	Netherlands	Uruguay
Egypt	New Zealand	USSR
El Salvador	Nicaragua	Vatican City
Ethiopia	Nigeria	Venezuela
Finland	North Korea (DPRK)	Vietnam (SRV)
France	North Yemen (YAR)	West Germany (FRG)
Gabon	Norway	Yugoslavia
Ghana	Oman	Zaire
Greece	Pakistan	Zimbabwe
Guatemala	Panama	Taiwan
Guinea	Paraguay	

APPENDIX C

Locations of International Terrorist Incidents Involving Foreign Diplomats

Afghanistan	Grenada	Pakistan
Albania	Guatemala	Panama
Algeria	Guineá	Papua New Guinea
Angola	Guyana	Paraguay
Argentina	Haiti	Peru
Australia	Honduras	Philippines
Austria	Hong Kong	Poland
Bahamas, The	Hungary	Portugal
Bahrain	Iceland	Qatar
Bangladesh	India	Romania
Barbados	Indonesia	Saudi Arabia
Belgium	Iran	Scotland
Benin	Iraq	Sierra Leone
Bolivia	Ireland	Singapore
Botswana	Israel	Somalia
Brazil	Italy	South Africa
Bulgaria	Ivory Coast	South Korea (ROK)
Burma	Jamaica	South Yemen (PDRY)
Burundi	Japan	Spain
Canada	Jordan	Sri Lanka
Central African Republic	Kampuchea	Sudan
Chile	Kenya	Suriname
China	Kuwait	Sweden
Colombia	Laos	Switzerland
Corsica	Lebanon	Syria
Costa Rica	Lesotho	Tanzania
Cuba	Liberia	Thailand
Cyprus	Libya	Trinidad and Tobago
Czechoslovakia	Luxembourg	Tunisia
Denmark	Malaysia	Turkey
Djibouti	Malta	Uganda
Dominican Republic	Martinique	United Arab Emirates
East Germany	Mexico	United Kingdom
Ecuador	Morocco	United States
Egypt	Mozambique	Upper Volta
El Salvador	Nepal	Uruguay
Equatorial Guinea	Netherlands	USSR
Ethiopia	New Zealand	Vatican City
Finland	Nicaragua	Venezuela
France	Nigeria	West Germany (FRG)
Gabon	North Yemen (YAR)	Yugoslavia
Ghana	Norway	Zambia
Greece	Oman	

APPENDIX D

Groups Allegedly Responsible for Terrorist Incidents Involving Foreign Diplomats, January 1968–April 1983

This list contains the names of organisations responsible either by claim or attribution for the incidents involving diplomats reflected in the statistics. Some of these events may have taken place without the approval or even the foreknowledge of the leaders of the organisations involved. Some claims of responsibility may be false, and some names may have been invented by organisations not wishing to link their own names with particular actions or by criminal or psychotic individuals who acted alone. In other cases organisations may have claimed credit for (or been blamed for) actions they did not commit.

Acilciler (Urgent Ones, part of TPLP-F)
Action Directe
Alacran (Scorpion)
Al Fatah
Al Jihad al Islami
Al Saiqa (Syrian controlled)
Ananda Marga
Anti-Imperialist Fighters for a Free Palestine
April 19 Movement (M-19)
Arab Communist Organisation
Armed Forces of National Liberation (FALN)
Armed Revolutionary Party of the People
Armenian Secret Army for the Liberation of
    Armenia (ASALA)
Army of National Liberation (ELN)
ASEAN Moslem Liberation Front
Bandera Roja
Basque Fatherland and Liberty (ETA)
Bazargan Brigades
Black Crescent
Black December Movement
Black June Organisation
Black September Organisation (associated
    with Al Fatah)
Charles Martel Group

Condor
Croatian Liberation Movement (emigres)
Democratic Front for the Liberation of
    Palestine (DFLP)
Dominican Popular Movement
Eagles of the Palestinian Revolution
El Condor
El Poder Cubano
Eritrean Liberation Forces
Eylem Birligi Faction of TPLP-F
Farabundo Marti Popular Liberation Forces (FPL)
Farug
February 28 Popular Leagues
Front for Liberation of Lebanon From Foreigners
Greek Anti-Dictatorial Youth
Greek Armed Group for Support of
    Northern Ireland
Guerrilla Army of the Poor (EGP)
Hammer (and) Sickle Group
Holger Meins Kommando (RAF subgroup)
Honduran Revolutionary Union (URP)
Honduran Socialist Party (PASO)
International Solidarity Command for Free
    Papua Movement
Invisible Ones
Iraqi Liberation Army-General Command
January 12 Liberation Movement
January 31 Popular Front
Japanese Red Army (JRA)
Jewish Defense League (Wrath of God)
June 2 Movement (2JM)
Justice Commandos for the Armenian Genocide (JCAG)
Kurdish Democratic Party
Latin American Anti-Communist Army
Lebanese Armed Revolutionary Brigades
Lebanese Armed Revolutionary Faction (LARF)
Lorenza Zelaya
Mano Argentine National Organisation Movement
Maruseido

Marxist-Leninist Armed Propaganda Unit
  (MLAPU, part of TPLP-F)
May 15 Organisation
Montoneros
Moro National Liberation Front
Mojahedin
Movement of the Revolutionary Left (MIR)
Muslim Brotherhood
National Liberation Alliance (ALN)
National Front for the Liberation of Congo (FLNC)
National Democratic Popular Front
New Armenian Resistance
October 1 Anti-Fascist Revolutionary Group (GRAPO)
Peoples Revolutionary Army
Peoples Army in Zaire (APOZA)
Peoples Strugglers
Petra Kraus Group
Polisario
Popular Front for the Liberation of Palestine (PFLP)
Popular Army Force (FAP)
Popular Forces of April 25 (FP-25)
Popular Liberation Army (EPL)
Popular Revolutionary Bloc
Popular Revolutionary Movement
Popular Revolutionary Vanguard (VPR)
Provisional Irish Republican Army (PIRA, Provos)
Quebec Liberation Front (FLQ)
Red Army Faction (RAF)
Revolutionary Armed Forces of Colombia (FARC)
Revolutionary People's Struggle
Revolutionary Cells (RZ)
Revolutionary Organisation of the People in
  Arms (ORPA)
Revolutionary Student Front (FER)
Revolutionary Youth Union (Dev Genc)
Soldiers of the Algerian Opposition Movement
Tupamaros
Turkish People's Liberation Army (TPLA)
Turkish People's Liberation Front (TPLF)
Uganda Freedom Movement

Ukrainian Nationalist Group
United Popular Action Front
United Liberation Front for New Algeria
Voice of the People (Halkin Sesi)
Workers Party of Guatemala (PGT-FAR)

APPENDIX E

Known or Presumed Terrorist Incidents in Australia Since 1970

1 January 1970	Planned bomb attack, Serbian Orthodox Church, Canberra
21 October 1970	Bombing, Yugoslav Consulate-General, Melbourne
17 January 1971	Bombing, USSR Embassy, Canberra
4 April 1971	Bombing, Serbian Orthodox Church, Melbourne
12 September 1971	Attempted arson, Serbian Orthodox Church, Melbourne
19 December 1971	Bombing, theatre in Sydney
11 January 1972	Bombing, Serbian Orthodox Church, Canberra
14 February 1972	Armed assault, Yugoslav Consulate, Perth
16 February 1972	Bombing, offices of two Yugoslav tourist agencies, Sydney
26 April 1972	Bombing, residence of pro-Yugoslav political figure, Melbourne
25 September 1972	Five Black September Organisation letter bombs, addressed to Israeli diplomats in Sydney and Canberra, detected in Australian post offices.
3 October 1972	Two letter bombs, addressed to Israeli officials in Sydney, detected by the Australian postal service
2 November 1972	Letter bomb sent to a prominent member of the Jewish community in Australia
8 December 1972	Bombing, Serbian Orthodox Church, Brisbane
24 January 1973	Letter bomb, addressed to a Jewish businessman in New South Wales, intercepted at a post office.
9 April 1973	Arson, premises of the editor of a Croatian newspaper, Melbourne
24 December 1974	Fire bombs, Pan Am ticket office, Sydney

25 May 1975	Bombing, 'Sunny Adriatic' Trade and Tourist Centre, Victoria
19 November 1975	Letter bombs, addressed to the Prime Minister and Premier of Queensland
29 August 1977	Arson, Indian High Commission, Canberra
31 August 1977	Arson, Australian Atomic Energy Commission, Sydney
15 September 1977	Kidnapping and wounding, Indian Defence Attache and wife, Canberra
19 October 1977	Armed assault, Air India employee, Melbourne
4 December 1977	Bombing, Yugoslav Airlines office, Melbourne
24 December 1977	Bombing, Statue of Yugoslav General Mihailovic, Canberra
13 February 1978	Bombing, outside Hilton Hotel, Sydney
25 March 1978	Bomb found in Indian High Commissioner's Residence, Canberra
13 November 1978	Poisoned sweets served to delegates at Assyrian Congress, Sydney
8 February 1979	Conspiracy to bomb Yugoslav targets and water pipelines discovered
17 December 1980	Assassination, Turkish Consul-General, Sydney
23 December 1982	Bombing, Israeli Consulate, Sydney
23 December 1982	Bombing, Hakoah Club, Sydney
12 November 1983	Bomb found and defused in Lucas Heights Atomic Research Establishment, Sydney
5 July 1985	Bombing, outside Union Carbide factory, Sydney
13 July 1985	Two shots fired at Vietnamese Embassy, Canberra
23 November 1986	Bombing, Turkish Consulate-General, Melbourne

APPENDIX F

Resolution Adopted by the General Assembly

Convention on the Prevention and Punishment of Crimes Against Internationally Protected Persons, Including Diplomatic Agents

The General Assembly,

Considering that the codification and progressive development of international law contributes to the implementation of the purposes and principles set forth in Articles 1 and 2 of the Charter of the United Nations,

Recalling that in response to the request made in General Assembly resolution 2780 (XXVI) of December 3, 1971, the International Law Commission, at its twenty-fourth session, studied the question of the protection and inviolability of diplomatic agents and other persons entitled to special protection under international law and prepared draft articles[1] on the prevention and punishment of crimes against such persons,

Having considered the draft articles and also the comments and observations thereon submitted by States, specialised agencies and other intergovernmental organisations[2] in response to the invitation extended by the General Assembly in its resolution 2926 (XXVII) of November 28, 1972.

Convinced of the importance of securing international agreement on appropriate and effective measures for the prevention and punishment of crimes against diplomatic agents and other internationally protected persons in view of the serious threat to the maintenance and promotion of friendly relations and cooperation among States created by the commission of such crimes,

Having elaborated for that purpose the provisions contained in the Convention annexed hereto,

1. *Adopts* the Convention on the Prevention and Punishment of Crimes against Internationally Protected Persons, including Diplomatic Agents, annexed to the present resolution;

2. *Reemphasizes* the great importance of the rules of international law concerning the inviolability of and special protection to be afforded to internationally protected persons and the obligations of States in relation thereto;

3. *Considers* that the annexed Convention will enable States to carry out their obligations more effectively;

4. *Recognizes also* that the provisions of the annexed Convention could not in any way prejudice the exercise of the legitimate right to self-determination and independence, in accordance with the purposes and principles of the Charter of the United Nations and the Declaration on Principles of International Law concerning Friendly Relations and

Co-operation among States in accordance with the Charter of the United Nations, by peoples struggling against colonialism, alien domination, foreign occupation, racial discrimination and *apartheid;*

5. *Invites* States to become parties to the annexed Convention;
6. *Decides* that the present resolution, whose provisions are related to the annexed Convention, shall always be published together with it.

2202 plenary meeting
14 December 1973

The States Parties to this Convention,

Having in mind the purposes and principles of the Charter of the United Nations concerning the maintenance of international peace and the promotion of friendly relations and cooperation among States,

Considering that crimes against diplomatic agents and other internationally protected persons jeopardizing the safety of these persons create a serious threat to the maintenance of normal international relations which are necessary for cooperation among States,

Believing that the commission of such crimes is a matter of grave concern to the international community,

Convinced that there is an urgent need to adopt appropriate and effective measures for the prevention and punishment of such crimes,

Have agreed as follows:

Article 1

For the purposes of this Convention:
1. "internationally protected person" means:
   (a) A Head of State, including any member of a collegial body performing the functions of a Head of State under the constitution of the State concerned, a Head of Government or a Minister for Foreign Affairs, whenever any such person is in a foreign State, as well as members of his family who accompany him;
   (b) any representative or official of a State or any official or other agent of an international organisation of an inter-governmental character who, at the time when and in the place where a crime against him, his official premises, his private accommodation or his means of transport is committed, is entitled pursuant to international law to special protection from any attacks on his person, freedom or dignity, as well as members of his family forming part of his household;
2. "alleged offender" means a person as to whom there is sufficient evidence to determine *prima facie* that he has committed or participated in one or more of the crimes set forth in article 2.

Article 2

1. The intentional commission of:
   (a) a murder, kidnapping or other attack upon the person or liberty of an internationally protected person;
   (b) a violent attack upon the official premises, the private accommodation or the means of transport of an internationally protected person likely to endanger his person or liberty;
   (c) a threat to commit any such attack;
   (d) an attempt to commit any such attack; and
   (e) an act constituting participation as an accomplice in any such attack shall be made by each State Party a crime under its internal law.
2. Each State Party shall make these crimes punishable by appropriate penalties which take into account their grave nature.
3. Paragraphs 1 and 2 of this article in no way derogate from the obligations of States Parties under international law to take all appropriate measures to prevent other attacks on the person, freedom or dignity of an internationally protected person.

Article 3

1. Each State Party shall take such measures as may be necessary to establish its jurisdiction over the crimes set forth in article 2 in the following cases:
   (a) when the crime is committed in the territory of that State or on board a ship or aircraft registered in that State;
   (b) when the alleged offender is a national of that State;
   (c) when the crime is committed against an internationally protected person as defined in article 1 who enjoys his status as such by virtue of functions which he exercises on behalf of that State.
2. Each State Party shall likewise take such measures as may be necessary to establish its jurisdiction over these crimes in cases where the alleged offender is present in its territory and it does not extradite him pursuant to article 8 to any of the States mentioned in paragraph 1 of this article.
3. This Convention does not exclude any criminal jurisdiction exercised in accordance with internal law.

Article 4

States Parties shall cooperate in the prevention of the crimes set forth in article 2, particularly by:
   (a) taking all practicable measures to prevent preparations in their

respective territories for the commission of those crimes within or outside their territories;

(b) exchanging information and coordinating the taking of administrative and other measures as appropriate to prevent the commission of those crimes.

Article 5

1. The State Party in which any of the crimes set forth in article 2 has been committed shall, if it has reason to believe that an alleged offender has fled from its territory, communicate to all other States concerned, directly or through the Secretary-General of the United Nations, all the pertinent facts regarding the crime committed and all available information regarding the identity of the alleged offender.

2. Whenever any of the crimes set forth in article 2 has been committed against an internationally protected person, any State Party which has information concerning the victim and the circumstances of the crime shall endeavour to transmit it, under the conditions provided for in its internal law, fully and promptly to the State Party on whose behalf he was exercising his functions.

Article 6

1. Upon being satisfied that the circumstances so warrant, the State Party in whose territory the alleged offender is present shall take the appropriate measures under its internal law so as to ensure his presence for the purpose of prosecution or extradition. Such measures shall be notified without delay directly or through the Secretary-General of the United Nations to:

   (a) the State where the crime was committed;
   (b) the State or States of which the alleged offender is a national, or if he is a stateless person, in whose territory he permanently resides;
   (c) the State or States of which the internationally protected person concerned is a national or on whose behalf he was exercising his functions;
   (d) all other States concerned; and
   (e) the international organisation of which the internationally protected person concerned is an official or an agent.

2. Any person regarding whom the measures referred to in paragraph 1 of this article are being taken shall be entitled:

   (a) to communicate without delay with the nearest appropriate representative of the State of which he is a national or which is otherwise

entitled to protect his rights or, if he is a stateless person, which he requests and which is willing to protect his rights; and
(b) to be visited by a representative of that State.

Article 7

The State Party in whose territory the alleged offender is present shall, if it does not extradite him, submit, without exception whatsoever and without undue delay, the case to its competent authorities for the purpose of prosecution, through proceedings in accordance with the laws of the State.

Article 8

1. To the extent that the crimes set forth in article 2 are not listed as extraditable offenses in any extradition treaty existing between States Parties, they shall be deemed to be included as such therein. States Parties undertake to include those crimes as extraditable offenses in every future extradition treaty to be concluded between them.
2. If a State Party which makes extradition conditional on the existence of a treaty receives a request for extradition from another State Party with which it has no extradition treaty, it may, if it decided to extradite, consider this Convention as the legal basis for extradition in respect of those crimes. Extradition shall be subject to the procedural provisions and the other conditions of the law of the requested State.
3. States Parties which do not make extradition conditional on the existence of a treaty shall recognize those crimes as extraditionable offenses between themselves subject to the procedural provisions and the other conditions of the law of the requested State.
4. Each of the crimes shall be treated, for the purposes of extradition between States Parties, as if it had been committed not only in the place in which it occurred but also in the territories of the States required to establish their jurisdiction in accordance with paragraph 1 of article 3.

Article 9

Any person regarding whom proceedings are being carried out in connection with any of the crimes set forth in article 2 shall be guaranteed fair treatment at all stages of the proceedings.

Article 10

1. States Parties shall afford one another the greatest measure of assistance in connection with criminal proceedings brought in respect of the crimes set forth in article 2, including the supply of all evidence at their disposal necessary for the proceedings.
2. The provisions of paragraph 1 of this article shall not affect obligations

Article 11

The State Party where an alleged offender is prosecuted shall communicate the final outcome of the proceedings to the Secretary-General of the United Nations, who shall transmit the information to the other States Parties.

Article 12

The provisions of this Convention shall not affect the application of the Treaties on Asylum, in force at the date of the adoption of this Convention, as between the States which are parties to those Treaties; but a State Party to this Convention may not invoke those Treaties with respect to another State Party to this Convention which is not a party to those Treaties.

Article 13

1. Any dispute between two or more States Parties concerning the interpretation or application of this Convention which is not settled by negotiation shall, at the request of one of them, be submitted to arbitration. If within six months from the date of the request for arbitration the parties are unable to agree on the organisation of the arbitration, any one of those parties may refer the dispute to the International Court of Justice by request in conformity with the Statute of the Court.
2. Each State Party may at the time of signature or ratification of this Convention or accession thereto declare that it does not consider itself bound by paragraph 1 of this article. The other States Parties shall not be bound by paragraph 1 of this article with respect to any State Party which has made such a reservation.
3. Any State Party which has made a reservation in accordance with paragraph 2 of this article may at any time withdraw that reservation by notification to the Secretary-General of the United Nations.

Article 14

This Convention shall be open for signature by all States, until December 31, 1974 at United Nations Headquarters in New York.

Article 15

This Convention is subject to ratification. The instruments of ratification shall be deposited with the Secretary-General of the United Nations.

Article 16

This Convention shall remain open for accession by any State. The instruments of accession shall be deposited with the Secretary-General of the United Nations.

Article 17

1. This Convention shall enter into force on the thirtieth day following the date of deposit of the twenty-second instrument of ratification or accession with the Secretary-General of the United Nations.
2. For each State ratifying or acceding to the Convention after the deposit of the twenty-second instrument or ratification or accession, the Convention shall enter into force on the thirtieth day after deposit by such State of its instrument of ratification or accession.

Article 18

1. Any State Party may denounce this Convention by written notification to the Secretary-General of the United Nations.
2. Denunciation shall take effect six months following the date on which notification is received by the Secretary-General of the United Nations.

Article 19

The Secretary-General of the United Nations shall inform all States, *inter alia:*

   (a) of signatures to this Convention, of the deposit of instruments of ratification or accession in accordance with articles 14, 15 and 16 and of notifications made under article 18;
   (b) of the date on which this Convention will enter into force in accordance with article 17.

Article 20

The original of this Convention, of which the Chinese, English, French, Russian and Spanish texts are equally authentic, shall be deposited with the Secretary-General of the United Nations, who shall send certified copies thereof to all States.

IN WITNESS WHEREOF the undersigned, being duly authorised thereto by their respective Governments, have signed this Convention, opened for signature at New York on December 14, 1973.

SELECT BIBLIOGRAPHY

1. DOCUMENTS AND OFFICIAL SOURCES

(a) Collections of Documents:

Brownlie, I. (ed), *Basic Documents in International Law* (Clarendon Press, Oxford, 1983).

Friedlander, R. A. (ed), *Terrorism: Documents of International and Local Control*, 3 vols. (Oceania Publications, Dobbs Ferry, 1979).

(b) Official (Australia):

Australian Federal Police Annual Report.

Australian Security Intelligence Organisation Annual Report (also *Report to Parliament*).

Consular, Trade and Other Official Representatives List.

Department of Administrative Services Annual Report (until 1981–82).

Department of Foreign Affairs Annual Report.

Department of the Special Minister of State Annual Report (from 1982–83).

Diplomatic List.

Protective Security Review: Report (Unclassified Version) Parliamentary Paper 397/1979 (AGPS, Canberra, 1979).

Report to the Minister for Administrative Services on the Organisation of Police Resources in the Commonwealth Area and Other Related Matters (AGPS, Canberra, 1978).

Review of Australia's Overseas Representation (AGPS, Canberra, 1986).

Royal Commission on Australia's Security and Intelligence Agencies, *General Report* (AGPS, Canberra, 1985).

Royal Commission on Australia's Security and Intelligence Agencies, *Report on the Australian Security Intelligence Organisation* (AGPS, Canberra, 1985).

Royal Commission on Intelligence and Security, *Intelligence and Security*, Four Reports, 5 vols., (AGPS, Canberra, 1977).

Australian Foreign Affairs Record
Backgrounder
Commonwealth Legislation
Ministerial and Departmental News and Media Releases
Parliamentary Debates (*Hansard*)

(c) Official (United States of America):

Lethal Terrorist Actions Against Americans, 1973–1985 (State Department, Washington, 1985).
Patterns of Global Terrorism: 1983 (State Department, Washington, 1984).
Patterns of International Terrorism: 1981 (State Department, Washington, 1982).
Public Report of the Vice President's Task Force on Combatting Terrorism (Washington, 1986).
Report of the Secretary of State's Advisory Panel on Overseas Security (State Department, Washington, 1985).
Terrorism and Security: The Challenge for Public Diplomacy, A Report of the United States Advisory Commission on Public Diplomacy (Washington, 1985).
Terrorist Bombings: A Statistical Overview of International Terrorist Bombing Incidents from January 1977 through May 1983 (State Department, Washington, 1983).
Terrorist Incidents Involving Diplomats: A Statistical Overview of International Terrorist Incidents Involving Diplomatic Personnel and Facilities from January 1968 through April 1983 (State Department, Washington, 1983).

Backgrounder
Congressional Record (*Hearings*, as given)
Current Policy
Department of State Bulletin
Gist
Official Texts

(d) Official (Other):

The Abuse of Diplomatic Immunities and Privileges: Report with an Annex; together with the Proceedings of the Committee; Minutes of Evidence taken on 20 June, and 2 and 18 July in the last Session of Parliament; and Appendices, First Report from the Foreign Affairs Committee, House of Commons, Session 1984–85 (HMSO, London, 1984).
Diplomatic Privileges and Immunities: Government Report on Review of the Vienna Convention on Diplomatic Relations and Reply to "The Abuse of Diplomatic Immunities and Privileges", The First Report from

the Foreign Affairs Committee in the Session 1984-85, Cmd.9497 (HMSO, London, 1985).

The Bomb Attack at the Martyr's Mausoleum in Rangoon: Report on the findings by the Enquiry Committee and the measures taken by the Burmese Government (Rangoon, 1984).

2. ARTICLES AND MONOGRAPHS

(a) Articles:

Adie, W. A. C., 'Australia and World Wide Terrorism', *IPA Review* 32:1 (January–March 1978).

Blackshield, A. R., 'The Siege of Bowral—The Legal Issues', *Pacific Defence Reporter* (March 1978).

Clifford, W., 'Terrorism: Australia's Quiet War', *Reader's Digest* (October 1981).

Clutterbuck, R., 'Diplomats Under Siege', *The Army Quarterly and Defence Journal* 111:2 (April 1981).

Doogan, C. M., 'Defence Powers Under the Constitution: Use of Troops in Aid of State Police Forces—Suppression of Terrorist Activities', *Journal of the Royal United Services Institute of Australia* 5:2 (October 1982).

Fairbairn, G., 'Terrorism and Defence', *World Review* 18:1 (April 1979).

Fawcett, J. E. S., 'Kidnappings versus Government Protection', *World Today* 26:9 (September 1970).

Fromkin, D., 'The Strategy of Terrorism', *Foreign Affairs* 53:4 (July 1975).

Gramont, S. de, 'How One Pleasant, Scholarly Young Man From Brazil Became a Kidnapping, Gun-Toting, Bombing Revolutionary', *New York Times Magazine*, 15 November 1970.

Hamer, J., 'Protection of Diplomats', *Editorial Research Reports* 11:3 (3 October 1973).

Hoffman, B., 'The Jewish Defense League', *Terrorism Violence and Insurgency Journal* 5:1 (Summer 1984).

James, A., 'Diplomacy and International Society', *International Relations* 6:6 (November 1980).

Jenkins, B. M., 'International Terrorism: Trends and Potentialities', *Journal of International Affairs* 32:1 (1978).

Kirkpatrick, J. J., 'Defining Terrorism', *Catholicism in Crisis* (September 1984).

'Legal and Constitutional Problems of Protective Security Arrangements in Australia', *Australian Law Journal* 52 (June 1978).

Mack, A., 'The Utility of Terrorism', *Australian and New Zealand Journal of Criminology* 14:4 (December 1981).

Madison, C. A., 'Coping With Violence Abroad', *Foreign Service Journal* (July/August 1985).

Merari, A. and Braunstein, Y., 'Shi'ite Terrorism: Capabilities and the Suicide Factor', *Terrorism Violence and Insurgency Journal* 5:2 (Fall 1984).

Milte, K., 'Terrorism and International Order', *Australian and New Zealand Journal of Criminology* 8:2 (June 1975).

Moynihan, D. P., 'Nuturing Terrorism', *Harper's* 268:1606 (March 1984).

Murphy, J. F., 'Report on Conference on International Terrorism: Protection of Diplomatic Premises and Personnel, Bellagio, Italy, March 8–12, 1982', *Terrorism: An International Journal* 6:3 (1983).

'Off The Champagne Trail: Diplomatic Security Abroad', *Australian Foreign Affairs Record* 54:5 (May 1983).

Poulantzas, N. M., 'Some Problems of International Law Connected With Urban Guerrilla Warfare: The Kidnapping of Members of Diplomatic Missions, Consular Officers and other Foreign Personnel', *Annals of International Studies* 3 (1972).

Rawson, D. W., 'Political Violence in Australia', *Dissent* 22 (Autumn 1968).

Reaburn, N. S., 'The Legal Implications in Counter-Terrorist Operations', *Pacific Defence Reporter* 4:10 (April 1978).

——'The Mark Report', *Pacific Defence Reporter* 4:11 (May 1978).

——'The Protective Security Review', *Pacific Defence Reporter* 6:11 (May 1980).

Selth, A. W., 'Romantic Ireland's Dead and Gone', *RUSI* (Journal of the Royal United Services Institute for Defence Studies) 128:1 (March 1983).

Shamwell, H. F., 'Implementing the Convention on the Prevention and Punishment of Crimes Against Internationally Protected Persons, Including Diplomatic Agents', *Terrorism: An International Journal* 6:4 (1983).

Sofaer, A. D., 'Terrorism and the Law', *Foreign Affairs* 64:5 (Summer 1986).

Stechel, I., 'Terrorist Kidnapping of Diplomatic Personnel', *Cornell International Law Journal* 5:189 (Spring 1972).

Stohl, M., 'National Interests and State Terrorism in International Affairs', *Political Science* 36:1 (July 1984).

Teichmann, M., 'Terror Australis', *Australian Penthouse* 2:8 (May 1981).

Thompson, W. S., 'Political Violence and the "Correlation of Forces"', *Orbis* 19:4 (Winter 1976).

Wardlaw, G., 'Perspectives on Terrorism', *Australian and New Zealand Journal of Criminology* 16:4 (December 1983).

——'Policy dilemmas in responding to international terrorism', *Australian Quarterly* 58:3 (Spring 1986).

——'The Armed Forces and Public Order Policing', *Pacific Defence Reporter* (October 1981).

—'The Mounting Threat of Terror', *Pacific Defence Reporter* 9:12 (June 1983).

—'Terrorism: State Involvement Adds New Dimension', *Pacific Defence Reporter*, Annual Reference Edition, (December 1984/January 1985).

—'The Year of the Bomb—And More to Come', *Pacific Defence Reporter*, Annual Reference Edition, (December 1983/January 1984).

'When Diplomats Are Targets', *US News and World Report* 75:3 (16 July 1973).

Wilkinson, P., 'After Tehran', *Conflict Quarterly* (Spring 1981).

—'Can a State be "Terrorist"?', *International Affairs* 57:3 (Summer 1981).

—'State-sponsored international terrorism: the problems of response', *The World Today* (July 1984).

Woods, C., 'The Problems of International Terrorism', *Australian Journal of Forensic Sciences* 12 (December 1979–March 1980).

Wright, Q., 'The Decline of Classic Diplomacy', *Journal of International Affairs* 17 (1963).

Yoder, A., 'The Effectiveness of UN Action Against International Terrorism: Conclusions and Comments', *Terrorism: An International Journal* 6:4 (1983).

—'United Nations Resolutions Against International Terrorism', *Terrorism: An International Journal* 6:4 (1983).

(b) Monographs:

Aston, C. C., *Political Hostage Taking in Western Europe*, Conflict Studies 157 (Institute for the Study of Conflict, London, 1984).

Bass, G. and Jenkins, B.M., *A Review of Recent Trends in International Terrorism and Nuclear Incidents Abroad*, Rand Note N–1979–SL (Rand Corporation, Santa Monica, 1983).

Brenchley, F., *Diplomatic Immunities and State-Sponsored Terrorism*, Conflict Studies 164 (Institute for the Study of Conflict, London, 1984).

Civil Violence and the International System, Adelphi Papers 82 (Part 1) and 83 (Part 2) (International Institute for Strategic Studies, London, 1971).

Clissold, S., *Croat Separatism: Nationalism, Dissidence and Terrorism*, Conflict Studies 103 (Institute for the Study of Conflict, London, 1979).

Gutteridge, W. (ed), *Libya: Still a Threat to Western Interests?*, Conflict Studies 160 (Institute for the Study of Conflict, London, 1984).

Jenkins, B.M., *Combatting Terrorism Becomes a War*, Rand Paper P–6988 (Rand Corporation, Santa Monica, 1984).

—*Diplomats on the Front Line*, Rand Paper P–6749 (Rand Corporation, Santa Monica, 1982).

—*Embassies Under Siege: A Review of 48 Embassy Takeovers, 1971–1980*, Rand Report R-2651-RC (Rand Corporation, Santa Monica, 1981).

—*High Technology Terrorism and Surrogate War: The Impact of New Technology on Low-Level Violence*, Rand Paper P-5339 (Rand Corporation, Santa Monica, 1975).

—*New Modes of Conflict*, Rand Report R-3009-DNA (Rand Corporation, Santa Monica, 1983).

—*Some Reflections on Recent Trends in Terrorism*, Rand Paper P-6897 (Rand Corporation, Santa Monica, 1983).

—*Talking to Terrorists*, Rand Paper P-6750 (Rand Corporation, Santa Monica, 1982).

—*The Lessons of Beirut: Testimony Before the Long Commission*, Rand Note N-2114-RC (Rand Corporation, Santa Monica, 1984).

Jenkins, B. M. and Johnson, J., *International Terrorism: A Chronology 1968–1974*, Rand Report R-1597-DOS/ARPA (Rand Corporation, Santa Monica, 1975).

Jenkins, B. M., Johnson, J. and Ronfeldt, D., *Numbered Lives: Some Statistical Observations from 77 International Hostage Episodes*, Rand Paper P-5905 (Rand Corporation, Santa Monica, 1977).

Wilkinson, P., *Terrorism: International Dimensions - Answering the Challenge*, Conflict Studies 113 (Institute for the Study of Conflict, London, 1979).

—*Terrorism versus Liberal Democracy—The Problems of Response*, Conflict Studies 67 (Institute for the Study of Conflict, London, 1976).

3. OTHER PUBLISHED WORKS

Aron, R., *Peace and War: A Theory of International Relations* (Praeger, New York, 1970).

Bassiouni, M. C.(ed), *International Terrorism and Political Crimes* (Charles Thomas, Springfield, 1975).

Baumann, C. E., *The Diplomatic Kidnappings: A Revolutionary Tactic of Urban Terrorism* (Martinus Nijhoff, The Hague, 1973).

Begin, M., *The Revolt* (W. H. Allen, London, 1951).

Bell, J. B., *A Time of Terror: How Democratic Societies Respond to Revolutionary Violence* (Basic Books, New York, 1978).

Bloomfield, L. M. and Fitzgerald, G. F., *Crimes Against Internationally Protected Persons: Prevention and Punishment: An Analysis of the UN Convention* (Praeger, New York, 1975).

Boyce, P. J., *Foreign Affairs for New States: Some Questions of Credentials* (University of Queensland Press, St Lucia, 1977).

Bull, H., *The Anarchical Society: A Study of Order in World Politics* (Macmillan, London, 1983).

Bull, H. and Watson, A. (eds), *The Expansion of International Society* (Clarendon Press, Oxford, 1984).

Christopher, W. *et al, American Hostages in Iran: The Conduct of a Crisis* (Yale University Press, New Haven, 1985).

Cline, R.S. and Alexander, Y., *Terrorism: The Soviet Connection* (Crane Russak, New York, 1984).

Clutterbuck, R., *Living With Terrorism* (Faber, London, 1975).

Debray, R., *Revolution in the Revolution? Armed Struggle and Political Struggle in Latin America* (Penguin, Harmondsworth, 1968).

Dobson, C. and Payne, R., *Terror! The West Fights Back* (Macmillan, London, 1982).

Eckstein, H. (ed), *Internal War: Problems and Approaches* (Collier-Macmillan, London, 1964).

Evans, A. E. and Murphy, J. F.(eds), *Legal Aspects of International Terrorism* (Heath and Co., Lexington, 1978).

Freedman, L. *et al, Terrorism and International Order* (Royal Institute for International Affairs, London, 1986).

Gore Booth (ed), *Satow's Guide to Diplomatic Practice* (Longman, London, 1979).

Grivas, G., *The Memoirs of George Grivas* (Longman, London, 1964).

Guevara, E., *Guerrilla Warfare* (Penguin, Harmondsworth, 1969).

Hall, R., *The Secret State: Australia's Spy Industry* (Cassell, Sydney, 1978).

Herz, M. F.(ed), *Diplomats and Terrorists: What Works, What Doesn't: A Symposium* (Institute for the Study of Diplomacy (Georgetown University), Washington, 1982).

Jackson, G., *Concorde Diplomacy: The Ambassador's Role in the World Today* (Hamish Hamilton, London, 1981)

Janke, P., *Guerrilla and Terrorist Organisations: A World Directory and Bibliography* (Harvester Press, Brighton, 1983).

Laqueur, W., *Terrorism* (Abacus, London, 1978).

——*The Terrorism Reader: A Historical Anthology* (Wildwood House, London, 1979).

Lodge, J. (ed), *Terrorism: A Challenge to the State* (Martin Robinson, Oxford, 1981).

Mao Tse-tung, *Selected Works of Mao Tse-tung* (Foreign Languages Press, Peking, 1967).

Marighela, C., *For the Liberation of Brazil* (Penguin, Harmondsworth, 1971).

Miller, J.D.B., *The World of States* (Croom Helm, London, 1981).

Molomby, T., *Spies, Bombs and the Path of Bliss* (Potoroo Press, Sydney, 1986).

Moss, R., *Urban Guerillas: The New Face of Political Violence* (Alister Taylor, Wellington, 1972).

Nicolson, H., *Diplomacy* (Oxford University Press, London, 1969).

Przetacznik, F., *Protection of Officials of Foreign States according to International Law* (Martinus Nijhoff, The Hague, 1983).

Schelling, T.C., *Arms and Influence* (Yale University Press, New Haven, 1966).

Schlesinger, P., Murdock, G. and Elliot, P., *Televising Terrorism: Political Violence in Popular Culture* (Comedia, London, 1983).

Semmel, B., *Marxism and the Science of War* (Oxford University Press, Oxford, 1981).

Sen, B., *A Diplomat's Handbook of International Law and Practice* (Martinus Nijhoff, The Hague, 1979).

Sterling, C., *The Terror Network: The Secret War of International Terrorism* (Holt, Rinehart and Winston, New York, 1981).

Stohl, M. (ed), *The Politics of Terrorism* (Dekker, New York, 1979).

'Sunday Times' Insight Team, *Siege! Princes Gate, London, April 30–May 5 1980* (Hamlyn, London, 1980).

Walter, E. V., *Terror and Resistance: A Study of Political Violence* (Oxford University Press, New York, 1969).

Wardlaw, G., *Political Terrorism: theory, practice and counter-measures* (Cambridge University Press, Cambridge, 1982).

Watson, A., *Diplomacy: The Dialogue Between States* (Eyre Methuen, London, 1982).

Wight, M., *Power Politics* (Leicester University Press, Leicester, 1978).

Wilkinson, P., *Terrorism and the Liberal State* (Macmillan, London, 1986).

Wilson, C. E., *Diplomatic Privileges and Immunities* (University of Arizona Press, Tucson, 1967).

4. UNPUBLISHED WORKS

Crenshaw, M., 'The International Consequences of Terrorism', Paper prepared for delivery at the 1983 Annual Meeting of the American Political Science Association, The Palmer House, 1–4 September 1983.

'International Terrorism', Address by the Head, Protective Services Coordination Centre, to the Joint Services Staff College, Canberra, 22 February 1983.

Stohl, M., 'Terrorism, States and State Terrorism: The Reagan Administration in the Middle East', Paper prepared for the Center for Contemporary Arab Studies—Georgetown University Seminar 'Terrorism and the Middle East: Context and Interpretations', 11 September 1986.

Wardlaw, G., 'State Responses to International Terrorism: Some Cautionary Comments', Paper prepared for a Symposium on International Terrorism, Defense Intelligence Analysis Center, Washington, 2–3 December 1985.

——'Strategic Aspects of Political Terrorism', Address to the Joint Services Staff College, Canberra, 29 February 1984.

——'The Terrorist Threat to Australia and the Region', Paper prepared for a seminar on 'International Terrorism and the Australian Experience', sponsored by the Australian Institute for Jewish Affairs and the Institute for Studies in International Terrorism, State University of New York, Melbourne, 8–9 June 1986.

Williams, C. O. G., *Terrorism: An Australian Perspective* (based on data available to 1 September 1980), Unpublished Master of Arts thesis, University of Melbourne, Melbourne, 1980.

INDEX